DG

MOUNTAIN
KINGS

AGONY AND EUPHORIA ON THE PEAKS OF THE TOUR DE FRANCE

D0552288

WITHDRAWN FROM STOCK

You
wv
Ple
O

Is
v
/

GILES BELBIN

COL D'ASPIN / 1490m

COL DE PEYRESOURDE / 1563m

COL DE MARIE-BLANQUE / 1035m

HAUTACAM / 1520m

LUZ-ARDIDEN / 1720m

PLA D'ADET / 1680m

COL DU TOURMALET / 2115m

COL D'AUBISQUE / 1709m

COL DE PORTET D'ASPET / 1069m

MONT VENTOUX / 1912m

PUY-DE-DÔME / 1415m

COL DE LA RÉPUBLIQUE / 1161m

ALPE D'HUEZ / 1850m

MOUNTAIN
KINGS

AGONY AND EUPHORIA
ON THE PEAKS OF THE
TOUR DE FRANCE

COL DE LA BONETTE / 2802m

COL DE L'ISERAN / 2770m

COL DE LA MADELEINE / 2000m

COL DU GLANDON/COL DE LA CROIX DE FER / 2067m

COL D'IZOARD / 2361m

COL DE JOUX-PLANE / 1700m

LA PLAGNE / 2080m

LES DEUX ALPES / 1650m

COL DE LA COLOMBIÈRE / 1613m

AVORIAZ / 1796m

COL DU TÉLÉGRAPHE / 1566m

COL DU GALIBIER / 2645m

This book copyright © Punk Publishing Ltd 2013
Text © Giles Belbin 2013
Photographs © Giles Belbin 2013 unless credited otherwise on p256

Published in the United Kingdom in 2013 by

Punk Publishing Ltd, 3 The Yard, Pegasus Place, London SE11 5SD
www.punkpublishing.co.uk

All rights reserved. No part of this publication may be reproduced, stored in a retrieval system, used in any form
of advertising, sales promotion or publicity, or transmitted in any form or by any means, electronic, mechanical,
photocopying, recording or otherwise, without prior permission in writing from the publishers.

Any copy of this book, issued by the publishers as a paperback, is sold subject to the condition that it shall not, by
way of trade or otherwise, be lent, resold, hired out or otherwise circulated, without the publishers' prior consent,
in any form of binding or cover other than that in which it is published, and without a similar condition including
these words being imposed on the subsequent purchaser.

A catalogue record of this book is available from the British Library.
ISBN 978-1906889593
10 9 8 7 6 5 4 3 2 1

8089624

CORK CITY
LIBRARIES

CONTENTS

CLIMBS / *RIDER PROFILES*

INTRODUCTION

July 17th 2006 was a watershed for me. The day before, I had flown into Geneva with three friends; we had brought our bikes with us. We drove south, anxiously glancing upwards at the fearsome peaks that towered above us.

After a night of fitful sleep in a nearby town, we drove to Valloire, at the foot of the frightening Col du Galibier. From there, having assembled our bikes, we slowly made our way up the climb. It was tough, far tougher than I had expected. On and on the road went, through lush meadows and into barren, rock-strewn desolation. Near the top, desperate for a few moments of respite, I pulled into a gravel lay-by and coasted to a standstill. Too tired to unclip from my pedals, I toppled over. I lay there for some time, at the point of exhaustion, humiliated. I still had three kilometres to go.

Eventually I gathered enough energy to pick myself up. I got back on the bike and slogged my way to the top. And there I stood: breathless and overjoyed; knackered and humbled. I had

made it. I had followed where the legends of the cycling world – Bartali and Coppi, Bobet and Anquetil, Merckx and Hinault – had led. I couldn't quite believe I had cycled the mighty Galibier. And what's more, despite the tiredness and the pain, despite the relentless leg-breaking effort, I'd loved it.

I had fulfilled a dream that had been born eight years earlier, when I had seen Channel 4's highlights of the Tour de France, and watched open-mouthed as Italian climber Marco Pantani lit up the race. From that moment I was smitten: by cycling, by the Tour and, in particular, by the mountains.

Year after year I returned to ride the climbs of the Tour and then to sit on the mountainside with thousands of others, waiting for the pros to race by. I was addicted. What other sport gives you an opportunity to do something like that? Can you go for a kick-about at Wembley hours before the cup final? No. Can you have a knock-up at Wimbledon just before Roger and

Rafa walk out? No. Can you go for a jog on the Olympic track while Usain warms up? No. Can you ride up Alpe d'Huez, or the Ventoux, or the Tourmalet, just hours before Contador, Wiggins and company do battle? Yes, you can. And make no mistake, these mountains are the most spectacular of sporting arenas.

This book tells you what it feels like to ride twenty-five of the Tour's greatest climbs, and recounts some of the great episodes associated with them. It is not exhaustive: how could it be, with over one hundred years of history to deal with? Not everyone will agree with my selection of climbs or the riders I have profiled. Many were obvious choices, others perhaps less so. Each of these mountains, though, indisputably offers a challenge and great rewards; and it's likewise incontestable that every rider featured in this book has played a major part in the story of the Tour.

In preparing this book, I have trawled through scores of publications, pored over maps and race routes and watched countless hours of footage. But Tour history, it must be said, can sometimes be elusive. Different sources often give different versions of events. Even the statistics of the Tour are more problematic than one might expect: distances and gradients of climbs, for example, vary from source to source. I have cited official Tour data wherever possible, but have also made use of the information

included on the website climbbybike.com, an invaluable resource for anyone wanting to tackle these mountains.

These climbs are tough, but they are not the preserve of the super-fit. I'm a slightly overweight guy in his late thirties who sits at a desk most days. My bike is a seven-year-old Giant with a triple chainset, a fact at which some will sneer, but I don't care – I'll use whatever it takes to get up the hills. I cycle to work but otherwise I'm rarely on my bike except when I go to the mountains, because it is there that I really want to ride. It's there where the history is, and the drama.

How do I go about it? Well, I take food and clothing for all eventualities, I drive to within 10km of the climb, then I get on my bike and ride up the mountain. I don't worry about how long it takes me, and I don't care if I have to stop. I just take my time, revelling in the glorious terrain. It is difficult, but that's the point: the pleasure is so much richer after a little suffering. And if I'm there to watch the Tour as well, I go as far as the gendarmes or the barriers allow, pull over, put on the radio (or find a nearby campervan with a TV), and settle down. Then, when I hear the TV helicopters approaching, I stand up, ready to watch the riders creating another chapter in the history of the Tour. For me it's the biggest thrill in the sporting world.

Giles Belbin, September 2012
Somerset

INTRODUCING THE TOUR

In 1903 a battle was raging in France. This battle was not being fought in the fields or in the hills, however – it was being fought in the printing presses of Paris and on the country's news-stands.

Bicycle races had been organised almost as soon as these self-propelled contraptions had appeared on the streets of Europe. Men wanted to test their speed against each other on these new machines, whether it be on the road or, eventually, on specially designed tracks. They wanted to test their endurance, too.

The first long-distance road race, Paris–Rouen, was held in 1868; it was won by an Englishman, James Moore. More one-day races followed, some over huge distances, such as the 1200km Paris–Brest–Paris and the 560km+ Bordeaux–

Paris. Some of the classics of today's cycling calendar were born around this time: Liège–Bastogne–Liège (1892), Paris–Roubaix (1896), Milan–San Remo (1907). The sport was still in its infancy, but it was developing a large and passionate following, as the public's imagination was fired by the unfathomable feats of fortitude achieved by these strongmen.

To sate and to stoke this appetite, the daily sports paper Le Vélo was created. Founded in 1892 by Pierre Giffard, Le Vélo established a trend by staging and sponsoring races in order to boost its circulation. It was Le Vélo that organised the very first one-hour record, taken by one Henri Desgrange, who rode 35.325km in the sixty minutes.

All was going well for Le Vélo when there came a

turn of events that, though seemingly unrelated, was to shape the future of cycle racing: the Dreyfus Affair.

Alfred Dreyfus, a Jew from the Alsace region, was an officer in the French army. In 1894 he was accused of, and ultimately jailed for, spying on his motherland for Germany. France was instantly divided into those people who believed Dreyfus to be a traitor and those who were convinced he was wrongly convicted, a victim of anti-semitism.

Giffard was firmly in the pro-Dreyfus camp, a stance he publicised through his paper. Unfortunately for Giffard, many of his backers, upon whom he relied for advertising and sponsorship revenues, were not of the same view. One of this group was Comte Dion, who owned a bicycle company. Dion pulled his money from Giffard's paper, and set about establishing his own. So it was that, in October 1900, *L'Auto-Vélo* was created. It was printed

on yellow paper and its editor was none other than Henri Desgrange, winner of the inaugural competition for the one-hour record. *L'Auto-Vélo* and *Le Vélo*, Desgrange and Giffard, were now going head to head.

Each organised races, sometimes on the same courses just weeks apart, as the two jostled for superiority, but neither could land a knockout blow. Until 1903, that is.

Picture the scene: November 20th 1902. Lunchtime in Montmartre, Paris. Sitting around the table are Desgrange and Géo Lefèvre. It's a brainstorming session, to concoct a way of putting one over on Gifford. Lefèvre suggests another race – the longest and hardest of them all. A race starting and finishing in Paris, but taking the riders right around the country, visiting every border, every coast. A loop around the country – a "Tour de France". Desgrange was persuaded, and approached the paper's financial controller, Victor Goddet, who gave

Desgrange the go-ahead. Years later, Goddet's son, Jacques, would succeed Desgrange as the race's director.

On January 16th 1903, *L'Auto-Vélo* became *L'Auto*, having been forced to remove the word "Vélo" from its title following legal action from Giffard. Three days later, the front page of *L'Auto* shouted: "The Tour de France: the greatest cycle race in the world."

Six stages were to take the riders from Paris to Lyon (467km), Lyon to Marseilles (374km), Marseille to Toulouse (423km), Toulouse to Bordeaux (268km), Bordeaux to Nantes (425km), and Nantes to Paris (471km). Initially, however, rival publications considered the Tour a ludicrous endeavour, and many of the riders of the day agreed. The race was due to depart Paris on May 31st and arrive back on June 5th, just six days later. A little over one month before the race's *grand départ*, only fifteen riders had signed up. A rethink was needed.

So the race start was put back a month, rest days were introduced, the entrance fee was halved, more prize money was made available and daily expenses were paid. This new-look Tour was more to people's liking. On the afternoon of July 1st 1903, sixty riders rolled out from the Cafe Réveil Matin, in the southern suburbs of Paris. Four hundred and sixty seven kilometres later, Maurice Garin rode into Lyon as the Tour de France's first stage winner. He would go on to become the first ever overall winner, nineteen days later in Paris (see p28).

The race captured French hearts at once. People rose from their beds to cheer on these iron-willed giants, as stories of their heroic deeds – proclaimed in the stirring prose of Desgrange and his team of scribes – spread around the country. Sales of *L'Auto* boomed, and *Le Vélo* was doomed. Desgrange had won the battle of the presses. The Tour had been born.

THE JERSEYS

Here's a brief guide to the four major Tour classifications and their respective jerseys.

THE YELLOW JERSEY (*maillot jaunc*) The most important jersey of the four, the *maillot jaune* is worn by the rider at the top of the General Classification – that is, the rider with the lowest overall aggregate time. The jersey was introduced in 1919 and is yellow because *L'Auto*, the sponsor of the Tour, was printed on yellow paper. The first rider to wear it was Eugène Christophe, although Philippe Thys claimed he was given one in 1913 but didn't put it on. Until the advent of the yellow jersey the leader of the race wore a green armband.

THE GREEN JERSEY (*maillot vert*) Worn by the rider who heads the Points Classification. Points are awarded at the end of every stage and at intermediate sprints along the way. The points competition was introduced in 1953 in celebration of the race's 50th anniversary. Fritz Schaer entered history as the first to wear the new jersey, and went on to win it in Paris.

THE POLKA-DOT JERSEY (*maillot à pois rouges*) Worn by the rider leading the King of the Mountains Classification. Points are awarded at the top of every classified climb, with the number of points on offer being relative to the difficulty of the climb. If the stage finishes at the top of a climb, the points are often doubled. The first winner of the King of the Mountains was Vicente Trueba, but the jersey wasn't introduced until 1975, when Lucien Van Impe of Belgium won it.

THE WHITE JERSEY (*maillot blanc*) Worn by the General Classification's best-placed rider under the age of 26.

THE MOUNTAINS

For many people, myself included, the mountains make the Tour. Some of Europe's most spectacular landscapes are to be found amid the summits of the Pyrenees and Alps, and it is on the slopes of these rugged masses of rock, where the riders fight each other and the worst that nature can throw at them, that the best stories of the Tour have been played out.

It took eight editions before the race entered the thin air of France's high peaks, though it had taken on some climbs before. The Col de la République, the first mountain over 1000m to feature, was tackled in the inaugural Tour (see p130). Then, in 1905, the Ballon d'Alsace was added. But although both the République and the Ballon are testing rides, neither bears any relation to what was unleashed on the peloton in the 1910 Tour.

The idea of introducing the Pyrenees into the Tour's route came from Desgrange's assistant at *L'Auto*, Alphonse Steinès. Desgrange may once have said that his ideal Tour would have

only one finisher and later demeaned the invention of the derailleur (it was only for people over 45, he remarked), but even he wasn't sure that mountains of this scale were such a good idea. Keen to convince his boss that racing in the Pyrenees was feasible, Steinès set out to traverse a proposed stage over the Col du Tourmalet. He started out from Sainte-Marie-de-Campan but his driver had to stop with 4km still to drive – snowdrifts made progress impossible. But Steinès, nothing if not determined, set out to tackle the final kilometres on foot, asking the driver to drive back through the valleys and meet him in Barèges, on the other side of the pass.

His concerned driver alerted *L'Auto*'s local correspondent, a Monsieur Lanne-Camy, who organised a search party. Steinès was eventually found stumbling towards the lights of Barèges, on the brink of hypothermia. After a bath and some sleep he had recovered enough to send a telegram to Desgrange. It said simply: "Crossed Tourmalet. Stop. Very Good Road. Stop. Perfectly Passable. Stop."

When the race route was published that April, not only was the Tourmalet included but also the Peyresourde, Aspin and Aubisque. All four in one stage. Then, once off the Aubisque, the riders had another 150km to cycle to the finish at Bayonne. Many people thought this was madness, and Desgrange himself had his doubts. "If we have trouble, there's the door," he reportedly told his assistant.

And so it was that stage 10 of the 1910 Tour de France set out from Luchon at 3.30am on July 21st. The 59 riders were about to take on the four climbs that were to become known together as the "Circle of Death". Octave Lapize and Gustave Garrigou quickly became engaged in a battle at the front of the race. Lapize headed everyone over the Peyresourde, the Aspin and the Tourmalet. With a nervous Desgrange deciding that it would be best if he were to absent himself from proceedings, Steinès and his colleague

Victor Breyer awaited the riders on the top of the last climb, the Aubisque. The clock ticked on, minutes became hours, and their concern grew. What had happened? Had there been a terrible accident? Then, at long last, the shape of a rider and his bicycle appeared in the distance.

Recounting the story years later, in the pages of *Sport et Vie*, François Brigneau wrote that the emerging rider came by in a daze, "his eyes out of his head, mouth open." But it wasn't Lapize, nor was it Garrigou. Breyer asked the rider who he was and whether he knew the whereabouts of the others. But the man said nothing in reply. "He just moaned and shook his legs." Eventually Steinès managed to identify the rider as an amateur from Bayonne called Lafourcade.

Fifteen minutes later, Lapize trudged up. At the top he turned towards Steinès and Breyer and uttered a single and now immortal word:

"Assassins". Yet, despite his obvious distress, Lapize would go on to win the stage in Bayonne. Incredibly, after more than 14 hours and 326km of racing, it came down to a sprint, with Lapize just pipping Pierino Albini to the line. Somewhat surprisingly, for the toughest stage in the Tour's short history, only thirteen men abandoned. The last to finish was Georges Cauvry. He arrived more than seven and a half hours down.

The experiment was deemed a success, and Desgrange, though ambivalent about being called an assassin, went to work on trying to top it. One year later the Tour entered the Alps: stage 5 of the 1911 Tour was a 366km slog from Chamonix to Grenoble, taking in the passes of the Megève, Aravis and Télégraphe before hitting the mighty Galibier, on a road that had been created only twenty years earlier with the blasting of a tunnel below the summit.

As well as having a penchant for making his riders suffer, Desgrange was known for his hyperbolic prose. As he sat on the Galibier that July day, watching the riders battle through two-metre-high walls of snow, often on foot, he wrote: "Are these men not winged, who today climbed to heights where even eagles don't go, and crossed Europe's highest summits? They rose so high they seemed to dominate the world!" The stage was won by Émile Georget. He took well over thirteen hours to get to Grenoble.

The introduction of the mountains to the Tour took the peloton into uncharted territory, and many were critical of Desgrange's new initiative. Garrigou, who would go on to win that 1911 Tour, branded him a "thug", while classics winner Eugène Christophe said: "This is no longer sport. It's not a race any longer. It is simply hard labour."

More than a hundred years later, a Tour without the mountains is inconceivable. The history of the race has been, and continues to be, written on the heights of France's great ranges. It is where the heroes of the sport have crafted their legends.

COL D'ASPIN

START POINT / Sainte-Marie-de-Campan
START ELEVATION / 865m
FINISH ELEVATION / 1490m
LENGTH OF CLIMB / 12.4km
AVERAGE GRADIENT / 4.8%
MAXIMUM GRADIENT / 8.3%
FIRST TOUR / 1910
APPEARANCES / 70

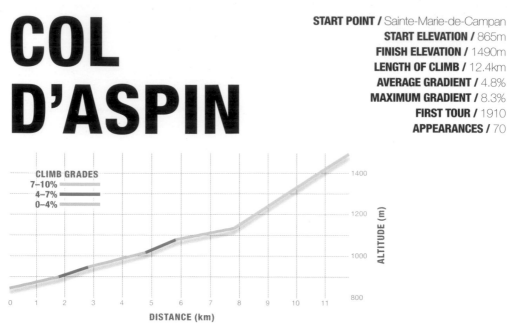

CLIMB GRADES
7–10%
4–7%
0–4%

ALTITUDE (m)

DISTANCE (km)

My first day in the Pyrenees dawns bright and clear, the pale sky turning an ever deeper shade of blue. The May sun slowly warms the air, softening the edges of a cool breeze that gives my bare arms goose pimples as I prepare for my first assault of a Pyrenean mountain: the Aspin.

I'm apprehensive. I've never visited this mountain range before and I've read that climbs here are harder than in the Alps – and I've always found the Alps plenty hard enough, thank you. While perhaps not quite as long as the average alpine ascent, the Pyrenean version is invariably steeper, less regular and, crucially, more poorly surfaced. I've read that the Pyrenees have roads that suck the energy right out from under your wheels, robbing the rider of all momentum. Well, today is the day I find out for myself.

Shortly before 9am I roll out of my B&B, in the hamlet of Saint-Roch in the Campan valley. Forty-five minutes later I roll out for the second time, having had to return to deal with some minor mechanical issues, and having forgotten to take the right size Allen key with me. An inauspicious start.

•••

Jean Robic holds the record for leading the peloton over the Col d'Aspin. Three times (1947, 1948 and 1953) the diminutive Frenchman rode over the summit at the head of the bunch. And it didn't matter to him which

way the race went up the climb. Whether it traversed its eastern or western slopes, Robic led the way.

In 1947 and 1953 he went on to win the stage and it was his 1947 ride, in the first Tour after the end of the Second World War, that set him on his way to his only Tour win.

In 1947 Robic, nicknamed "leather-head" because of the leather helmet he was forced to wear after fracturing his skull during a crash at the 1946 Paris–Roubaix, was over 23 minutes down on race leader René Vietto going into stage 15, from Luchon to Pau. It was a stage that would take in climbs of the Peyresourde, Aspin, Tourmalet and Aubisque. Despite his deficit, Robic still thought he could win the Tour, saying that he felt "unstoppable".

However, the stage over the Aspin represented one of the few opportunities left to make up the huge time gap, and Robic knew it. He was aggressive right from the start of the stage, attacking first on the Peyresourde, where – along with the Italian rider Pierre Brambilla – he distanced Vietto. Then, on the Aspin, Robic struck out alone. No one was able to match his pace. A classic Pyrenean pursuit ensued, but Robic was too strong. At the top of the Aspin he had a lead of nearly seven minutes over Vietto, and by the time he rode into Pau it had ballooned to nearly eleven. That, coupled with the time bonuses he had earned over the four giant Pyrenean peaks, meant that he had gained over fifteen

ITS SITUATION MEANS THAT IT ACTS AS EITHER THE STARTING POINT OR FINISHING POINT OF TWO OF THE MOST USED CLIMBS IN TOUR HISTORY.

minutes during the course of one day. It was an impressive display, but it wasn't enough to put him in yellow. He was still eight minutes down.

Four days later, Robic grabbed a handful of that time back in a mammoth 139km time trial. The Frenchman came in second, crucially ten minutes ahead of Vietto, who fell to fourth overall. But again Robic missed out on the yellow jersey – instead it went to Brambilla, his initial companion on the Peyresourde. The Italian now had a lead of nearly three minutes, which he maintained going into the last stage.

These days a truce is normally called on the last day of the Tour and the yellow jersey is allowed to ride into Paris unchallenged. Not in 1947. Not if Robic had anything to do with it. He attacked on the only gentle rise of the final stage, got a lead over Brambilla, convinced Édouard Fachleitner, a fellow Frenchman, to work with him (the 100,000 francs he reportedly promised probably did it), and rode into Paris over thirteen minutes ahead of the yellow jersey. Robic had won the Tour on the final day, becoming the first person to win without ever wearing the yellow jersey on the roads of France, a feat matched only by Jan Janssen, in 1968.

● ● ●

I ride to the village of Sainte-Marie-de-Campan. This tiny place has secured a berth right at the top of Tour de France legend, thanks principally to its location at the foot of both the Col d'Aspin and the Col du Tourmalet. Its situation means that it acts as either the starting point or finishing point of two of the most used climbs in Tour history. In fact, only on eleven occasions has the Tour not passed through this village since the race started visiting the Pyrenees in 1910. The village's most

famous story comes from 1913 and concerns Eugène Christophe, who would go on to become the first rider to wear the fabled yellow jersey when it was introduced six years later. In 1913 Christophe found himself in a forge in Sainte-Marie, fashioning some new forks, watched by eager-eyed Tour officials. But that story belongs to the Col du Tourmalet and so must wait for now (see p76).

I swing left in the village and immediately I am on the Aspin. From Sainte-Marie the road climbs gently and I settle into an easy rhythm. The kilometre signs drift by, telling me how far I have left to go and the average gradient of the next kilometre. These early averages are nothing to get alarmed about: 2%, 4.5%, 3%. But the signs don't tell the whole truth. The gradients are averages and, like interest rates on a savings account, gradients can go down as well as up. That's what happens on the early slopes of the Aspin: periods spent gaining altitude are wiped out in a blink of an eye when the road sends you back downwards. At first I welcome these sections – it's a chance to rest the legs and enjoy the scenery, so what's not to like? Until it dawns on me that, at some point, I will have to regain that lost elevation, meaning effectively I have to ride to the same height twice. Downhill sections on a mountain climb are the cyclist's enemy, masquerading as an ally.

● ● ●

In 1950, the Aspin again played a decisive role in determining the outcome of the Tour, but this time in very different circumstances.

The Tour had been dominated by Italy since Robic's win in 1947. Gino Bartali had triumphed in 1948, and his rival Fausto Coppi in 1949. In 1950 the Italians entered not one but two teams: the national team, with Bartali as its leader, and a B team. As the race entered the Pyrenees a Frenchman, Bernard Gauthier, was leading the race, but Italian riders had already claimed five out of ten stages. With the Pyrenees and Alps still to come, Bartali and the Italian team were primed to make their move.

Sure enough, on the stage from Pau to Saint-Gaudens, Bartali and his team-mate Fiorenzo Magni were in the leading group as the race went over the Tourmalet. The spectators at the side of the road were restless and started shouting abuse at the riders. They had seen enough of Italian riders heading the Tour and were anxious for a Frenchman to win. Even with Gauthier in yellow, their real hopes lay with Bobet and Robic, both of whom were in the same lead group.

Things deteriorated further on the Aspin. Near the top, with the crowds swarming all over the roads, Bartali and Robic touched wheels. Both went down, with Robic suffering damage to his front wheel. Some of the crowd went to their aid, others took the opportunity to berate Bartali, swearing, punching and throwing stones and bottle tops at the Italian. Later Bartali even accused one spectator of coming at him with a knife, although it now seems generally accepted that the alleged assailant had just forgotten to put down a pen-

knife he was using to slice some meat for a sandwich. It took the intervention of Jacques Goddet, the race director, to push the throng back, allowing Bartali and Robic to continue. Enraged, Bartali flew down the other side of the Aspin and to the stage win. His team-mate Magni took yellow. To the fury of France, Italy was on course for another successful race.

But that night Bartali could not get the events of the day out of his head. He was concerned for his safety and called his team manager, Alfredo Binda, to his room. There he told Binda that he was abandoning the Tour and that all the Italian riders should follow suit. Prolonged discussions followed. In the book, *La Fabuleuse Histoire du Cyclisme*, Pierre Chany describes Bartali holding court with journalists and officials late into the night, smoking cigarette after cigarette, vehemently defending his decision. "We are victims of abuse", he said. "No Italian will ride tomorrow."

And no Italian did ride. All left the Tour in support of their leader, some with greater reluctance than others. It was particularly tough on Magni, who was leading the race and had been encouraged by many to ride on. Magni refused, saying "I can't stay on while Bartali has withdrawn... What would I be taken for? A usurper!"

With the Italians gone, the yellow jersey moved to Ferdi Kübler. The Swiss rider held it all the way to Paris.

• • •

I approach the small resort of Payolle, riding alongside a torrent of meltwater cascading from the peaks. Situated on a plateau, Payolle comes 6km from the top of the Aspin. It is a nondescript place that owes its existence to cross-country skiing and other outdoor pursuits. I press on, watched by a herd of donkeys.

It is quickly apparent that it is from this point that the Aspin gets serious. The gradient is unrelenting, hovering around 8% for the remaining 5km. The sun is getting hotter, the road is getting steeper and my legs are getting weaker. The road, now rising in a series of hairpins, is flanked by pine trees on both sides, affording only the occasional glimpse of the surrounding mountains as a diversion.

When the trees do fall away it gives a rare opportunity to enjoy panoramic views. At one point I glance back over my shoulder and am startled to see the Pic du Midi astronomical observatory, built in the 1880s as a weather station and later used by NASA, standing high on a rocky outcrop, perched against a backdrop of azure sky.

With just under 3km to go my heart feels like it's going to burst through my chest, my legs are burning and my lower back is beginning to make it known that it isn't

particularly happy with whatever is happening today. I expected this. While the Aspin is one of the easier climbs I will face, it is still a first category ascent. Plus I am not exactly over-trained.

I ride on, and for the first time I can see the top of the pass. I round the last hairpin and I am on the final approach. Suddenly, I can see nothing beyond the pass itself, just the road, a meadow and the mountains to either side. Then, as I near the top, the view beyond the pass slowly starts to reveal itself – a summit here, a peak there, and at last a joyous vista is unveiled.

I sit and rest, happily munching my lunch and gazing out at my reward. I'm happy with my day's work. More cyclists arrive, some having to dodge wayward cattle that have wandered on to the road. Then, just as I'm about to make my way back down, I catch sight of an eagle soaring high above me. It's the cream on the pudding, topping off a fantastic first day. These Pyrenees, they're going to be okay, aren't they?

WITH JUST UNDER 3KM TO GO MY HEART FEELS LIKE IT'S GOING TO BURST THROUGH MY CHEST.

MAURICE GARIN

WHILE LEADING THE DINANT–NAMUR–DINANT, GARIN SUFFERED A PUNCTURE. FOCUSED SOLELY ON HIS BID FOR VICTORY, HE SIMPLY LEFT HIS BIKE AND GRABBED THE BIKE OF ANOTHER RIDER'S SOIGNEUR DESPITE HIS PROTESTS.

The first name on the list of immortals that is the official record of Tour de France victors is that of Maurice Garin. Next to Garin's name come the letters "(FRA)" to denote his nationality. So, the first winner of the Tour de France was French. But, as is so often the case with the Tour de France and its history, all is not quite as it seems. For Maurice Garin was actually born in Italy, and how he came to live in France, and exactly when he became a French citizen, is something of a mystery.

Garin was born in Arvier, in the Aosta valley of north-west Italy, on March 3rd 1871, to a farm labourer and a hotel worker. Maurice Clement and his wife, Maria Teresa, had a large family – four daughters and five sons, of whom Maurice was the eldest – and their life was tough. In 1885 the couple decided to make the move over the border into France.

There is some conjecture as to whether the Garins made the journey as a family, individually or in a bigger group. It's said that the young Maurice was exchanged for some cheese by his father, probably to a recruiter of chimney sweeps, who took the youngster to northern France. This may sound implausible, but it's known that officials in the Aosta valley were at that time warning people about the activities of unscrupulous outsiders who were trafficking in child labourers. By whatever means he got there, by 1892, now aged 21, Garin was a regular sight as he rode around the French town of Maubeuge, close to the Belgian border. He entered his first race at the behest of the secretary of the local cycling club and showed instant promise, finishing fifth in the 200km Maubeuge–Hirson–Maubeuge. The result prompted Garin to embark on a serious training programme, while continuing his work as a chimney sweep.

His first victory, in 1893, did not come without incident. While leading the Dinant–Namur–Dinant, Garin suffered a puncture. Focused solely on his bid for victory, he simply left his bike and grabbed the bike of another rider's *soigneur* despite his protests. Garin would win by more than ten minutes; he later returned the borrowed bike and recovered his own.

His entry into the professional ranks came in 1894, after a curious turn of events at a race at Avesnes-sur-Helpe, 25km from Garin's home. Upon arrival at the start line he was dismayed to find that the race, and the 150 francs prize, was for professional riders only. The organisers flatly refused to allow him to enter. Showing the sort of bloody mindedness that would serve him well later in his career, Garin simply waited until the professionals had left and then set off after them in hot pursuit. He caught and passed every single one, even gaining enough time to survive a couple of falls. While the crowd was ecstatic, the organisers were less than impressed, refusing to pay him the prize money. Not that it mattered. The crowd took it upon themselves to right that wrong with a swift whip-round. Garin went home that night with 300 francs in his pockets, double what the organisers were offering.

Soon after, Garin turned professional. In 1896 he came third in the inaugural Paris–Roubaix, a race that also featured eventual Tour de France founder Henri Desgrange, who abandoned. The following year Garin would win in Roubaix, a feat he matched in 1898.

A lean patch followed, with no wins in 1899 or 1900. But Garin, now known as "the little chimney sweep", returned to form in 1901, claiming the almost unimaginably long 1200km Paris–Brest–Paris in a staggering time of just over 52 hours, and securing one of the two 1902 editions of Bordeaux–Paris. It was this talent for long-distance racing that had Garin installed as the firm favourite ahead of the first Tour de France in 1903. A billing that he more than matched.

Of the six stages that comprised that first Tour, Garin won three. He took the race lead on the initial 467km leg from Paris to Lyon and never relinquished it. Before the race, his biggest rival was thought to be Hippolyte Aucouturier (nicknamed The Terrible), who had won the 1903 editions of Paris–Roubaix and Bordeaux–Paris. However, Aucouturier quit on stage 1 and thus was resigned to competing only for later stage wins – riders in those days were allowed to start the next stage regardless of whether they had completed the previous one, but if they failed to complete a stage they were removed from the battle for the overall win. Aucouturier would win the next two stages, into Marseille and Toulouse, but these wins did not affect Garin's position at the top of the classification.

Garin rolled into Paris with a time of 94 hours 33 minutes and 14 seconds. He had cycled around the country at an average of 25.679km/h. His winning margin over second-placed Lucien Pothier was 2 hours 59 minutes 2 seconds.

So it was that on July 18th 1903 Maurice Garin entered the record books as the first winner of the Tour de France. The following year, Garin would secure another place in the history books. He would become the first rider to be stripped of a Tour de France title.

"THE TOUR DE FRANCE IS OVER AND ITS SECOND CELEBRATION WILL ALSO, I DEEPLY FEAR, BE ITS LAST. IT WILL HAVE BEEN KILLED BY ITS OWN SUCCESS, BY THE BLIND PASSIONS THAT IT UNLEASHED, AND THE SLURS AND THE FILTHY SUSPICIONS WORTHY ONLY OF THE IGNORANT AND MALICIOUS."

In 1904 Garin again secured the initial stage victory, again from Paris to Lyon. Despite not winning another stage, he was able to retain his lead throughout the race, entering Paris with a lead of 3 minutes 28 seconds, again over Pothier. But the race was mired in controversy. Riders had been fined for drafting behind cars and disqualified for taking lifts. Garin himself and Italian rider Giovanni Gerbi had been attacked by followers of Antoine Fauré. Supporters of another rider, Ferdinand Payan, had formed an angry mob when he was thrown out of the race for drafting. More than once the organisers were forced to fire shots into the air to dispel gangs who were hell-bent on securing wins for their favourites. In short, the 1904 Tour was a disaster, and almost as soon as Garin had rolled into Paris, Desgrange was announcing that the 1904 edition would be the Tour's last, writing: "The Tour de France is over and its second celebration will also, I deeply fear, be its last. It will have been killed by its own success, by the blind passions that it unleashed, and the slurs and the filthy suspicions worthy only of the ignorant and malicious."

But worse was to come. Garin's win was deemed provisional by the Union Vélocipédique de France until December. Only then, more than four months after the end of the race, did the Union announce that Garin, along with the riders who finished second (Pothier), third (César Garin – brother of Maurice) and fourth (Aucouturier) were to be disqualified and suspended for what were termed "*violation des réglements*". Garin, it was alleged, had at one point jumped on board a train. The win was instead awarded to Henri Cornet, who had finished fifth in Paris.

Publicly Garin denied the allegations of rulebreaking until his death, but Les Woodland, in *The Unknown Tour de France*, writes that Garin, in old age, did finally admit to the caper. He died in 1957, aged 85 years.

And so to the issue of his nationality. Until relatively recently it was thought that Garin had adopted French citizenship in 1892, upon reaching the age of 21. However, in 2004, Italian author Franco Cuaz wrote that, in researching the life of Garin, he had uncovered the document that certified Garin's naturalisation. It was dated 1901, nine years later than thought. Though not affecting his Tour win, it does mean that he won his first races as an Italian, not as a Frenchman.

It seems that some secrets Garin did take to the grave.

MAURICE GARIN SELECTED RESULTS:

1893:	1st Dinant–Namur–Dinant 1st 800km de Paris	**1898:**	1st Paris–Roubaix 1st Valenciennes–Nouvion–Valenciennes
1894:	1st 24h de Liège	**1899:**	3rd Bordeaux–Paris
1895:	1st 24h des Arts Libéraux 1st Guingamp–Morlaix–Guingamp	**1900:**	2nd Bordeaux–Paris 3rd Paris–Roubaix
1896:	1st Paris–Le Mans 1st Liège–Thuin	**1901:**	1st Paris–Brest–Paris
		1902:	1st Bordeaux–Paris
1897:	1st Paris–Roubaix 1st Paris–Cabourg 1st Paris–Royan	**1903:**	1st overall and 3 stage wins Tour de France

CORK CITY LIBRARIES

COL DE PEYRESOURDE

CLIMB GRADES
7–10%
4–7%
0–4%

ALTITUDE (m)

1600
1400
1200
1000
800
600

DISTANCE (km)
0 1 2 3 4 5 6 7 8 9 10 11 12 13 14 15

At the top of the Col de Peyresourde there is a café. It serves fresh crêpes for 50 cents. I buy two. Well, it's the least I deserve for riding the 15km up here from Bagnères-de-Luchon in the pouring rain.

Earlier, as I had assembled my bike in a car park in the centre of Luchon, with the rain already falling heavily, the wind buffeting my ears and the mountains above rapidly gaining a thin coating of fresh snow, a man had walked by with his dog. He looked at me with pity in his eyes and glanced skyward. "It's a bad day to be on a bike," he said helpfully. I looked at him but offered no reply. Tell me something I don't already know, I thought.

• • •

With Luchon providing a perfect start/finish town at the foot of the Peyresourde, the mountain has been used by the Tour many times over the years, often in concert with the Aspin, Tourmalet and Aubisque. In that combination, the Peyresourde is always either the first or the last mountain to be scaled, meaning it can either act as the perfect springboard for a day-long attack, or as the mountain upon which gains made earlier in the day can be consolidated, or lost.

In 1924 Henri Pélissier, the winner the previous year, was one of the favourites for the win, but it was one of his team-mates who lit up the race right from the start. Ottavio Bottecchia won the opening stage from Paris to Le Havre and took the yellow jersey. Pélissier, who had admitted that Bottecchia was "head and shoulders above the rest of us", quit the race on stage 3 with his brother Francis, after a row with the organisers over a discarded jersey (riders were meant to finish a stage with everything that they had started with). The way was now clear for Bottecchia.

Stage 6 was the classic Pyrenean stage, from Bayonne to Luchon: a four-peaked monster over the most famous climbs the Pyrenees could offer. Bottecchia was still in yellow, but was just three minutes ahead of Hector Tiberghen and Giovanni Brunero, who were tied in second place.

Bottecchia attacked on the first serious climb of the day, the Aubisque, and never looked back. At the bottom of the Tourmalet his lead was four minutes; by the time he crested the summit, it had shot up to over eleven; at the top of the Aspin it was sixteen minutes. Bottecchia was in the process of securing the Tour. But he didn't let up. On the slopes of the Peyresourde he maintained his solo assault, continuing to eke out time with every revolution of his pedals. He flew up the Peyresourde

START POINT / Bagnères-de-Luchon
START ELEVATION / 630m
FINISH ELEVATION / 1563m
LENGTH OF CLIMB / 15km
AVERAGE GRADIENT / 6.1%
MAXIMUM GRADIENT / 9.8%
FIRST TOUR / 1910
APPEARANCES / 63

and, by the time he reached the top, his lead was nearly eighteen minutes. He then descended like a madman, taking yet more time on the road down to Luchon. He powered over the finish line 15 hours 24 minutes and 25 seconds after he had left Bayonne, nearly nineteen minutes ahead of Lucien Buysse. His lead overall had gone from three minutes to over half an hour.

In Paris he took the race win by 35 minutes over Nicolas Frantz. Bottecchia had become the first Italian to win the Tour de France, and he had done it in style, wearing yellow every day, from stage one until the finish.

Bottecchia would go on to win the Tour again in 1925 before he died in strange circumstances while on a training ride in Italy, with his skull fractured and bones broken but his bike undamaged. His death was never truly explained.

I'm sweating like a pig within minutes of climbing out of Luchon. Because of the wet and the wind, and the high probability that the rain would turn to snow as I approached the pass, I had decided to clad myself head to toe in proper wet-weather gear. So I'm wearing a heavy waterproof jacket and a thick pair of waterproof cycling trousers. No slinky Lycra for me today.

According to the profile, the early stages of this climb should be relatively easy. Three kilometres of less than 4% gradient, save for a small section of just over 6.5%. I should be flying up, but my legs feel empty and my

heartbeat is far higher than it should be. I can't work out whether it's the dismal conditions, the heavy clothing or the fact that I had the day off the bike yesterday and haven't done much of a warm-up. Whatever the reason, I need to ride my way out of it quickly, otherwise the Peyresourde is not going to make for a pleasant ride.

Approaching the village of Saint-Aventin I begin to feel a little better. The legs are turning more easily and my breathing has settled down a little. The problem is, I really have no idea how far into the climb I am. Unlike many of the famous climbs the Tour uses, the Peyresourde appears to place kilometre markers very sparingly – I haven't seen one since the sign denoting the start. I deliberately ride without any form of GPS tracking system because, if I did, I know I would become obsessed with the thing, looking down all the time at what the gradient was, or at how many metres I'd covered since the last time I'd looked down, instead of just enjoying the ride and really experiencing the mountain. Still, right now, in the rain and in the cold, I admit it would be good to know how far I've come.

And then, as I exit the village, I find out: the top of the Col de Peyresourde is another 10km away. I'm one third through.

Just three years after Bottecchia's romp through the mountains, the man who finished second in Paris to the Italian that year, Luxembourg's Nicolas Frantz, repeated the feat.

The 1927 Tour was a peculiar beast. Eager to shake things up a little, organiser Henri Desgrange introduced more stages (24 as opposed to the previous year's 17) and made 16 of them team time trials. Setting off 15 minutes apart, teams would ride together, although each rider would be awarded his actual time. In theory, at least, a rider could break away from his own team to get a faster time.

Desgrange's motivation for the change came from his belief that the early stages of the Tour counted for little when it came down to the final reckoning in Paris. For him the Tour was becoming predictable: generally won in the Pyrenees, generally on the Bayonne–Luchon stage.

In Bayonne, at the start of stage 11, one of the few to be run as a normal road stage, Frantz was over 23 minutes down on yellow jersey Hector Martin. The stage started at midnight in poor weather. A relatively unknown Italian rider, Michele Gordini, riding as an independent without a team, went on the attack, unnoticed by the main contenders. At the bottom of the Aubisque, Gordini had a lead of nearly an hour, making him the leader of the Tour. Unfortunately for him the peloton got wind of his escapade and set off on a high-speed pursuit. With the teams of the favourites in full flight behind him, Gordini slowed as his explosive start and a series of problems with his bike wore him down.

Gordini still led over the Aubisque but he had been caught by the time he reached the summit of the next climb. Frantz led them over the Tourmalet and then continued alone, determined to ride himself into the overall lead. Over the Aspin and Peyresourde he rose before dropping into Luchon over eleven minutes ahead of the next rider. More importantly, he had arrived nearly two hours before Martin, securing the yellow jersey that he would wear all the way to Paris.

Desgrange's experiment hadn't worked. Despite his tinkering the Tour was still won in the Pyrenees, in the mountains between Bayonne and Luchon. *Plus ça change*.

• • •

I reach the tiny village of Garin and immediately wonder whether the place is named after the first winner of the Tour, or whether it's just a coincidence. I take time to ride up the short, steep road to the village square to see if I can find a monument to him. I can't. A coincidence it is, I conclude.

The gradient on the Peyresourde is constantly changing, which is a good thing, for me at least. As opposed to mountains where the road rises monotonously at a regular pitch, I prefer climbs where the road clambers up the mountain in a series of short but tough sections,

interspersed with periods where the gradient relaxes. And the Peyresourde does exactly that. Just when I think that a section of tough riding is getting too difficult, the road slackens off a bit. It doesn't have to be much, just enough to let the legs spin with a little less resistance. It's as if the road is saying to me: "There you go Giles, that last bit was hard wasn't it? Take a short breather now. You're doing okay."

After Garin the road splits. To the left is the ski station of Peyragudes, to the right is the pass. Shortly after I turn off towards the pass, I hear voices behind me. I haven't seen another cyclist all day so, as I turn my head, I am startled to see two riders clothed in the kit of the Rabobank team, a car crawling slowly alongside them and a man leaning out giving instructions. Clearly it's a couple of professionals out training. They fly by me, one giving me a withering glance. With a sodden, awkward jacket and full, baggy waterproof trousers, I must look a complete sight to them. I scrabble around in my bag, anxiously trying to find my camera but I'm too late. By the time I retrieve it they are long gone. Luckily later I will still be riding up when they come back down, giving me a chance to rattle off some shots of them descending.

AS I CREST THE PASS I FEEL A REAL SENSE OF JUBILATION. NOT ONLY HAVE I CONQUERED THE CLIMB BUT I'VE DONE IT IN REALLY TOUGH CONDITIONS.

After the turn-off the ride really changes character. I'm now cycling along an exposed traverse towards the pass. Off to the right, nestled in a plain below, are a couple of small villages. It's wild and windswept and, while the rain has temporarily ceased, clouds are gathering with menace anew.

Three kilometres to go and I can at last see the summit. The last approaches are via a series of steep hairpins. One last challenge before salvation. I feel myself racing to get to the top and have to force myself to go slower. I'm eager to get this climb in the bag, but a kilometre or two can be a long way at the top of one of these mountains.

As I crest the pass I feel a real sense of jubilation. Not only have I conquered the climb but I've done it in really tough conditions, dressed like an Arctic explorer. It feels good and I'm ready for my reward.

A couple of walkers appear out of the gloom and I follow them into the café, where the owner quizzes us on our nationalities and what we are doing up a mountain on a day like this. The walkers are from Wales, here to tackle the GR10, but the weather has forced them lower. They now face a 15km walk down into Luchon that will surely take them most of the afternoon. I, on the other hand, have a thirty-minute ride, albeit one so cold that I will find my teeth chattering and my fingers numb as I near the bottom. As I down my coffee, bid my farewells and prepare to go on my way, for the first time today I find myself glad I'm on two wheels.

VICENTE
TRUEBA

THE SPANIARD HAD A TENDENCY TO FLY UP CLIMBS BUT THEN LOSE ALL THE TIME HE HAD GAINED GOING DOWN THE OTHER SIDE.

In 1933, Spanish rider Vicente Trueba became the first official winner of the Tour de France's best climber classification, then called the Grand Prix de la Montagne. Small and slight, at only 1.58m (5 feet 2 inches) and 60kg (8 stones 2 pounds), Trueba was ideally suited to the high peaks of the Alps and the Pyrenees. With a terrific turn of speed that he was able to maintain far longer than his rivals, he could climb better than almost anyone, a fact well illustrated by the great Alfredo Binda, five-time winner of the Giro d'Italia, who once chose to describe his own climbing prowess in comparison to that of the Spaniard, saying: "Nobody can stop me in the mountains, not even the legendary Trueba." To have Alfredo Binda describing you as "legendary" was high praise indeed.

Trueba was born in Torrelavega, Cantabria, in 1905. It was an expanding town in a poor, largely rural part of Spain where nothing came without hard graft. The young Trueba worked in the potato fields, and managed eventually to save enough money to buy a bike. With his older brother, José, already riding and encouraging his younger sibling to follow him into the sport, Trueba entered his first race in 1924, aged 19 years. He finished second.

Enthused by his result, he continued to race with his brother and soon their performances were garnering attention. In 1925 Vicente won his first race, the Copa Directivos, which included a number of professional riders. It was here that the first real display of his potential came, with an impressive ascent of the Braguía setting the foundation of his win.

As Vicente progressed, so he began to outshine his brother. Both were to turn professional, Vicente in 1928 and José in 1929, when they rode together as the Cantabra SC. But their fortunes were soon to diverge, with José remaining a professional for just two years.

Wins in 1929 (Circuito Ribera del Jalón) and 1930 (Gran Premi Pascuas), paved the way for Trueba's first Tour de France appearance, when he was selected to ride for the Spanish national team. Although the Spanish team in general did not perform well, with no stage wins and Salvador Cardona their best-placed rider at 16th, Trueba offered glimpses of his climbing talent, notably during stage 16, 331km from Grenoble to Évian, where he rode the slopes of the Col du Galibier in the company of Learco Guerra, Pierre Magne and Benoît Fauré, all of whom were challenging Leducq for the race lead. Trueba would finish 24th in Paris, more than three hours down, but his ability to soar over peaks had captured the attention of the French public, who christened him *La Pulga de Torrelavega* – the Flea of Torrelavega.

Trueba rode the Tour again in 1932, this time as a *touriste-routier*, an independent rider without a team – indeed, Trueba was the only Spaniard in the race. He recorded a string of top-ten stage results on his way to finishing 27th overall, just over two hours behind André Leducq, who took the second of his two Tour victories.

It was in 1933, however, that Trueba would enter the record books of the Tour.

By the time the Tour entered its fourth decade it had been clear for some time that the public had become transfixed by the exploits of the riders in the high mountains. The race organisers were aware that the climbers were winning the hearts of the spectators and so, in 1933, they

devised an official classification for the mountain men – the Grand Prix de la Montagne. With points awarded at the top of each major climb on the route, it was a prize for which Trueba, a terrific climber but a hopeless descender, was ideally placed to challenge. The Spaniard had a tendency to fly up climbs but then lose all the time he had gained going down the other side. His inability to descend quickly meant that he was never able to contest stage wins, because at that time summit finishes had yet to enter the Tour. Understandably, Trueba viewed the new prize with much interest.

AS HE RODE INTO THE PARC DES PRINCES, IN FRONT OF 50,000 PEOPLE, THEY ROSE AND SHOUTED: "BEHOLD THE MORAL VICTOR OF THE TOUR DE FRANCE."

One hundred and twenty riders started the 1933 Tour, which ran clockwise around the country, with the Alps preceding the Pyrenees. Trueba, again riding as an independent, made his intentions clear as soon as the road tilted upwards. On stage 4, as the race tackled the Ballon d'Alsace, the first of that year's twenty big climbs, Trueba went to the head of the bunch and held his position over the summit, grabbing maximum points. On stage 7, from Aix-les-Bains to Grenoble, Trueba again showed his climbing class, leading the peloton over the Télégraphe and the Galibier, before taking maximum points again two days later at the top of the Vars.

But it was in the Pyrenees that Trueba confirmed his superiority in the mountains, claiming top points on the Peyresourde and Aspin (stage 17) and then again on the Tourmalet and Aubisque (stage 18). In all, Trueba claimed maximum points on nine of the major climbs that featured in 1933, winning the inaugural mountains prize with a total of 126 points. The next best-placed rider was Antonin Magne, nearly 50 points behind. Trueba would also record his highest overall finish in the Tour, coming sixth.

Indeed, 1933 could have been even better for Trueba. While the record books show his placing as sixth, back in 1933 there were many who thought he should have been recognised at the race winner. On stage 10, from Digne to Nice, Trueba was one of only four riders to have finished the stage within the time limit, calculated as a percentage of the winning time. Had the normal rules been applied, all the other riders would have been eliminated. However, because of the large numbers affected, the organisers flexed the rules so that the majority of the peloton could be allowed to continue. Trueba finished in Paris as the highest-placed rider of the four that had actually finished within the allotted time, a fact not unnoticed by the public. As he rode into the Parc des Princes, in front of 50,000 people, they rose and shouted: "Behold the moral victor of the Tour de France."

His career never again quite reached the heights of 1933. In the 1934 Tour he picked up two top-three stage placings, finishing tenth overall and second in the mountains competition. A number of top-ten stage finishes in the Vuelta a España followed between 1935 and 1938, then in the following year he retired, returning to the town of his birth to open a restaurant and factory. Both proved to be astute investments.

Vicente Trueba died in 1986, aged 80. Upon his death, Spanish cycling writer Simon Rufo described him as "the forerunner of the great climbers" and, citing Dalmacio Langarica (the winner of the 1946 Vuelta a España), referred to the "Trueba style" – "it was he who caused his opponents to react again and again… and who responded with a new attack and then another and another… to blast away at his pursuers". It's a description that could also be applied to the Tour's most recent Spanish super-climber, Alberto Contador.

VICENTE TRUEBA SELECTED RESULTS:

1929: 1st Circuit Ribera del Jalón
1930: 1st Gran Premi Pascuas
1931: 1st Circuit Ribera del Jalón
1933: 1st mountains classification Tour de France

COL DE MARIE-BLANQUE

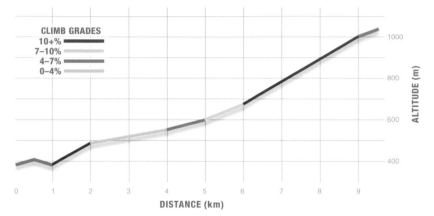

CLIMB GRADES
10+%
7–10%
4–7%
0–4%

ALTITUDE (m)

1000

800

600

400

DISTANCE (km)

For some reason I used to like the Col de Marie-Blanque. Then I rode up it.

I don't know why I liked it. I've never been there before nor have I watched any stages of the Tour tackle it – the climb often features too early in a stage for TV coverage. But I'd read stories about it, looked at pictures of it and for some reason I can't quite fathom it resonated with me. It struck a chord somewhere in my psyche in a way that other, more famous, more iconic climbs didn't. Perhaps it was the name: the Marie-Blanque. To me it has always sounded romantic yet mysterious. I used to imagine that a glamorous woman of yesteryear had tragically fallen from its slopes in suspicious circumstances, bestowing upon the pass the honour of carrying her name forever.

Three kilometres from the top and it's time to reassess my thoughts. I hate the Marie-Blanque.

The western ascent starts in the village of Escot, the eastern ascent from Bielle. As with all passes, I have a choice. Should I start from Bielle, which is closer to my base, or Escot, which would add thirty minutes to my drive and which, though shorter than the eastern side, looked significantly harder?

A quick glance at the history of the climb settled things. If I was to stay true to the spirit of the Tour I would need to ride the western side – of the times the Tour has visited the climb, all but two have ascended from Escot.

•••

I USED TO LIKE THE COL DE MARIE-BLANQUE. THEN I RODE UP IT.

First used in 1978, the Marie-Blanque has been climbed thirteen times by the Tour. Belgian Michel Pollentier led the peloton over the climb that first year, but his Tour was soon to unravel. Pollentier went on to cross the line first at Alpe d'Huez, one week later, to put himself in yellow. However, at the subsequent anti-doping control he was found to have a condom full of "clean" urine strapped to his body, complete with an elaborate system of tubes. In his book *Blazing Saddles*, Matt Rendell describes Pollentier as being "caught like an apprentice bagpiper as he attempted to squeeze urine... into the sample bottle." Pollentier was dumped from the Tour.

In 1987 the Tour scaled the Marie-Blanque not once but twice. On stage 13, 219km from Bayonne to Pau, the route took the peloton over the Col de

START POINT / Escot
START ELEVATION / 327m
FINISH ELEVATION / 1035m
LENGTH OF CLIMB / 9.3km
AVERAGE GRADIENT / 7.6%
MAXIMUM GRADIENT / 11%
FIRST TOUR / 1978
APPEARANCES / 13

Burdincurutcheta, Col de Soudet and then finally the Col de Marie-Blanque.

Over the Soudet, Frenchman Robert Forest led in a solo breakaway. Forest would go on to lead over the Marie-Blanque two years later, but in 1987 he was caught by a pursuing group that contained Erik Breukink, Jean-François Bernard, Pablo Wilches and the pocket-sized Colombian climber Luis "Lucho" Herrera.

I CHECK IF THE TYRES ARE FLAT, I CHECK THE CHAIN. I CHECK EVERYTHING. EVERYTHING IS FINE. IT'S JUST ME THAT'S THE PROBLEM. AND THE ROAD.

With Forest dropped, Herrera, who was fifteen minutes down overall, made a bid to escape on the steep slopes of the Marie-Blanque, but was gradually pulled back near the top. Still, the Colombian had enough energy to take the maximum King of the Mountain points as he went over the climb in first place. With a descent and flat run-in to Pau to come, the slight Herrera was never considered a serious prospect for the stage win, and when he pulled up on the descent of the climb with mechanical problems it looked like he was already out of the reckoning.

But, remarkably, he managed to get back to the leading group, and Herrera, Breukink, Bernard and Wilches were still together as they entered the streets of Pau. Then, with less than one kilometre to go, Breukink launched his attack. No one went with him, leaving him to solo to the win. Behind, the three riders splintered. To the surprise of nobody, Herrera came in fourth out of that leading group. Still, he had picked up valuable mountain points, and in a fortnight's time Herrera would stand on the podium wearing the polka-dot jersey of the King of the Mountains, repeating his 1985 win in that competition.

The next day the route again took the riders over the Marie-Blanque en route to a summit finish at Luz-Ardiden. The stage was won by Dag-Otto Lauritzen of the 7-Eleven-Hoonved team, but for the people of the Pyrenees the day belonged to Gilbert Duclos-Lassalle. Duclos-Lassalle, a future two-time Paris–Roubaix winner, lived in the nearby town of Oloron-Sainte-Marie. He attacked early on the stage, leading the peloton through his home town and over the Marie-Blanque before falling away as he rode towards the Aubisque. Duclos-Lassalle would arrive at Luz-Ardiden over eight minutes down on Lauritzen but would forever be remembered for leading the peloton over his home climb.

•••

The day is hot, humid and sticky. Tonight will bring the first thunderstorms of the summer to the Pyrenees but, as I tackle the first few kilometres, those storms are still brewing. I'm hemmed in by trees on both sides, giving the climb a claustrophobic feel. The going is decidedly slow. The lack of perspective means that, to my eye, the road is barely rising, yet I'm crawling along.

I glance back down the slope. This climb doesn't really feel like a "proper" mountain. Because it's relatively low you don't get the sweeping views that normally come with riding in the mountains. Instead it feels like I'm on a loop, continuously riding up a very long hill back home in Somerset.

As I'm resting I spot another cyclist. So far only one rider has passed me on the way up today, but here comes the second. But he's walking, pushing his bike, beaten by the Marie-Blanque. He nods a greeting and trudges on. I have to admit to a slight glow of satisfaction as I cycle past him a minute or so later. I may have stopped, but I haven't walked.

• • •

In 2006 the Marie-Blanque was the final climb on a 190km stage from Cambo-les-Bains to Pau. In the first big day in the mountains, the Soudet, as in 1987, was to be tackled before the Marie-Blanque.

At the start of the stage Cyril Dessel, who ended his career in 2011 with a handful of victories to his name, had eyes on the polka-dot jersey. He got himself in the day's early break, which quickly became just two riders: himself and Juan-Miguel Mercado. Dessel led over the Soudet but, as the pair descended, they were caught by the remnants of the early breakaway. A group of seven riders were now riding along the valley towards the Marie-Blanque.

Once the group hit the upper slopes of the climb, Dessel attacked. Dragging Mercado with him, Dessel crested the Marie-Blanque in the lead, picking up the maximum points. It was enough to propel the Frenchman into the polka-dot jersey. But it was a jersey he never got to wear.

A by-product of Dessel's escape was a huge lead over the peloton, and in particular Serhiy Honchar, who had

I decide something must be wrong and dismount. I spin the wheels to make sure my brake blocks aren't rubbing (that's happened to me before – I once rode up the Col du Petit Saint-Bernard with my rear brake virtually locked on). I check if the tyres are flat, I check the chain. I check everything. Everything is fine. It's just me that's the problem. And the road.

I ride on, I hear a woodpecker drilling into a tree and consider stopping to look for it (any excuse) but decide against it. I have a feeling I'll be stopping a little bit later on. Two cyclists descending swoop past me with a pitying nod of their heads. They know what lies ahead.

I grind by the 4km-to-go sign. The average gradient for the next kilometre is 11% and it won't drop below that marker for the rest of the way. From this point the Marie-Blanque is unrelenting. There are no hairpins, just long sections of road meandering up the slope through a series of short bends that you can't quite see beyond until you get to them. Every time I approach one of these bends I'm sure that the gradient will relax a bit. Then I go round it and see another impossibly steep stretch.

And it continues to get steeper. At the 2km sign the Marie-Blanque throws more at you. A kilometre of 13%. It's almost too much and, for the first time, I genuinely fear I might not make it. My legs feel hollow and my brain is telling me that it really would be much quicker to walk. But I refuse to give in to this climb. I start to sing a song, just to try to take my mind off the pain but it quickly turns into the incoherent ramblings of the delirious. I stop to rest.

started the day in yellow, almost three minutes ahead of Dessel. Coming off the Marie-Blanque, Dessel and Mercado had gap of over nine minutes on the bunch. Dessel was the better placed of the two riders on the overall classification. All of a sudden his attention switched from the polka-dot jersey to the yellow.

Into the final few kilometres Dessel drove hard, using every ounce of energy in his bid to secure the leader's jersey. At the finish Mercado took the stage win but Dessel had done more than enough to take over the race lead. That night he had two jerseys hung in his room but it was the one coloured yellow that he would wear for the next three days.

● ● ●

After the final kilometre marker the road flattens slightly and I come to another bend. Round this corner

must be the top I think, but no, beyond the corner is actually another steep section of road. With no summit in sight, I unclip my shoes and slump dejectedly onto my handlebars. I just can't believe this climb.

Then the walking cyclist approaches again. "Fini," he says.

I look at him, trying to summon the energy to reply.

"Non," I sigh, and point up the road.

"Ah non, c'est le fini..." And he gestures as if to say that the finish is just round the next corner.

And then, as I remount for one last push, I realise that the walking cyclist knows this climb. He's been here before, he knows what it is like. He knows how tough those last kilometres are and he knows that he'll have to push his bike. Yet still he came back.

I'm not sure I will.

Robert Millar's cycling career was book-ended by national championships: in 1978 he announced his entry into the sport by winning the amateur national road race, and in 1995 he signed off by claiming the elite national title on the Isle of Man. In the seventeen intervening years Millar rewrote the record books for British riders in the Grand Tours. At the Tour the Scot became the first British rider to wear the polka-dot jersey, the first (and to date only) Brit to win the King of the Mountains competition and the first to infiltrate the top five placings. He finished runner-up at the Giro and the Vuelta (twice), recording the highest-ever placing of a British rider in a Grand Tour, a record that stood until matched by Chris Froome at the Vuelta in 2011 and then was finally beaten by Bradley Wiggins at the 2012 Tour.

Born in September 1958, Millar was raised in the tough Gorbals area of Glasgow before the family moved to Pollokshaws on the southern side of the city. In his teens Millar joined the Glenmarnock Wheelers, participating in their weekend rides into the surrounding countryside – "the green bits", as he would call them. It was on these rides that Millar's somewhat solitary nature would reveal itself. In his biography of the rider, *In Search of Robert Millar*, Richard Moore describes the young man wandering away from the group when they stopped for the traditional "drum-up" – the lighting of a fire to brew tea before turning for home – in order to light his own fire.

Having claimed the amateur national title in 1978, Millar headed to the continent, joining the renowned amateur club ACBB (Athlétic Club de Boulogne-Billancourt) for the 1979 season. It was a tough but successful union. With little money and poor relations between the French and foreign riders, life was not easy, but the results flowed and he ended the season with the prize awarded to France's top amateur cyclist.

He turned professional the next year, joining Peugeot, where he stayed for six seasons. During his early years in the professional ranks wins were conspicuous by their absence, a second place overall in the 1982 Tour de l'Avenir being his stand-out result.

ROBERT MILLAR

That all changed in 1983 when he took to the Tour's start line for the first time. Stage 10 that year was the traditional hard Pyrenean day, over the Aubisque, Tourmalet, Aspin and Peyresourde into Bagnères-de-Luchon. Millar found himself in the leading group and then, on the Tourmalet, he escaped with Colombian rider Patrocinio Jiménez, also a Tour novice. Jiménez led over the Tourmalet and Aspin. Then, in the last kilometre of the ascent of the Peyresourde, with Pedro Delgado closing in ominously, Millar attacked. Behind him, Delgado was bearing down, but he couldn't catch the Scot. Millar crossed the line with just six seconds' advantage. The man from Glasgow had triumphed in the highest mountains against the top riders in the race.

The following year came his best Tour, when another stage win in the Pyrenees, at Guzet-Neige, sent him on his way to the King of the Mountains title and fourth overall. He came closest to winning a Grand Tour at the 1985 Vuelta. Millar held a slender lead over Francisco Rodriguez Maldonado, a Colombian, going into the penultimate day of the race, the last real chance for anyone to gain time. There were three climbs to tackle and Millar was with Rodriquez as they finished the day's climbing. All looked set for a Millar win.

But, unbeknown to Millar or his team manager, Pedro Delgado had slipped away. Delgado was over six minutes behind overall but quickly his lead on the bunch grew. No one told Millar what had happened. By the time he realised, Delgado had nearly five minutes. With no team-mates with him and the predominately Spanish pack unwilling to help, Millar was helpless. As the rain fell and the wind blew at the stage finish in Segovia, he crossed the line nearly seven minutes down. Pedro Delgado had won the Vuelta by 36 seconds. "Every one of them was against me," Millar said.

More stage wins at all three Grand Tours followed, as did an overall win at the Critérium du Dauphiné, his greatest stage race victory. Millar rode his last race in 1995, winning the Manx Trophy which, that year, doubled up as the national championships.

He spent a short time working as a coach before disappearing from view. Millar remains out of the public eye, although he resurfaces every once in a while. During the 2012 Tour he wrote a series of insightful articles for the website cyclingnews.com, sharing his unique perspective on Wiggins' ride to glory. After all, he is one of few British riders who knows what it feels like to contend for a Grand Tour.

ROBERT MILLAR SELECTED RESULTS:

1978: 1st amateur national championships
1st Tour of the Peaks

1979: 1st overall Route de France U23
1st amateur national championships

1980: 2nd overall Tour du Vaucluse

1982: 2nd overall Tour de l'Avenir

1983: One stage win Tour de France
2nd overall Critérium du Dauphiné

1984: One stage win, 1st mountains classification and 4th overall Tour de France
One stage win Tour de Romandie

1985: 1st overall Volta Ciclista a Catalunya
2nd overall Vuelta a España

1986: 2nd overall and one stage win Vuelta a España

1987: 2nd overall, 1st mountains classification and one stage win Giro d'Italia
One stage win Tour Méditerranéen

1988: 3rd Liège–Bastogne–Liège

1989: One stage win Tour de France
One stage win Critérium du Dauphiné
One stage win Tour de Romandie
1st overall Tour of Britain

1990: 1st overall Critérium du Dauphiné
One stage win Tour de Romandie

1991: One stage win Tour de Suisse

1993: 2nd overall Vuelta a los Valles Mineros

1995: 1st national championships

HAUTACAM

START POINT / Ayros-Arbouix
START ELEVATION / 487m
FINISH ELEVATION / 1520m
LENGTH OF CLIMB / 14.4km
AVERAGE GRADIENT / 7.2%
MAXIMUM GRADIENT / 11%
FIRST TOUR / 1994
APPEARANCES / 4

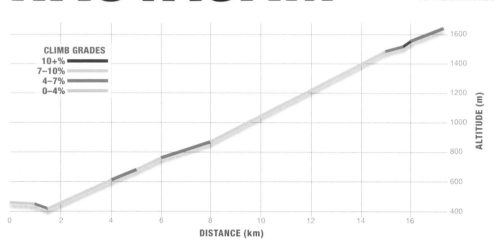

CLIMB GRADES
10+%
7–10%
4–7%
0–4%

ALTITUDE (m)

DISTANCE (km)

There's always someone, isn't there? Someone who'll take your achievement and trump it. Someone who will make you reflect on what you've done and question quite why you were so proud of it. Whether they mean to or not.

Take today, for example. There I am, happily descending from Hautacam after a torrid ride up – a ride that had me sweating so much that my hands kept slipping off the handlebars; a ride that had my heartbeat echoing in my head and left my legs so bereft of feeling that I collapsed on the grass at the top – when who do I see riding up the other way, but a man on a bike, towing his child in a trailer. Yes, where most parents might opt to take their young ones out for a ride along a canal towpath, this guy opts for the Hautacam, one of the toughest mountain ascents in the Pyrenees. I can't quite believe it when he waves cheerily as he passes.

A few moments later and here's his wife. She is towing a trailer full of camping equipment and has two dogs on leads. She waves as well, happy as can be.

Yes, there's always someone who'll see your ride and raise it.

• • •

Hautacam has featured on the Tour itinerary on only four occasions, but it has always brought drama, and not only during the stages that have been fought out on its strenuous slopes. It has winners with amazing stories of adversity overcome, winners who come with a whiff of scandal, and winners who come complete with whole stink-bombs of shame.

The first winner on Hautacam was Luc Leblanc in 1994. It was the first mountain stage on that year's itinerary and it was a long one: 263.5km.

As the riders hit the early slopes of Hautacam, a five-man breakaway was caught, having been chased down by the Spanish ONCE team. The peloton was not complete for long, for almost as soon as the break had been caught, Italian climber Marco Pantani, who had swapped bikes in preparation for the climb, sped off up the road. With the 1994 Tour particularly mountainous (it featured seven tough mountain stages and five summit finishes, one of which would eliminate nearly half the field until race organisers waived the time-limit), Pantani, an expert in the mountains, was a real threat to the yellow jersey of Miguel Indurain, who was looking for his fourth straight Tour win.

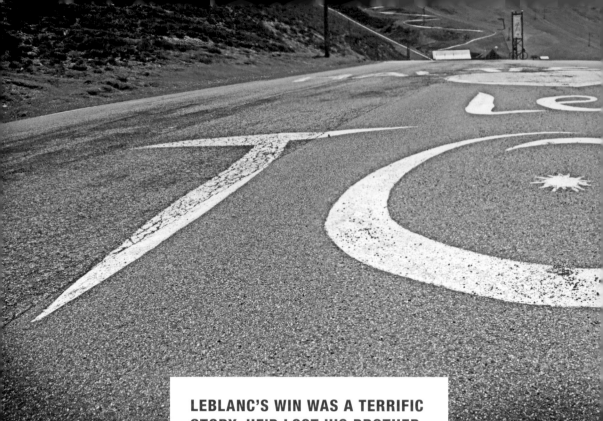

LEBLANC'S WIN WAS A TERRIFIC STORY. HE'D LOST HIS BROTHER AT A YOUNG AGE, WHEN BOTH OF THEM WERE HIT BY A CAR WHILE OUT CYCLING. THE ACCIDENT LEFT LEBLANC UNABLE TO WALK AND WITH ONE LEG SHORTER THAN THE OTHER.

So Indurain launched the pursuit of the Italian, leading a group of about twenty riders halfway up the climb before his speed split them all over the mountain. Pantani had a lead of 26 seconds with 5km to go, but it was not enough. Indurain, setting a ferocious pace, with Festina rider Luc Leblanc on his wheel, continued to make inroads into the Italian's lead.

As the riders entered the mist that covered the upper slopes of the mountain, and with Leblanc now helping Indurain, the pair finally caught Pantani. And then the roles were reversed. No sooner had they caught the Italian than Leblanc powered past Indurain. Now it was Leblanc alone at the front, and Pantani on Indurain's wheel trying to chase him down. By the time the riders reached the 1km banner, Indurain had caught Leblanc and dropped Pantani. The fight was on for the stage win, with Indurain pulling out all the stops, his face contorted in pain, sweat coursing down his face.

In the final metres, though, Leblanc came around the Spaniard to cross the fog-bound finish line first. It was Leblanc's first Tour stage win (he would win again in 1996 at Les Arcs, ironically the stage in which Indurain's reign was finally ended by Bjarne Riis), but Indurain retained yellow and would go on to win the Tour.

Leblanc's win was a terrific story. He'd lost his brother at a young age, when both of them were hit by a car while out cycling. The accident left Leblanc unable to walk and with one leg shorter than the other. Eventually he learned to walk again and incredibly managed to forge a career in cycling. That's the triumph over adversity bit. Then came the scandal. In 1998 he became embroiled in the Festina affair (see p179) and in 2000 admitted to using performance-enhancing drugs during his time with Festina. He would not be the only one with a chequered history to win on Hautacam. Far from it.

So it is that, five minutes later, I cross the river and start the long haul up to Hautacam, with an overstuffed rucksack on my back.

• • •

Enthralled by the dramatic racing in 1994, the Tour returned to Hautacam just two years later. In 1996 it was the turn of Bjarne Riis to win, en route to his sole Tour triumph. A win he would later confess was fuelled by the performance-enhancing drug EPO.

At the time it was seen as an incredible performance by the Dane. He attacked not once, not twice but three times on the lower slopes. Each strike gradually whittled down the lead group until there was no one left who could go with him. On two occasions he deliberately slowed, so he could survey the damage he was doing, before making his way back to the front with consummate ease and then attacking again. After the last of his attacks he was left with just three riders tracking him. Then Riis just systematically rode them off his wheel. No sudden acceleration, just a gradual ramping up of speed that took him away from everyone and on to victory. He would win the stage by 49 seconds and the yellow jersey in Paris, 1 minute 41 seconds ahead of his team-mate and 1997 winner, Jan Ullrich. Years later it would become a triumph tarnished, when Riis held a press conference in Copenhagen and admitted taking EPO and other drugs. "My [yellow] jersey is at home in a cardboard box," he said. "They are welcome to come and get it."

• • •

I'd been warned about Hautacam. The reading that I'd done had uncovered a common theme – that I shouldn't be fooled by the profile of the climb, or the quoted average gradient of 7.2%. This is one testing mountain, with gradients varying wildly all the way to the summit. Its fearsome reputation was confirmed when I met Paddy Sweeney, who owns a cycling company in Saint-Savin, close to a number of Pyrenean giants. I asked him which he considered to be the toughest climb in the Pyrenees. "Hautacam," he said, without hesitation.

I park in the town of Argelès-Gazost, just across the Gave river from the climb. As I am busy preparing myself and the bike, a man pulls up in his car, digs around in the passenger footwell and brings out an armful of spare parts. He then proceeds to try to convince me to buy some of them, telling me that they are far less expensive than what I'll find in any shop. On the back seat, his kids are eyeballing the contents of my car boot. Eventually he goes away. It's possibly all very innocent. Perhaps he just drives around the town pouncing on cyclists, of which there are many, trying to flog them stuff they don't need. Whatever the case may be, I spend a paranoid ten minutes wondering if he's going to come back when I'm gone and break into my car. I really don't want to pack the bike up and re-park, so there's really only one answer – to take anything of value with me.

After days of rain and murky riding conditions, today is a complete contrast. I'm cycling underneath pure blue skies without a hint of wind. The sun illuminates the surrounding peaks and, as the road makes its way up the west side of the mountain, I'm rewarded with great views of Argelès-Gazost, the Luz valley and the mountains beyond, towards the Col du Soulor.

The first part of the climb takes me through some small and attractive villages. Arbouix, Souin and Artalens all go by, providing a least some distraction from the pain that my legs are beginning to feel. With 5km still to go, I'm in some difficulty. I've been in my lowest gear since the start of the climb but it feels like every revolution of the pedals is driving an over-sized cog made of lead. I look down just to make sure I really am in the lowest gear. Unfortunately, I am.

• • •

The Tour visited Hautacam for the third time in 2000. Again the stage was the first summit finish of the race and again the rider who wore the yellow jersey at the end of it (Lance Armstrong) would go on to stand on the top step in Paris.

The winner, though, was Spaniard Javier Otxoa. In dreadful conditions he managed to get in an early breakaway and then rode on alone on the slopes of the Col d'Aubisque. Riding for the Kelme team, Otxoa just managed to stay away for the win in front of the rampaging Armstrong, who was riding into yellow behind him.

RIIS HELD A PRESS CONFERENCE IN COPENHAGEN AND ADMITTED TAKING EPO AND OTHER DRUGS. "MY [YELLOW] JERSEY IS AT HOME IN A CARDBOARD BOX," HE SAID. "THEY ARE WELCOME TO COME AND GET IT."

The next year, in an eerie echo of what had happened as a child to Luc Leblanc, the first winner on Hautacam, Otxoa and his brother Ricardo were hit by a car while on a training ride. Ricardo lost his life and Javier suffered massive injuries to his head and chest, lying in a coma for nearly five weeks. Eventually he recovered enough to compete in the Athens 2004 and Beijing 2008 Paralympics, going on to win two gold medals and two silvers. Once more a Hautacam winner had triumphed over adversity.

But then, in 2008, as in 1994 and 1996, Hautacam would once more provide a winner whose reputation was to be ruined by drugs. This time it was Leonardo Piepoli of Saunier Duval.

Part of a small leading group on the early slopes of the climb, Piepoli jumped on to the wheel of Fränk Schleck when Schleck attacked with about 10km to go. Piepoli was then joined by team-mate Juan Jose Cobo, and together they worked over Schleck, finally distancing him. The two Saunier Duval riders rode the

rest of the climb alone, Cobo sitting back to allow Piepoli to take the win. The day ended with a one-two for the Spanish team, with another of their riders, Ricardo Riccò, in the polka-dot jersey.

However, everything was soon to come crashing down around the team. Just three days later the team withdrew from the race after Riccò had tested positive for CERA, a form of EPO. The following day, the team sacked both Riccò and Piepoli. In October it was confirmed that Piepoli had tested positive at the Tour for the same product as Riccò. In 2009 he admitted he had used CERA in "a moment of weakness". He then urged others not to follow his path saying: "Don't dope because you'd trample on your conscience and dignity. Forever."

• • •

I start to ignore the kilometre markers. Pretty much all the way up they've been stating averages of 8–10%. More often or not they appear on relatively flat or modest uphill sections. If you're riding on a flat section and pass a sign that says the next kilometre averages 10%, that can only mean one thing – that a world of pain is literally just around the corner. And that's what happens on Hautacam. Rather too often for my liking.

So instead I just give myself small goals to reach. It's the only way I can deal with it. "I'll just get to that butterfly sunbathing, now just to that stone by the side, now to that squashed *something…* " and so on as I inch my way up the road.

This tactic gets me through some really difficult riding between the 5km and 2km markers. It's then that I realise that although there are only 2km left of this climb, there appears to be no sight of the ski resort.

I follow a hairpin round to the left. Above me, about 500m away through a series of steep ramps, I can now see the 1km marker. Away to my right I glimpse a small building. I don't know it yet, but that building *is* the ski resort of Hautacam.

Just a thousand metres left to go but every fibre of my body is screaming at me to stop. My tongue is hanging out as I gasp for air. Eventually I drag myself to the top, finally ending the torture, I muster the strength to dismount and collapse on the ground, exhausted. I lie there all alone for some minutes, wondering if a rucksack full of clothing, tools, cameras, phones and sat-nav systems could double up as a nice soft pillow for a while.

Hautacam is a stunning climb. Hard but rewarding. Let's hope that the next winner atop this demanding yet beautiful mountain listens to what Piepoli said in 2009, because Hautacam deserves more deserving winners.

LUIS OCAÑA

If luck had been on his side, Luis Ocaña's career could have turned out very differently. Instead of a single Tour victory, one Vuelta a España title and a handful of other stage-race successes, he could have ended up a multiple Tour champion. He amassed a list of wins that would be the envy of the vast majority of professional peloton, but Ocaña could have had so much more. His was a life beset by poor luck and tragedy. A life that was ended by his own hand, when he was just 48 years old.

Luis Ocaña Pernia was born in 1945 in Priego, central Spain, to a poor family. His mother and father sometimes struggled to put food on the table for the young Luis and his three siblings. As his sister Amparo recalled: "At teatime my mother would lock us inside the house so we wouldn't see the other kids eating."

In search of better times, Ocaña's family moved over the border to France. There Luis discovered he had a talent for cycling and realised that a career on the bike represented his best chance of escaping poverty. His father disapproved, but Ocaña persisted despite the obstacles thrown up by his family, and at the age of 17, while working as a carpenter, he started to race. Two years later he applied to join Stade Montois, a renowned amateur club. Pierre Cescutti, president of the club and a figure who would guide Ocaña throughout his career, found him a room and job in Mont de Marsan, the club's home town, and in 1965 Ocaña began riding in a Stade Montois jersey.

Over the next couple of years Ocaña forged a reputation as a good climber and a strong time trial rider, recording a string of good results, both regionally and nationally. His stand-out result as an amateur came in 1967 when he won the amateur version of the Grand Prix des Nations.

HE AMASSED A LIST OF WINS THAT WOULD BE THE ENVY OF THE VAST MAJORITY OF PROFESSIONAL PELOTON, BUT OCAÑA COULD HAVE HAD SO MUCH MORE.

That, coupled with a sixth place in the difficult Grand Prix du Midi-Libre stage race, led to an offer from the Spanish Fagor-Fargas team for the 1968 season. Ocaña had achieved what he had dreamt of – he was now a professional cyclist.

Wins in national championships and week-long stage races followed, as well as stage victories at the Vuelta a España. In 1970, now riding for the Bic team, he took the overall win at the Vuelta as well as the prestigious Critérium du Dauphiné.

Ocaña soon became one of the few riders that cycling's colossus, Eddy Merckx, genuinely feared. As his career developed, Ocaña took it upon himself to challenge the all-conquering Merckx, even naming his dog after the great champion so he could boss "Merckx" around. But ill-fortune and ill-health would prevent the Spaniard from ever truly dethroning the Belgian. He came closest in the 1971 Tour, when a devastating attack in the Alps put him in the lead by over eight minutes, only for a terrible crash to force him out of the race (see p88).

The 1972 Tour de France was set to be a great showdown between the two, who indulged in a nasty war of words in the run-up to the race. Both were in good form: Merckx had just taken his third Giro d'Italia and Ocaña his second Critérium du Dauphiné.

The Tour entered the Pyrenees on stage 7, with Ocaña just 51 seconds behind Merckx. Once more bad luck came Ocaña's way and he fell while descending the Soulor in rain. He picked himself up, making it to the finish just under two minutes behind the Belgian. Theoretically he was still in contention, with seven more mountain

stages to come, but the crash had taken its toll. Ocaña contracted a lung infection and steadily began to lose time. By the end of stage 14 he was more than twelve minutes behind. Finally worn down by illness and the ravages of the world's toughest race, Ocaña abandoned.

Ocaña's greatest moment came in 1973, when he won the Tour. He stated his intentions early, when he joined a stage 3 breakaway on the cobble-stoned flatlands of northern France (hardly his favoured terrain), and unexpectedly gained more than two minutes on his rivals. It wasn't enough

to give him the yellow jersey but it set him up nicely for the mountains.

Sure enough, after the first day of climbing, Ocaña had taken control of the race. But it was on day two in the Alps that he tightened his grip. Stage 8 was a monster, taking the riders over the Madeleine, Télégraphe, Galibier and Izoard en route to a summit finish at Les Orres. At the start Ocaña held a lead approaching three minutes. By the time his work was done at Les Orres, his lead would have trebled.

IN ALL OCAÑA WOULD WIN SIX STAGES IN 1973 AND WIN BY NEARLY SIXTEEN MINUTES. IT WAS AN ALL-CONQUERING DISPLAY, WITH MORE THAN A HINT OF MERCKX ABOUT IT.

Ocaña's biggest rival that day would turn out to be fellow Spanish climber José-Manuel Fuente. On the slopes of the Télégraphe, Fuente tried to distance Ocaña and the other leaders, including Frenchman Bernard Thévenet. With 6km to go to the summit of the Galibier, Fuente attacked again, this time decisively. Only Ocaña could match him, and the two progressed alone at the head of the race. By the top of the Galibier they had opened a gap of more than one minute.

The two rode together over the Izoard, but Fuente was now refusing to share the work with Ocaña, content instead to merely shadow the yellow jersey. On the climb to Les Orres, Fuente suffered a puncture and Ocaña sprinted to take the stage win by a little under a minute. Only five riders arrived within fifteen minutes of him. His overall lead was now more than nine minutes, with Fuente – who had started the day outside the top ten – now lying second.

In all Ocaña would win six stages in 1973 and win by nearly sixteen minutes. It was an all-conquering display, with more than a hint of Merckx about it. The only caveat? Merckx wasn't there, choosing instead to ride the tours of Italy and Spain (where he beat Ocaña by over three minutes). Ocaña had won the Tour, but he still hadn't vanquished the mighty Belgian.

Ocaña retired to his farm with his wife Josiane in 1977, having never again reached the heights of his 1973 season. He continued to suffer ill-health during his retirement and was diagnosed with hepatitis C, then with cancer. He drank heavily, and on May 19th 1994, with certain death from his illnesses not far away, Luis Ocaña took a gun, went into his office and shot himself.

LUIS OCAÑA SELECTED RESULTS:

1967: 1st amateur Grand Prix des Nations

1968: 1st national championships
Three stage wins Vuelta a Andalucía

1969: Mountains prize, 2nd overall and three stage wins Vuelta a España
1st overall Grand Prix du Midi-Libre

1970: One stage win Tour de France
1st overall and one stage win Critérium du Dauphiné
1st overall and two stage wins Vuelta a España
2nd overall Paris–Nice

1971: Two stage wins Tour de France
1st overall and one stage win Volta Ciclista a Catalunya
1st overall and one stage win Vuelta Ciclista al País Vasco
1st Grand Prix des Nations

1972: 1st national championships
1st overall and two stage wins Critérium du Dauphiné

1973: 1st overall and six stage wins Tour de France
1st overall Critérium du Dauphiné
1st overall and one stage win Vuelta Ciclista al País Vasco
1st overall and one stage win Setmana Catalana de Ciclismo

1974: 3rd overall Vuelta Ciclista al País Vasco

1975: One stage win Vuelta Ciclista a la Rioja
One stage win Vuelta a Andalucía (Ruta del Sol)

1976: 2nd overall Vuelta a España
3rd overall Paris–Nice

LUZ-ARDIDEN

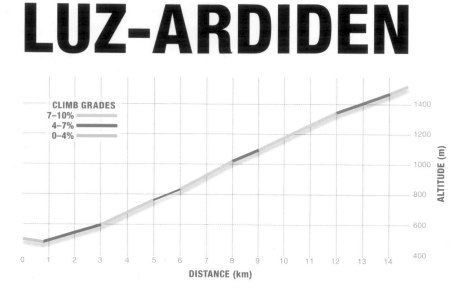

CLIMB GRADES
7–10%
4–7%
0–4%

ALTITUDE (m)

DISTANCE (km)

Apparently, the views on the climb to the tiny ski resort of Luz-Ardiden are spectacular, offering vistas of valleys, mountain towns and magnificent Pyrenean peaks. I know because when I was preparing for my ride I read numerous comments and reports to that effect. Here's an example, from the website bestofthepyrenees.com: "[Luz-Ardiden] offers soaring eagle's-eye views of the town and valley of Luz-St-Sauveur." And another from "Cumbrian Cyclist" on climbbybike.com: "When the climb opens out the views are fantastic."

I've absolutely no reason to doubt those accounts, but I'm afraid that I can't confirm them for you. You see, my ride was undertaken in thick cloud and mist. To put it mildly, visibility was poor. If I hadn't passed a sign every kilometre informing me that I was still on the road to Luz-Ardiden, and that the gradient was still going to be punishing, I could have been anywhere.

• • •

The climb was introduced by the Tour in 1985, the year that French legend Bernard Hinault was riding to become only the third man to win the race five times. And the stage to Luz-Ardiden was the first of three days in the Pyrenees that were to play a huge part in Hinault's quest.

Hinault had taken yellow at the end of the first week, following a devastating display in the long time trial to Strasbourg, but as the race approached the Pyrenees disaster struck: in the closing moments of stage 14 into Saint-Étienne, Hinault was involved in a high-speed crash that left him with a broken nose and a couple of black eyes.

Battered and bruised, Hinault set off for Luz-Ardiden with a lead of 3 minutes 38 seconds over his team-mate Greg LeMond. Over the penultimate climb of the day, the Tourmalet, Hinault was struggling: barely able to breathe, he trailed LeMond by 1 minute 18 seconds. It was a torturous ascent for the Breton rider, but Hinault was never a quitter.

On to the climb of Luz-Ardiden. LeMond and Stephen Roche, who was third overall, still held a lead over Hinault. On the early slopes LeMond was feeling powerful and thought that he could overhaul Pedro Delgado, who was up the road leading the stage. What happened next was one of the Tour's great controversies.

According to LeMond, he was told by his team that Hinault was only forty seconds behind and that he was to wait for him. But Hinault wasn't forty seconds behind. The gap was more like three minutes. In an interview with Bryan Malessa, LeMond recounted:

START POINT / Luz-Saint-Saveur
START ELEVATION / 736m
FINISH ELEVATION / 1720m
LENGTH OF CLIMB / 13.3km
AVERAGE GRADIENT / 7.4%
MAXIMUM GRADIENT / 10%
FIRST TOUR / 1985
APPEARANCES / 8

"Paul Köchli [the team director], came up and started talking to me, saying 'You cannot ride with Roche, you can't attack. Hinault's coming up. You need to wait for him. We want to insure our first and second place'... So I waited... I wait and I wait... I wait and I wait... By the time I finished the stage, he was still a minute and fifteen seconds down and I'd waited minutes for him!"

As LeMond sees it, the decision of the team cost him a first Tour victory. Perhaps not surprisingly, Köchli tells it differently. In Richard Moore's book *Slaying the Badger*, Köchli tells Moore that LeMond had been given the green light to attack, so long as he definitely dropped Roche – but LeMond didn't then attack. Köchli draws the conclusion that LeMond didn't feel strong enough to distance Roche.

Whatever the truth of what happened on the first visit to the slopes of Luz-Ardiden, LeMond and Roche exited the Pyrenees still trailing Hinault, who would go on to win his fifth Tour.

• • •

My climb to Luz-Ardiden was an uncomfortable one. Low cloud hung just above me as I set off, and as soon as I was through the village of Sazos I was riding in dense mist. With visibility reduced to 50m or less, I could only concentrate on the road right ahead of me. I could see nothing else, no summits, no valleys, no meadows, nothing. Just the road and the trees that flanked it. It was spooky and silent. I only saw one person, a farmer cutting branches from trees. His debris was all over the road, blocking it. My appearance out of the mist startled him and he quickly had to clear a way through with a nod of apology.

• • •

Like Hinault in 1985, Lance Armstrong was in the middle of his bid to win five Tours when the race came to Luz-Ardiden in 2003. Like Hinault, Armstrong had

STILL AHEAD WAS ULLRICH. DECISION TIME. HIS HEAD MUST HAVE BEEN SCREAMING AT HIM TO STOMP ON THE PEDALS AND RIDE TO TOUR GLORY, WHILE HIS HEART WAS TELLING HIM THAT CYCLING ETIQUETTE DEMANDED HE WAIT.

secured the yellow jersey at the end of the first week. And like Hinault he was having a torrid time defending it.

The day after taking yellow Armstrong only just avoided crashing with Joseba Beloki as they were chasing an escape by Alexandre Vinokourov on the descent of the third-category Rochette. Beloki, who had finished on the Tour podium in 2000, 2001 and 2002, hit the road hard, breaking his leg and wrist. He was never the same rider again. For his part, Armstrong was forced off the tarmac and took a detour over a field before rejoining the race. It was a narrow escape.

Then, in the time trial between Gaillac and Cap Découverte, a stage he would have expected to dominate, Armstrong was beaten by the man he feared most – Jan Ullrich. Ullrich took more than 90 seconds out of the American, jumping up the classification from sixth to second. Ullrich eked out more time the following day, as did Vinokourov the next. The result was that, as the Tour headed up to Luz-Ardiden, just 18 seconds separated the top three riders: Armstrong, Ullrich and Vinokourov.

Stage 15 took the riders to Luz-Ardiden via the Aspin and Tourmalet. A series of attacks over the Tourmalet had softened the Texan up. The leaders were back together by the time they reached the final climb but Armstrong had already expended considerable effort. For the first time in five years he looked vulnerable.

When the first attack came it was not from Ullrich but instead from the Spanish climber Iban Mayo, who was four-and-a-half minutes behind the yellow jersey. Armstrong snuffed that one out, with Ullrich on his wheel. Then he went himself. Armstrong gained a few metres but Ullrich and Mayo looked to have the move comfortably covered when Armstrong got his handlebars caught in a spectator's bag and fell heavily, taking Mayo with him. Ullrich just avoided the crash and carried on. The road ahead was clear for the German to launch his own attack and make a bid for

Tour victory. Behind, Armstrong and Mayo clambered to their feet and remounted. A team-mate, José Luis Rubiera, arrived at Armstrong's side to pace him back. Then Armstrong's shoe came out of its pedal, causing a painful-looking collision between groin and top tube. Still ahead was Ullrich. Decision time. His head must have been screaming at him to stomp on the pedals and ride to Tour glory, while his heart was telling him that cycling etiquette demanded he wait.

Ullrich's heart won out. The German waited, along with the rest of the leaders. Eventually Armstrong came back to the group, towed to the front by Rubiera. Then, after a brief period of calm, the skirmishes continued. Again Mayo attacked. Again Armstrong negated the move and then launched his own. Fuelled by the adrenaline still coursing through him after his crash, Armstrong's acceleration unhinged Ullrich easily. With Mayo still tracking him, the Texan ramped up the pace, riding the Spaniard off his wheel.

His face rigid with determination, Armstrong danced his way up the slopes of Luz-Ardiden, riding with such ferocity that he brought back the lone leader, Sylvain Chavanel, who at one point had enjoyed a gap of nearly four minutes on the climb. Armstrong rode up to Chavanel, patted him on the back, and zipped off up the mountain.

On one of the Tour's most dramatic days, Armstrong went on to win the stage by 40 seconds. Six days later he won his fifth Tour by just 1 minute and 1 second over the German. Without that fall on Luz-Ardiden and the subsequent surge of aggression, it is a strong possibility that Armstrong would not have stood on the top step in Paris in 2003.

● ● ●

The road continued all the way to the summit at a fairly consistent pitch. I found it more difficult than I expected. Maybe it was the disappointment of having to ride in those conditions, maybe it was the absence of any other defining features, but for me Luz-Ardiden was a bit of a drag.

I had been looking forward to the last four kilometres of this climb. While the pretty much the whole route is a series of hairpins, the last few kilometres open up, allowing you to view in full the sequence of switchbacks that you've negotiated to reach the top. I'd seen pictures of it and I was eagerly anticipating seeing it for myself. Unfortunately, the low cloud meant it was not to be.

At last the top came. Sheep milled about as I took a quick look before heading back down into the murk. It was not a day to be hanging around. I noticed what looked like new chairlifts, a children's snow park and a toboggan run. It seemed that every available bit of space had something mechanical bolted to it. As far as I could see (which admittedly was not very far) there was nothing left untouched here. Nothing natural. Maybe it feels different when you can see the full splendour of the surrounding mountains.

I left feeling a little deflated. It had been a hard ride with little to show for it in terms of memories. Then, on the way back down, I spotted a marmot for the first time. It looked at me nervously before dashing back inside its burrow, only to emerge again, cautiously eyeing my every move. I stopped and watched it for a while. Even on the gloomiest, most depressing of days in the mountains, something always happens to lighten the mood.

BERNARD
HINAULT

WHO STOOD WITH A CHIN OF GRANITE, SHOULDERS BROAD AND PROUD, HANDS CLASPED BEHIND HIS BACK, HEAD HELD HIGH IN DEFIANCE? HINAULT, OF COURSE.

For me, if there is one image that captures the essence of Bernard Hinault, it comes from the 1978 Tour. But it is not a picture of him racing.

The peloton was not happy during the 1978 Tour. Spread over 25 days, the race had a number of two-stage days, meaning the riders were early to the day's first start line and late under its final finishing banner. That, coupled with the poor timing of some long transfers, had left the riders angry. It all came to a head at Valence d'Agen. Having already started one 158km stage that morning, the riders faced another 96km stage into Toulouse, followed by a 200km transfer to the next day's start in Figeac. It was too much. A riders' strike was called.

This was Hinault's first Tour. He was fast gaining a fearsome reputation, having already won the Critérium du Dauphiné, Liège–Bastogne–Liège and the Vuelta a España, but so far his record in the Tour was a blank page. He was a Tour virgin.

But he didn't act like one. As the day's first stage approached the finish town of Valence d'Agen, the riders dismounted and just stood there. And who was at the head of proceedings? Who stood with a chin of granite, shoulders broad and proud, hands clasped behind his back, head held high in defiance? Hinault, of course. While the other riders are pictured milling around, hands on hips, having a chat, fiddling with caps and peering over one another's shoulders to see what's going on, there is Hinault: dressed in the jersey of the French national champion, rock-steady, mouth folded into a picture of grim determination, an immovable object.

Although Hinault would later deny he was the ringleader, it was the first demonstration of his absolute authority over the Tour. And he was still only 23 years old. Hinault would go on to stand on the final podium, dressed in yellow for the first time. It was something he would repeat on another four occasions. It was also the first of three Grand Tour doubles (he had already won the Vuelta in April – the Vuelta didn't move to its current August slot until 1995). Yes, in 1978, a new *patron* of the peloton had arrived.

The young Hinault was raised in Brittany. Born in 1954, he showed early athletic promise, initially as a runner. Eventually he switched to the bike, winning his first race and impressing on the local scene. Aged 17 he went national, winning the junior championships in 1972, adding his name to a list that included Raphaël Géminiani, a multiple Tour stage winner and two-time podium finisher.

A move to the professional ranks came in October 1974, when he joined Lucien Van Impe's Sonolor-Gitane team, having finished second in the U23 Route de France. A first win in a stage race followed a year later (Circuit Cycliste Sarthe) and was backed up in 1976 with wins in both the Tour du Limousin and the Tour de l'Aude.

Hinault's breakthrough into the top league came in 1977, when he won the one day classic races Gent–Wevelgem and Liège–Bastogne–Liège, as well as the Critérium du Dauphiné stage race. Hinault was gaining a reputation as a tough rider who could duke it out on the short, snappy climbs of northern Europe, as well as more than hold his own on the longer, more gradual ascents of the higher mountains. And he was no slouch in a time-trial either, winning the 1977 edition of the Grand Prix des Nations.

Hinault could do it all and so it was no surprise when he won his first Grand Tour at the 1978 Vuelta and followed it by winning his maiden Tour de France just two months later. Hinault wore the yellow jersey for the first time just three days before Paris, after winning the mammoth 72km time trial between Metz and Nancy by over one minute and turning a 14-second deficit to race leader Joop Zoetemelk into a 3 minute 56 second advantage by the time night fell. That margin would remain exactly the same in Paris. Afterwards Hinault said: "I feel so good I could race another three months like that, I'm feeling better and better every day." It was a prophetic indication of the stranglehold he was about to have on the Tour and the sport in general.

Those three days that Hinault spent in yellow in 1978 were the first of a total of 78 that he spent in the leader's jersey over the course of nine years. His best year was 1981 when, after having to retire from the 1980 edition with a knee injury, he returned with a vengeance, winning the opening time trial, briefly relinquishing the race lead for five days when his team was beaten in the team time trial, before grabbing it back on stage 7. He then held it for the final 18 days in a row. He won every individual

time trial that year as well as the stage from Bourg d'Oisans to Le Pleynet, over five categorised alpine climbs. His overall winning margin over his former team-mate Van Impe was more than 14 minutes.

While his exploits in the Grand Tours ensured he would be ranked only below Eddy Merckx in the number of wins to his name (Hinault has ten compared to Merckx's eleven), some of Hinault's greatest rides came away from the rigours of three-week stage races.

HE SPED ON, OVER PERILOUSLY ICY ROADS, ALL THE WAY TO LIÈGE. HIS TEAM-MATES, HAVING LONG SINCE ABANDONED, WATCHED AGHAST FROM THE COMFORTS OF THEIR HOTEL AS THEIR LEADER REWROTE THE HISTORY BOOKS.

Three races, held over the course of two years, perhaps define the mental and physical toughness of the Breton rider, the man who would become known as the Badger, that most tenacious of animals, better than any other.

The 1980 edition of Liège–Bastogne–Liège has gone down in history as one of the toughest one-day classics ever held. The race, known as La Doyenne, or the old lady, is the oldest of all the classics (it was first held in 1892), but its riders have rarely experienced the conditions that greeted them that April morning in 1980.

Things got underway in the middle of a blizzard. Hinault soon dropped back to announce he was quitting, before being convinced by his team to tough it out until the race turned at Bastogne. Other riders were not so hardy and were abandoning in droves. Over half had gone with little over an hour raced. Pretty soon many teams barely had a single rider left, leaving the organisers concerned that they would soon be without a race. Hinault struggled on, reached Bastogne and, revealing his true spirit, began the homeward leg.

The Frenchman found himself leading a small group up the Stockeu, a couple of minutes behind the leader Rudy Pévenage. Hinault was freezing, but with 80km still to ride he ramped up his pace and went out alone. By the next climb he had passed Pévenage. Hinault was leading the race.

He sped on, over perilously icy roads, all the way to Liège. His team-mates, having long since abandoned, watched aghast from the comforts of their hotel as their leader rewrote the history books. Enduring some of the worst conditions ever faced in a bike race, Hinault rode into Liège alone to win by nearly ten minutes. It took him weeks to recover the sensation in his index and middle fingers, and it has been reported that even today he still has no feeling in one of his fingers. That only 21 of the 174 riders who started the race made it to the finish pays testimony enough to Hinault's heroics.

Later that same year, Hinault was again at the forefront. This time in one of the toughest world championships the sport has ever seen. The 1980 world championships were held in Sallanches, in the French Alps. The 268km route took the riders over the Côte de Domancy twenty times. A short 2.5km climb it might be, but it has a maximum gradient of 16% and was to act as the springboard for a number of attacks.

The opening laps brought a flurry of attacks, counter-attacks and breakaways. However, by the time the race started the thirteenth of the 20 laps, the favourites were all together and the main action was about to start. An attack by Belgium's Michel Pollentier was marked by Hinault. They were joined by two Italian riders and a Dutch rider, Johan van der Velde. Over the course of the next six laps the formation of the breakaway changed until, with one lap remaining, just two riders were left at the front: Hinault and Italy's Gianbattista Baronchelli.

The final lap was a cagey affair, with Hinault leading and constantly looking back over his shoulder at his Italian companion. Baronchelli barely shared any of the work, either unwilling or unable to help. The French crowds were out in force, desperate to see one of their riders win the world title for the first time in eighteen years and, to their sheer delight, on the last section of the climb, just where the road ramped up, Hinault went alone.

"*Et voilà!* Now he attacks! Attack! Bernard Hinault!" shouted the TV commentator as the Badger growled his way up the final climb. Baronchelli couldn't respond and in no time at all Hinault had opened an unassailable lead. The noise from the thousands lining the road rose into a crescendo. "Hinault! Hinault! Hinault!" they chanted as their hero rode into history under leaden alpine skies.

Hinault crossed the line in 7 hours 32 minutes and 16 seconds, just over one minute ahead of Baronchelli. Of the 107 riders that took to the start line, only fifteen finished.

If those two races in 1980 demonstrated his physical strength, then his capacity to be mentally strong, to pick himself up off the floor when all seemed lost, was ably illustrated the following spring, when he won the Paris–Roubaix.

Following his triumph in Sallanches, Hinault took to the start line wearing the rainbow jersey of the world champion. Paris–Roubaix is a unique challenge, over 250km of racing on flat roads, with a significant proportion of the last 100km or so over *pavé*: cobblestoned, bone-jarring "roads" of the kind that break your bike and mash your head. If the weather is dry, a huge, choking dust cloud envelops the peloton as the riders rampage across the cobbles. Worse still, if it is wet the cobblestones become roads of filth, smothered in mud and animal waste, rendering them as precarious as ice; the riders emerge caked in crap, resembling miners more than bike-riders. This race is not dubbed "The Hell of the North" for nothing.

Hinault had ridden three Paris–Roubaix races prior to 1981, each year steadily improving: 13th in 1978, 11th in 1979 and 4th in 1980. Perhaps this was the year for Hinault finally to get the win. But the race didn't go well for him: the race report stated that he crashed no fewer than seven times. His last crash was on the final section of cobbles when he swerved to avoid hitting a small dog on a corner while in the leading group. Hinault had the fortitude to dust himself off, get back on his bike, stomp on the pedals, rejoin the leaders who had motored on without him and, as if to demonstrate that he was unaffected by his tumble, go straight to the front.

Into the outdoors velodrome where the race traditionally ends, Hinault was with five other riders, including multiple Paris–Roubaix winners Roger De Vlaeminck and Francesco Moser. Traditional tactics would have every rider hanging back, looking for someone else to take the lead so to gain an advantage from their slipstream. Not Hinault. He led the group round the final laps of the track before exploding on the final banking to take the win by a wheel. Six months after becoming the first French world champion in eighteen years, Hinault became the first French winner of the country's greatest one-day race in a quarter of a century. How did the famously forthright Frenchman react? "Paris–Roubaix est une connerie," he said – "Paris–Roubaix is bullshit."

Hinault won his fifth and final Tour title in 1985 but, with the emergence of his team-mate Greg LeMond as a genuine Tour threat, his win was clouded by infighting within the team. The team turmoil continued the following year until he (eventually) turned *domestique*, helping LeMond to his first Tour win (see p138). Hinault retired in 1986 to work his farm in Brittany. In recent years he has returned to the Tour in an official capacity, always present for the post-stage protocol, helping with the jersey presentations and introducing riders to local dignitaries. His passion and temper remain undimmed, though. In scenes reminiscent of the Paris–Nice race of 1984, when he threw a haymaker of a punch at an unlucky shipbuilder who had been participating in a protest that had forced the stage to stop, in 2008 he literally threw an interloper off the podium before calmly carrying on with introducing stage winner Samuel Dumoulin to the great and the good of Nantes.

The Badger lives on.

BERNARD HINAULT SELECTED RESULTS:

1972: 1st junior national championships

1974: 2nd U23 Route de France

1975: 1st overall Circuit Cycliste Sarthe

1976: 1st overall and one stage win Circuit Cycliste Sarthe

1st overall Tour du Limousin

1977: 1st overall and one stage win Critérium du Dauphiné

1st Gent–Wevelgem

1st Liège–Bastogne–Liège

1978: 1st overall and three stage wins Tour de France

1st overall and five stage wins Vuelta a España

1st national championships

1979: 1st overall, 1st points competition and seven stage wins Tour de France

1st La Flèche Wallonne

1st Giro di Lombardia

1st overall and three stage wins Critérium du Dauphiné

1980: 1st overall and one stage win Giro d'Italia

1st world championships

1st Liège–Bastogne–Liège

3rd overall and one stage win Giro d'Italia

Three stage wins Tour de France

1981: 1st overall and five stage wins Tour de France

1st overall and four stage wins Critérium du Dauphiné

1st Paris–Roubaix

1st Amstel Gold Race

1982: 1st overall and four stage wins Tour de France

1st overall and four stage wins Giro d'Italia

1st GP des Nations

1st overall and one stage win Tour du Luxembourg

1983: 1st La Flèche Wallonne

1st overall and two stage wins Vuelta a España

1984: 1st GP des Nations

1st Giro di Lombardia

2nd overall and one stage win Tour de France

1985: 1st overall and three stage wins Tour de France

1st overall and one stage win Giro d'Italia

1986: 2nd overall, 1st mountains classification and three stage wins Tour de France

PLA D'ADET

START POINT / Saint-Lary-Soulan
START ELEVATION / 819m
FINISH ELEVATION / 1680m
LENGTH OF CLIMB / 10.7km
AVERAGE GRADIENT / 8%
MAXIMUM GRADIENT / 13.5%
FIRST TOUR / 1974
APPEARANCES / 9

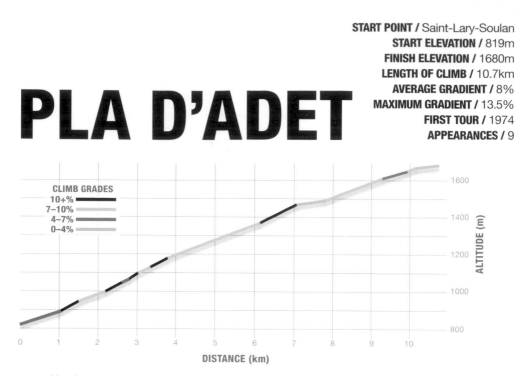

It is cold today in Saint-Lary-Soulan, the town where the climb to the ski resort of Pla d'Adet starts. A passerby is watching me put on layer upon layer of clothing. Curiosity pricked, he wanders over and asks if I'm cold. My simple "Oui, Monsieur" is enough for him to realise that I am not a native French speaker.

"You riding to Pla d'Adet?" he asks, in perfect English.

I nod.

"You won't be cold for long then."

I compliment him on his English. Marc has lived all his life in Saint-Lary. "It's a shame but not many English come here," he tells me. "I can't practise very often."

I tell him he doesn't need to practise. He shrugs happily, gives me directions to the start of the climb and waves me off with a heartfelt: "Enjoy!"

Enjoy Pla d'Adet? Maybe his English does need a bit of work after all.

• • •

The climb first featured in the Tour in 1974. On that occasion Raymond Poulidor, a rider dubbed the Eternal Second for featuring on the podium of the Tour eight times but never winning the yellow jersey, took the stage. He was by far the strongest rider that day but, by the time he crossed the finish line for his first and only stage win that year, he was too far behind Eddy Merckx to vie for the race lead. Poulidor would again come second that year, more than eight minutes behind Merckx.

But Poulidor's exploits on the road to Pla d'Adet had impressed the race organisers and the race returned for the next two years. Holland's Joop Zoetemelk took the stage in 1975 but it was in 1976 that the climb had its first major impact on the race, acting as the springboard for possibly the greatest climber of all time – Lucien Van Impe (see pp74–75) – to take his one and only overall Tour victory.

Going into the stage, which tackled the Mente, Portillon and Peyresourde before the final climb to Pla d'Adet, the Belgian was lying second in the overall classification. He was 2 minutes 41 seconds behind the yellow jersey of Raymond Delisle, team-mate of pre-race favourite Bernard Thévenet, who had won the race the year before and thereby ended the reign of Eddy Merckx.

On the Portillon, with a breakaway up the road, Spanish climber Luis Ocaña struck out alone in pursuit of the

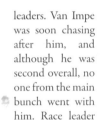

ZOETEMELK, REALISING TOO LATE THAT HE HAD BACKED THE WRONG HORSE IN FOLLOWING DELISLE, NOW ATTACKED ON THE LAST CLIMB, BUT HE COULD NOT CATCH VAN IMPE. THE BELGIAN CLIMBER WON THE STAGE BY MORE THAN THREE MINUTES.

leaders. Van Impe was soon chasing after him, and although he was second overall, no one from the main bunch went with him. Race leader Delisle didn't have the strength to follow and everyone else, most notably Zoetemelk, was content to stick with the yellow jersey. By the time the two climbing specialists had reached the top of the Peyresourde they had caught the breakaway and were leading the stage.

The two riders co-operated on the descent and, in the valley, Ocaña came into his own, working tirelessly for Van Impe. Despite not being a team-mate, Ocaña led the younger man to the foot of the climb. Maybe it was some sort of climber's union. Maybe it was because Ocaña thought that Zoetemelk had never contributed to his battles with Merckx over the years and so was now meting out a little retribution. Whatever the reason, on the lower slopes of Pla d'Adet, a grateful Van Impe knew his time had come. He launched himself up the mountain, easily distancing Ocaña.

Zoetemelk, realising too late that he had backed the wrong horse in following Delisle, now attacked on the last climb, but he could not catch Van Impe. The Belgian climber won the stage by more than three minutes and had an overall lead of 3 minutes 18 seconds. It was a lead that would grow further on the way into Paris, where Van Impe was crowned as the winner of the Tour. Zoetemelk's time would come, but he'd have to wait another four years.

• • •

I cross the Neste river before turning right on to the climb. Immediately the road shoots up and I pass the first sign telling me that the first of the 10km to the resort is at an average of 9%.

I click down through the gears as I pass a postman out on his morning deliveries. "Bonjour. Bonne chance!" he says, as I go by slowly. I must look like I need luck.

The road, hacked out of the rock face, does not mess about. There's no: "Hello, how are you feeling? Let's just spend a few kilometres getting the legs going." No, the climb to Pla d'Adet is more like "WHAM! Take that, sucker. Wanna carry on? There's another 9km of this."

I labour on. The sun at last starts to pierce the overcast sky. Above and over to my left is my destination, the ugly ski station of Pla d'Adet. The resort will stay in sight now for pretty much all of the rest of my ride. It looks almost too close at this stage, but it is the other side of a valley and the road must continue until it is high enough to cross. It gives an odd perspective, as if I'm riding a separate climb. If anything it seems like I'm twisting away from my target.

After 5km I enter the village of Soulan. It's a tiny place, nothing more than a collection of old houses, a church and a fountain. It has been a real slog to this point and the last kilometre to the village was really tough. I am merely crawling along. If the village weren't so empty, I'd half expect someone to walk past me with a nod. That said, the views back down towards Saint-Lary and ahead to the Massif de Néouvielle, freshly dusted after last night's snow, are diverting enough.

Beyond Soulan the gradient temporarily relents, but the slope is still nudging 8%. And then it ramps up again.

I battle to keep the legs turning. My muscles are shouting at me to stop, and I'm constantly going from being too hot when the sun is out, to too cold when the sun retreats behind cloud or the road turns me away from its rays. I'm starting to really suffer when I see the 3km-to-go mark. It says 5%. I could kiss it.

● ● ●

The most recent ascent of Pla d'Adet was in 2005. Stage 15 was a monster day in the Pyrenees, over five climbs, four of them first category, before the haul up to the finish.

The day was defined by a long breakaway. Fourteen riders got away early on the stage, including George Hincapie, team-mate of yellow jersey wearer Lance Armstrong. At one point the group had a lead of nineteen minutes. By the time the leaders went over the penultimate climb of the day, the Col de Val Louron-Azet, the group had shrunk to six, with Hincapie still there, having sat at the back of the group, marking the moves, all day long.

Early on the climb to Pla d'Adet there was a flurry of attacks that whittled the leading group down further. With 6km to go only four were left out front: Michael Boogerd, Oscar Pereiro, Pietro Caucchioli and, bringing up the rear, George Hincapie. Pereiro attacked; Hincapie followed. And then there were two.

In front of the huge crowds lining the road, with barely a cycle's width of tarmac to ride on, Pereiro led the whole way up the rest of the climb. That is, until they passed the 200m marker. Then Hincapie, having played a shrewd tactical game, finally came to the front and sprinted away for his biggest win in a stage race.

● ● ●

I cross the valley. It's amazing how easy 5% feels after 7km of 10%. My legs don't know themselves and start spinning freely. I am rewarded with some fantastic views back down the valley and over the road with which I've been battling for the last hour or so. To see it from this aspect is really quite startling. At one point the road just seems to dive down the mountain. I can't quite believe I rode up it not thirty minutes ago.

The resort itself is as grim close up as it is far away. There is literally no one around. Every shop, hotel, restaurant, fast-food shack and bar is shut. I linger, though, because the views are spectacular, stretching to the giant peaks of the border with Spain. Even after two straight weeks in this most bewitching of mountain ranges, the panorama from the top of Pla d'Adet is pretty special. I just need to ignore the buildings immediately around me. Then, with the cold wind picking up, there's really nothing more to do but button up and retrace my route back to Saint-Lary.

Lucien Van Impe was one of the best climbers that the Tour has ever seen. He was also one of its most consistent. In a professional career that lasted from 1969 to 1987 he competed in fifteen Tours, finishing eight of them in the top five and never once abandoning. He won nine stages, took home the best climber prize six times and, most importantly of all, won one yellow jersey.

Van Impe was born in Mere, Belgium, in 1946, and it was on the flatlands and short, punchy hills of Flanders that he learnt to ride. Having won regularly as an amateur, he turned professional in 1969, signing for the Sonolor-Lejeune team on June 26th. He was promptly thrown into the deep end – just two days later he was in Roubaix for the start of the Tour. Such an introduction to the professional ranks would be unthinkable today, but Van Impe rode impressively, finishing four stages in the top ten and coming an incredible 12th overall.

His first King of the Mountains title came in 1971, when he also finished third in Paris. Those achievements came without a stage win, something he put right the following year when he won at Orcières-Merlette after escaping with Joaquim Agostinho before the final climb, just pipping the Portuguese to the line. Again he won the King of the Mountains. A third KoM title came in 1975, when he became the first rider to win the now iconic polka-dot jersey – until then, no specific jersey had been awarded.

LUCIEN VAN IMPE

"I OWE A LOT TO BAHAMONTES," HE IS QUOTED AS SAYING, "SO MUCH THAT WHEN I'D WON THE KING OF THE MOUNTAINS TITLE SIX TIMES, AS HE HAD, I DIDN'T TRY TO WIN IT AGAIN."

His sole Tour win came in 1976, when he put on the yellow jersey for the first time after the climb to Alpe d'Huez, though the stage was narrowly won by Joop Zoetemelk (see p143). Although he lost the jersey a few days later, he regained it following his win at Pla d'Adet (see p70), and eleven days later he stood on top of the Paris podium.

Two of Van Impe's nine stage wins came on time trials to Avoriaz. In 1977 he won by 20 seconds ahead of Thévenet, and in 1983 by 36 seconds ahead of Stephen Roche. That 1983 win, on his way to his sixth and final King of the Mountains title, was to be his last Tour stage victory. His idol was Federico Bahamontes and once he had equalled the Spaniard's record of six mountain titles he was content. "I owe a lot to Bahamontes," he is quoted as saying, "so much that when I'd won the King of the Mountains title six times, as he had, I didn't try to win it again."

Van Impe constructed his entire career around the high peaks of the Tour, and was sometimes criticised for narrowing his focus so much. But whenever he did widen his sights to include other mountains, he invariably met with success, taking stage wins in both the Vuelta a España and Giro d'Italia, plus two mountain classification wins in the latter.

He retired in 1987, having spent some eighteen years at the top of the sport.

LUCIEN VAN IMPE SELECTED RESULTS:

1968: One stage win Tour de l'Avenir

1969: 1st overall Vuelta Ciclista a Navarra

1971: 3rd overall and 1st mountains classification Tour de France

1972: One stage win and 1st mountains classification Tour de France

1973: One stage win Tour de France
One stage win Grand Prix du Midi-Libre
One stage win Tour de Romandie

1975: Two stage wins and 1st mountains classification Tour de France
1st overall and two stage wins Tour de l'Aude

1976: 1st overall and one stage win Tour de France
One stage win Grand Prix du Midi-Libre
One stage win Tour de l'Aude

1977: One stage win and 1st mountains classification Tour de France
One stage win Critérium du Dauphiné
Two stage wins Tour de Suisse

1979: One stage win Tour de France
Two stage wins Vuelta a España

1981: One stage win and 1st mountains classification Tour de France

1982: 1st mountains classification Giro d'Italia

1983: One stage win and 1st mountains classification Tour de France
One stage win and 1st mountains classification Giro d'Italia

1986: 1st overall and one stage win Vuelta a los Valles Mineros

COL DU TOURMALET

START POINT / Sainte-Marie-de-Campan
START ELEVATION / 847m
FINISH ELEVATION / 2115m
LENGTH OF CLIMB / 17.1km
AVERAGE GRADIENT / 7.3%
MAXIMUM GRADIENT / 10%
FIRST TOUR / 1910
APPEARANCES / 81

It took me two attempts to reach the top of the Col du Tourmalet. It wasn't my fault that the first had to be aborted. It was because of a meteorological moment.

My first trip started under low cloud. I stood outside my accommodation near Campan and spoke to the first person I saw coming from the direction of the Tourmalet. I was eager to find out what conditions were like on the road up. The lady with wild hair told me that, while a couple of kilometres of the road were shrouded in cloud, the route from 10km to go until the top was clear and that because of low-lying cloud in the valley, some killer shots were on offer. And that there was a llama about. So off I went, camera at the ready.

The cloud started to swirl around me after 5km. Steadily it got denser until visibility was under 50m. I could hear cars coming down the mountain long before I could see them. I was getting no feel for the mountain: I had no views, and just bleak silence as I rode in a thick blanket of cloud.

Five hundred metres from the ski resort of La Mongie, a cyclist, gingerly making his way back down, passed me. I shouted and gestured, asking if the cloud stayed this thick all the way to the top. I didn't fully catch his answer as he disappeared into the gloom but it sounded very much like "Oui, c'est grave." Whether that was really what he said or not I'll never know,

but upon reaching La Mongie I decided enough was enough and turned back. Llama or no llama. I wasn't enjoying it and it felt too dangerous to be riding up a mountain I didn't know with zero visibility.

Those clouds that forced me back down the mountain with under 4km to ride would that night dump enough snow at the top of the climb to close the pass for five full days.

● ● ●

The Col du Tourmalet was first used by the Tour in 1910, when the race introduced the high peaks of the Pyrenees into the race itinerary. Along with the Aubisque to the west, and the Aspin and Peyresourde to the east, it forms what is ominously known as the "Circle of Death".

The first rider to crest the Tourmalet in 1910, despite his protestations to the race organisers about the inclusion of the mountains (see pp18–19), was Octave Lapize, who would go on to win that year's race.

The Tourmalet's most famous story occurred just three years later. In 1913 stage 6 took the peloton back into the Circle of Death, this time heading west to east, with the Aubisque first to be tackled followed by the Tourmalet, Aspin and Peyresourde. Heading into the

stage Eugène Christophe – a Frenchman from the outskirts of Paris who had placed second the year before – was in second place, just under five minutes behind race leader Odile Defraye. But Christophe had eyes on the race lead and was looking to pounce on this, the toughest of all stages.

INITIALLY THINGS WENT WELL FOR CHRISTOPHE, AND HE TOPPED THE MIGHTY TOURMALET COMFORTABLY ON THE WHEEL OF PHILIPPE THYS OF BELGIUM. UNFORTUNATELY FOR THE FRENCHMAN, HOWEVER, HIS MACHINE WAS NOT AS STURDY AS HIS LEGS.

Sure enough by the time they rose over the Aubisque, Christophe was leading the stage. In addition Defraye had abandoned, having fallen behind by more than two hours. The Parisian was the new leader of the Tour de France. That was until they hit the slopes of the Tourmalet.

Initially things went well for Christophe, and he topped the mighty Tourmalet comfortably on the wheel of Philippe Thys of Belgium. Unfortunately for the Frenchman, however, his machine was not as sturdy as his legs.

Shortly after passing over the summit, Christophe noticed something was wrong with his bike. His forks had broken. So famous is the story of what happened next that in 1960, in celebration of fifty years of the Tour racing in the Pyrenees, the monthly magazine *Sport et Vie* managed to get Christophe to recreate the astonishing tale.

"I did not crash," Christophe said. "I had time to see my fork bend before me. I am telling you now but back then, to avoid poor publicity for my sponsors, I did not want to reveal it." Christophe told the magazine how he had found himself alone, watching as his fellow riders passed him one by one, before deciding he had no option but to heave his bike up onto his shoulders and walk the 12km down the mountain to Sainte-Marie-de-Campan where a woman showed him to a blacksmith's forge.

At the forge Christophe proceeded to repair his broken forks. A despatch the next day from a *L'Auto* correspondent described the scene:

"After descending from the summit of the Tourmalet with his bicycle on his back, a man arrives, masked in tragedy. Like a madman, he asks after a blacksmith. This man knows that he should have won the Tour, that the die has rolled for him. He has one desire left: to take his machine back to Paris, with the other seven riders of the Peugeot team... Christophe sets to work, so weary that he struggles to lift his machine, and his cries fill the smoky, dirty space of the forge. He has finished the piece and, refusing all help, tries to insert it into the tube; it won't fit. He has to start again."

Eventually Christophe successfully repaired the bike and set off from the forge towards the Aspin and the Peyresourde. He rolled into Luchon 3 hours and 50 minutes behind stage winner Thys, who would go on to win that year's Tour. To rub salt into an already cavernous wound, the race organisers saw fit to dock Christophe another three minutes because a boy had pumped the bellows for him during the repair; this at a time when all outside assistance to riders was expressly forbidden. That penalty may pale into insignificance when compared with the hours he lost elsewhere but, even so, it seems cruel, given the extreme efforts to which he went just to remain in the race.

Amazingly, despite this huge setback, Christophe did not finish last on the stage, although he was now out of overall contention. He would finish seventh in Paris but, thanks to his broken bike, his place in Tour history was secure for all time – a place further

cemented in 1919 when he became the first wearer of the newly introduced yellow jersey. Oh, and he broke his forks again.

• • •

Six days after my first attempt I'm back in Sainte-Marie-de-Campan, preparing the bike for a second assault on this most mythical of mountains. The day couldn't be more different: clear blue skies and not a hint of cloud. I can feel the heat rising from the road, through my feet and into my body. I stop by the forge where Christophe repaired his forks back in 1913, now commemorated with a plaque. It's a tiny place, little more than a stone shack really, but it means much to be so close to the place where one of the Tour's most famous episodes was played out.

The early going is relatively simple. Kilometres click by easily, just a gentle rise through tiny hamlets. The sun is beating down remorselessly. Rather stupidly, I've set off just before 11.30am, meaning I am now riding with the sun at its highest. If the Tourmalet doesn't sap my spirit, the sun just might.

A fellow cyclist approaches from behind, a Frenchman with good English, wearing fluorescent Agritubel kit. He rides alongside me for a while. He is staying in Bayonne and has already ridden over the Aspin today, which means he must have got out of bed much earlier than me. He's on his way to meet his wife at the top of the Tourmalet. "After that I stop," he laughs. "It is too hot. And I'm meant to be on holiday." He goes on his way.

• • •

At 5745km, the route of the 1926 Tour remains the longest there has ever been. Held between June 20th and July 18th, it comprised 17 stages. Stage 10 took the riders from Luchon to Bayonne, a 326km ride through the "Circle of Death". It was to be a day that would never be forgotten.

The conditions that greeted the riders in the early hours of July 6th were horrific. A gentle drizzle at the start of the stage soon turned into torrential lashings of freezing rain and sleet. Thunder and lightning echoed around the peaks, and an icy fog veiled the valleys and masked the mountains. The roads, little more than dirt tracks, turned rapidly into swamps. It is described by

Dominique Kérébel in the book *Le Tour de France et les Pyrénées* as a "*stage Dantesque*".

Going into the day, Belgian Lucien Buysse was over twenty minutes behind the race leader, Gustaaf Van Slembrouck. Buysse had always intended to use this stage to launch his assault on the lead and wasn't about to let the hateful conditions stop him. He attacked on the Aubisque and was followed by fellow Belgians Albert Dejonghe and Omer Huyse. As the race approached the foot of the Tourmalet, the three of them were all alone.

Three soon became two when Huyse fell away quickly on the slopes of the Tourmalet. The riders were battling their way up the mountainside in any way they could. The unrelenting rain meant that, stuck in the mud, they were sometimes forced to continue on foot, dragging their mud-laden machines with them as they fought against the mire.

Buysse and Dejonghe were then joined by three other riders, including Odile Taillieu, who led them over the Tourmalet. But then Buysse upped his pace, striking out for victory and cresting the Aspin and Peyresourde alone. Buysse crossed the line in Luchon 17 hours, 12 minutes and 4 seconds after he had left Bayonne. He finished over 25 minutes ahead of second-placed Bartolomeo Aimo and took hold of the yellow jersey by over 36 minutes from Taillieu.

Behind, riders abandoned in droves. Only 54 completed the stage, the last of them arriving in Luchon over 22 hours after the stage had started. At midnight search parties were sent out to find riders who were still on the road or had taken shelter in bars.

It was a day when the forces of nature were unleashed on the Tour's peloton, a day best summed up by Charles-Anthoine Gonnet who, in the pages of *L'Auto*, painted a picture of a mountain without trees; of roads running with mud and water and ice; of never-ending hairpins; of broken-down cars; of a piercing wind that "cuts your face"; and of the "innumerable sufferings that assailed our men."

Buysse went on to win the 1926 Tour and his win is commemorated with a bust at the top of the Aubisque. In fact, for Buysse, the stage from Bayonne to Luchon was far from his biggest ordeal. During the race his daughter had died, and it was only through the encouragement of his family that he continued.

● ● ●

The road ramps up once I'm through the village of Gripp and things start to get altogether trickier. As if that isn't enough the local highways authority has decided that today is a good day to resurface part of the road. I've read before that riding up a mountain can feel like riding through molten tar. Well now I know what it feels like to actually ride through molten tar at the same time as riding up a mountain. And I can tell you, it doesn't feel nice.

I hear a disturbing "schliippp" as my wheels strain to disengage themselves from the newly laid road surface. What's more, my tyres are steadily gaining an ever-growing film of tar, with the result that they are picking up every stone that comes near my wheels. I'm paranoid about punctures anyway and often, even without this sort of problem, will stop and spin the wheels of my bike, running my hands over them to remove any stone chippings. Now I've got more gravel glued to my wheels than is on my mum's driveway. I try to get rid of some of it but to no real avail. I press on, anxiously waiting for what I now consider to be the inevitable hiss as a stone buries itself into an inner tube. A road worker looks at me with pity. "It's just 2km," he says. That's okay then, I think.

But mercifully no puncture comes. As I ride through the tar and chippings I find myself imagining the very early days of the Tour, when riders spent their careers cycling over far worse surfaces than I'm trawling through now. I'm sure they would've given their right arms for a group of workmen to be out resurfacing the roads of the mountains.

A sharp hairpin just after the Garet waterfall introduces the second part of the climb: the long stretch up to the ski-station of La Mongie. It's 4km of monotonous riding, with no views to speak of, just an interminable drag up to the drab resort. From now on the gradient won't dip much below 8%. Other cyclists are passing me regularly as my pace has slowed markedly. Whether it's the heat, the mountain or the tar I don't know, but I am struggling.

• • •

By stage 17 of the 1969 Tour Eddy Merckx, riding his first Tour, already had the race pretty much sewn up. After four stage wins he was leading by over eight minutes from Raymond Pingeon. All he had to do was ensure he lost no time over the next seven stages, and his maiden Tour was in the bag.

But such an approach went against the grain for Merckx. His nickname would not become The Cannibal for nothing. As stage 17 tackled the upper slopes of the Tourmalet, Merckx attacked, dropping his rivals and gaining a gap of a few seconds. Now, with the Tour all but won and a precipitous and dangerous descent into the Pau valley to come, most riders would be more concerned with staying upright and would take it relatively easy. Not Eddy.

He dropped from the summit of the Tourmalet like a lead weight tossed from the rock-strewn peak. By the bottom his gap of a few seconds had grown to over a minute. Through the valley his lead continued to grow and, by the time he got to the foot of the next climb, the Col du Soulor, his lead was over three minutes.

In all Merckx, wearing yellow, spent 130km of the 214.5km stage alone at the head of the race in the sort of escapade that has rarely been seen before or since. Certainly in the modern era such an act of bravado is simply unthinkable. Journalist and author Pierre Chany likened Merckx to a matador, "thirsty for blood."

Merckx crossed the finish line in Mourenx nearly eight minutes ahead of second-placed Michele Dancelli and increased his overall lead to over sixteen minutes. "Never again," wrote Jacques Goddet, "will we be able to say that the Tour is not won until Paris." Merckx went on to win the 1969 Tour by nearly eighteen minutes. He also won the points classification and the mountains prize: the only time a single rider has claimed all three competitions.

• • •

One kilometre to go to La Mongie and I see Agritubel man, talking on a mobile phone as his wife towels down his legs. I can't believe he has been to the top and back down in the time it has taken me to get here. It helps me to think that perhaps he hasn't, that perhaps it was too much and he called it day here, before La Mongie. But deep down I know that isn't the case. It's a dispiriting thought.

Not quite as dispiriting as La Mongie itself. Perhaps in the winter, with snow and happy skiers and snowboarders filling the slopes and bars, it looks different. Today it just looks depressed and lonely. The road steepens through the town, hardening my feelings to it even more as I start the final leg of the climb. Four kilometres to the col.

• • •

In 2010 the organisers of the Tour brought the race here twice. It was the centenary of the first stages in the Pyrenees and it was to be commemorated with four days of racing in the mountain range, including ascents

of both sides of the Tourmalet. The highlight of the celebrations was a summit finish, only the second time that a stage has ended at the top of the pass.

The scene was set for a battle royal between the two big protagonists of the 2010 Tour, Andy Schleck and Alberto Contador. Three days earlier, on the Port de Balès, Schleck, while leading the Tour from Contador by 31 seconds, had gone on the offensive, eager to gain more time ahead of the final time trial in five days' time. At first it had appeared that Contador couldn't react, but then disaster struck for Schleck when his chain slipped off. While the Luxembourger battled with his bike, Contador sped off up the road. Unwritten etiquette normally means that riders do not seek to take advantage when a rival, particularly one wearing the yellow jersey, suffers a mechanical problem, but Contador continued, eventually gaining 39 seconds

on Schleck and taking the yellow jersey. That night an apologetic Contador posted a video online saying he had made a mistake.

Now, three days later, Schleck was ready to take the battle to Contador once more. On the slopes of the Tourmalet, which was concealed with a thick cover of fog, Schleck attacked as he said he would. Contador marked the move and the two went toe to toe all the way up the mountain. Schleck led the whole way and tried several moves to shake off the Spaniard, but it was no use – Contador was unflappable. The intense drama was played out all the way up to the murky summit, where Schleck at least took the stage win. But Contador was still in yellow and he would retain the jersey until Paris. His winning gap over Schleck? Thirty-nine seconds – exactly what he had gained when Schleck's chain got caught.

But the drama was not over yet. It was later announced that Contador had tested positive for small traces of

It's a barren landscape now as well, strewn with boulders and rocks. Two huge peaks rise above me menacingly. Suddenly the Tourmalet feels quite unfriendly. A series of final hairpins take me painstakingly to the top. I pass a group of Australian women busy painting names on the road in support of their loved ones who are further down the mountain. I ask them to take my photo. "Don't worry love, the top's just around the corner," says one, clearly concerned at my appearance. "Do you want a push love?" says another. I would love a push, but I politely refuse. I don't want any asterixes against this climb. "Giles Belbin; Col du Tourmalet 2012*. Was pushed for last 100m by an Australian woman." No thanks.

Clenbuterol (see p237), and he was eventually stripped of his 2010 title. The record books now show Andy Schleck as the winner of the 2010 Tour.

And finally the top is reached with, I have to admit, an involuntary clench of my fist. There I am, greeted by a statue of Jacques Goddet, director of the Tour from 1936 to 1987, plus a terrific view out over the western descent.

•••

BEHIND, RIDERS ABANDONED IN DROVES. ONLY 54 COMPLETED THE STAGE, THE LAST OF THEM ARRIVING IN LUCHON OVER 22 HOURS AFTER THE STAGE HAD STARTED. AT MIDNIGHT SEARCH PARTIES WERE SENT OUT TO FIND RIDERS WHO WERE STILL ON THE ROAD OR HAD TAKEN SHELTER IN BARS.

After twenty minutes or so at the top I head back down the way I have come, which means another battle with fresh tar and loose chippings. If anything it is far worse on the descent. Stones fly up, stinging my legs, while others simply cling on to my tyres. And how do I spend my afternoon after a hard ride up the Tourmalet? Do I bask in the glory with a cold beer or two, reflecting on what an achievement it is to conquer this giant of the Tour. No. I spend it painstakingly cleansing my tyres of Tourmalet chippings. Chippings that, had they not been picked by my rubber, could've witnessed as yet unwritten Tourmalet tales.

I can see the pass now, high above me, the windscreens of campervans twinkling in the sun. I realise that this last stretch is going to be hard. I still have a lot of altitude to gain and not far to gain it in. And my legs hurt. A lot.

EDDY
MERCKX

IN 1966 EDDY MERCKX CAME ALONG TO THE TOP TABLE OF PROFESSIONAL CYCLING. AND THINGS WERE NEVER QUITE THE SAME AGAIN.

"I mean, how were we supposed to know?" Felice Gimondi tells author Daniel Friebe in his book *Eddy Merckx: The Cannibal*. "I had won the Tour de France in my first year as a pro, I was about to win another Giro. Everything was going well… Who knows how many more Giri d'Italia I'd have won if he hadn't come along. But he did come along. And we didn't realise for months, years."

In 1966 Eddy Merckx came along to the top table of professional cycling. And things were never quite the same again.

Édouard Louis Joseph Merckx, or Eddy Merckx, as he is known to the world, was born on June 17th 1945 in Meensel-Kiezegem, Belgium. When he was still young he moved with his family to Sint-Pieters-Woluwe, a suburb of Brussels, where his parents took ownership of a grocery store.

Merckx started riding aged eight and grew up idolising the Belgian rider Stan Ockers. Ockers was a world champion and multiple classics winner, and had twice picked up stage wins in the Tour de France in 1950 and 1954, as well as taking the points competition in 1955 and 1956 and finishing runner-up overall in 1950 and 1952. The Belgian ace died on the track in 1956 after colliding with a Derny motorcycle. The incident is said to have deeply shocked the young Merckx.

Merckx's first race win came in 1961 in Petit-Enghien. Aged 16 and still relatively small, he wasn't considered a threat in a race in which most of the riders were at least two years older. But, in a style that would later become all too familiar, Merckx sped away from the pack to upset the odds and take the race.

His first win of note came three years later in 1964 at Sallanches when, at the age of 19, he won the amateur road race world championship. It was a race for which he very nearly wasn't entered,

after a medical test carried out by Belgium's cycling federation apparently uncovered a fault with his heart. However, a series of phone calls between Merckx's mother and various doctors and officials revealed a possible plot: it seemed that the Belgian team selector didn't want Merckx to race in Sallanches, probably because he hailed from Brussels and not Flanders, and had used the supposed test results as a pretext. Eddy was duly reinstated and paid his mother back for her efforts by winning the race from fellow countryman Willy Planckaert, who would go on to win stages of the Tour de France and Giro d'Italia as well as winning the points classification at the 1966 Tour. But the issue of problems with Merckx's heart would resurface four years later.

In 1965 Merckx turned professional with the Solo-Superia team. He suffered an inauspicious start: having punctured in his first race, the semi-classic La Flèche Wallonne, he was forced to abandon when he couldn't get back to the bunch. A little under two weeks later, with lessons learnt, Merckx picked up his first professional victory at Vilvorde. It may not have had the prestige of La Flèche Wallonne, but it was a maiden victory taken within a month of turning professional. Seven more wins came that year and, at the end of the season, Merckx moved to Peugeot, home of Roger Pingeon and Tom Simpson.

On March 20th 1966, Eddy Merckx took the first of what would eventually become a staggering haul of classics wins. Entering the final kilometres of Milan–San Remo, Merckx was part of an eleven-man breakaway that had a lead of over thirty seconds. Later Merckx admitted that

he had no idea when he started the sprint for the line that he would be in with a chance of victory. Friebe writes that Merckx said after the race: "I didn't know my rivals, but I'd have played my cards in a sprint anyway. I tried and it turned out well. I'm as happy today as when I pulled on the rainbow jersey in Sallanches. No, actually, I'm even happier."

It was Merckx's single big win that year. Victories in smaller races followed (he picked up 19 wins in all in 1966), but second in that autumn's Giro di Lombardia represented his next best result in a major race.

Merckx remained with Peugeot for 1967 and looked to build upon his maiden classics victory. That spring he took wins in two stages of Paris–Nice, won Gent–Wevelgem, La Flèche Wallonne and a second Milan–San Remo, as well as finishing second in Liège–Bastogne–Liège and third in the Tour of Flanders. Now firmly established as a one-day rider of some repute, he turned his attention to the Giro d'Italia and his first Grand Tour appearance.

The 1967 Giro started in Treviglio. By his future standards Merckx had a quiet start, although he finished in the top ten on no fewer than seven occasions during the early stages. However, it was on stage 12 that he announced his Grand Tour potential. Until that stage to Blockhaus, despite finishing sixth on Mount Etna five days earlier, Merckx had never shown quite what he was capable of in the mountains.

Going into stage 12, 220km from Caserta to Blockhaus, Merckx was well placed within the top five. But the route took in climbs of the Macerone, Rionero Sannitico and Roccaraso, as well as the summit finish on the Blockhaus. This was going to be a brutal examination of his abilities to climb against the best mountain men in the business, deep into the second week of a punishing three-week schedule.

At the foot of the Blockhaus climb, after nearly 200km of racing, the peloton was still pretty much together, but it soon splintered as the road reared upwards. Merckx, however, was able to stay with the leading group, riding close behind the climbing specialist Italo Zilioni, and unleashed an annihilating turn of speed with a little under 1km to ride. He won the stage by ten seconds, ahead of the distraught Italian. It may have been a slender victory, but Merckx

OFF MERCKX WENT UP THE ROAD, CHASING DOWN A BREAK THAT, AT ONE POINT, HAD NINE MINUTES ON HIM, OVERTAKING THEM WITH EASE, SECURING THE STAGE WIN AND THE PINK JERSEY, AND LEAVING SOME OF HIS FELLOW RIDERS WITH TEARS OF DISBELIEF IN THEIR EYES.

had won his first summit finish in a Grand Tour and, at the same time, had issued a huge statement of intent. He had stayed with, and beaten, the best climbers the Giro had to offer on one of the race's toughest climbs.

The Italian media were incredulous. They were used to Merckx winning one-day races on the (relative) flat in the spring, but this was something different. *La Gazzetta dello Sport* ran the headline: "Italian disappointment: Belgian sprinter wins in the mountains." As if to make things worse, Merckx would win again two days later in Lido degli Estensi. On the flat. In a sprint.

While Merckx finished the 1967 Giro in ninth position overall, over eleven minutes down on winner Gimondi, there could be no doubting now that he would soon be a serious contender in the Grand Tours – a fact confirmed beyond all doubt just twelve months later.

Merckx had won the world championships in the late summer of 1967 and so, for the majority of the 1968 season, he had the rainbow jersey on his shoulders. Early in 1968 Merckx, now at the Faema team, had already won three stage races: the Giro di Sardegna, the Volta Ciclista a Catalunya and the Tour de Romandie, as well as the classic Paris–Roubaix. So far so Eddy. Now for a second stab at the Giro.

Such was Merckx's insatiable appetite for victory that experienced rider Vittorio Adorni was detailed to look after the exuberant Belgian during the three-week haul through Italy. Merckx duly won the first stage and took hold of the leader's pink jersey, and Adorni promptly told him to lose it again – it was too much to take the lead now and have to defend it for 21 days. Though it went against every fibre in his being,

Merckx finally relented and gave up the race lead two days later. Now it was just a matter of when to win it back.

But behind the scenes another drama was being played out. While visiting the Faema team, a professor at the Italian Institute of Sports Medicine named Giancarlo Lavezzaro was invited to take a cardiogram of Merckx. The results were unexpected, to say the least. They were of a man having a heart attack, not those of someone as healthy as Merckx appeared to be. They repeated the test. The result was the same. It was like 1964 again, although now there was no suspicion of ulterior motives. The decision was made to allow Merckx to keep riding, although Lavezzaro was convinced that he was on the brink of collapse.

No collapse came. Merckx, under the tutelage of Adorni, was instead waiting impatiently to re-assume the lead. The moment finally came on stage 12, a summit finish to Tre Cime. On a day of rain and snow and ice, and with Merckx straining at the leash, Adorni finally let his charge go. Off Merckx went up the road, chasing down a break that, at one point, had nine minutes on him, overtaking them with ease, securing the stage win and the pink jersey, and leaving some of his fellow riders with tears of disbelief in their eyes. The era of Merckx domination had arrived.

Merckx would win five Giri d'Italia over the course of his career. He would also claim five Tours de France, the first coming in 1969 (see p81) and the last in 1974 (the chances are he would have won six but for an injury inflicted by a supporter – see p122), and one Vuelta a España. He won countless classics: Milan–San Remo

seven times, Liège–Bastogne–Liège five times, Paris–Roubaix three times, the Tour of Flanders twice, the Giro di Lombardia twice. He claimed three world championships; he held the world hour record; the list goes on and on. That the majority of these wins come after he suffered a crash in 1969 that inflicted serious injury on him, and killed his Derny-riding pacer, makes his story all the more incredible.

There are countless tales of Merckx's daring escapades and seemingly suicidal solo attacks. His 1969 Tour of Flanders win is a case in point. In atrocious weather Merckx led a breakaway of some 22 riders and carried them for over 60km before splintering the group on the Muur de Grammont and going it alone. With over 70km to ride until the finish, Merckx's team director was incredulous, shouting from the team car: "Are you nuts? You'll die in the headwind, wait for the group." Merckx's reply was to drive on into the wind, fuelled by anger at his director's lack of faith and his opponents' unwillingness to share in the work. He won by over five minutes.

Merckx's hunger for success has been the topic of much debate. What was the source of his desire to dominate so crushingly? It appeared that winning, and winning well, was not enough for him – only absolute supremacy would do. Whole books have been written trying to answer this question, but what should not be forgotten is that, unlike some sportsmen, Merckx never had a "win at all costs" attitude. His sense of fair play was well and truly intact.

An incident from the 1971 Tour illustrates the point. Spanish rider Luis Ocaña (see pp54–57) was one of the few riders who could challenge Merckx at his peak. At the 1971 Tour, Merckx had held the yellow jersey for twelve days before surrendering it to Joop Zoetemelk on stage 10. Ocaña was in second place overall, just a single second behind, with Merckx now one minute down.

Stage 11 was a ride through the Alps, taking in the Laffrey and Noyer on the way to a summit finish at Orcières-Merlette. Ocaña lit up the race with an incredible solo attack that no one could answer, and by the finish he had put well over eight minutes into Merckx and Zoetemelk to take over the race lead. Merckx was magnanimous, telling *L'Equipe*: "What he did was extraordinary, believe me; he really was head and shoulders above the rest of us. You can only bow down before a champion of his calibre."

It looked like Merckx was going to be beaten in the Tour for the first time, but fate cruelly intervened for Ocaña. Three days later, on the stage to Luchon, Merckx went on the attack, desperately trying to shake of the Spaniard and take back time. As the leaders fought on the roads of the Pyrenees a storm settled over them. Rain and hail battered the riders, making the road surfaces treacherous. On the descent of the Col de Mente riders began to fall. First Merckx, then Ocaña went down. Merckx remounted but Ocaña was not so fortunate. Zoetemelk, who had been following, crashed into the yellow jersey with such force that Ocaña was unable to continue.

IT APPEARED THAT WINNING, AND WINNING WELL, WAS NOT ENOUGH FOR HIM – ONLY ABSOLUTE SUPREMACY WOULD DO.

The result was that Merckx took the race lead but his sense of winning fairly had been insulted. He refused to wear the yellow jersey the next day out of respect for Ocaña and even considered abandoning the race. Eventually he decided to continue, going on to win his third straight Tour.

In 1978 Merckx retired with an incredible 525 victories to his name. He is without question the greatest cyclist who ever raced a bike. His attitude to winning is best summed up in a response he is said to have given to a journalist who once asked him after a race if he had planned to be victorious.

"Why do you think I'm here?" he replied. "To watch the others win?'

EDDY MERCKX SELECTED RESULTS:

1964: Amateur world championships

1966: 1st Milan–San Remo
1st Trofeo Baracchi

1967: 1st Milan–San Remo
1st Gent–Wevelgem
1st La Flèche Wallonne
1st world championships
Two stage wins Giro d'Italia

1968: 1st Paris–Roubaix
1st overall and one stage win Tour de Romandie
1st overall and three stage wins Giro d'Italia

1969: 1st overall and six stage wins Tour de France
1st overall and three stage wins Paris–Nice
1st Milan–San Remo
1st Tour of Flanders
1st Liège–Bastogne–Liège
Four stage wins Giro d'Italia

1970: 1st overall and six stage wins Tour de France
1st overall and three stage wins Paris–Nice
1st Gent–Wevelgem
1st Paris–Roubaix
1st La Flèche Wallonne
1st overall and three stage wins Giro d'Italia

1971: 1st overall and five stage wins Tour de France
1st world championships

1st overall and three stage wins Paris–Nice
1st overall and two stage wins Critérium du Dauphiné
1st Milan–San Remo
1st Liège–Bastogne–Liège
1st Giro di Lombardia

1972: 1st overall and six stage wins Tour de France
1st Milan–San Remo
1st La Flèche Wallonne
1st Liège–Bastogne–Liège
1st overall and three stages Giro d'Italia
1st Giro di Lombardia

1973: 1st Gent–Wevelgem
1st Amstel Gold
1st Paris–Roubaix
1st Liège–Bastogne–Liège
1st overall and six stage wins Vuelta a España
1st overall and six stage wins Giro d'Italia

1974: 1st overall and nine stage wins Tour de France
1st overall and two stage wins Giro d'Italia
1st world championships

1975: 1st Milan–San Remo
1st Amstel Gold
1st Liège–Bastogne–Liège
1st Tour of Flanders
Two stage wins Tour de France

1976: 1st Milan–San Remo

COL D'AUBISQUE

START POINT / Argelès-Gazost
START ELEVATION / 457m
FINISH ELEVATION / 1709m
LENGTH OF CLIMB / 29km
AVERAGE GRADIENT / 4.2%
MAXIMUM GRADIENT / 8.5%
FIRST TOUR / 1910
APPEARANCES / 72

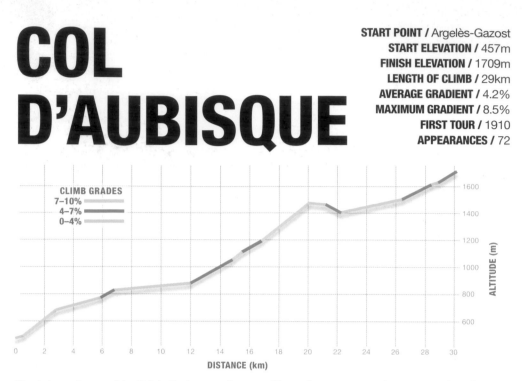

CLIMB GRADES
7–10%
4–7%
0–4%

ALTITUDE (m)

DISTANCE (km)

I'm sitting at the top of the Col du Soulor, munching a *pain aux raisins*, staring at the one stretch of road I have feared since I planned this trip. I'm joined by four or five sheep as I eat and ponder the next few kilometres. Even the sheep appear apprehensive, looking at me as if to say "we're really not sure you should be heading down there."

I am looking at the corniche of the Cirque de Litor, which runs between the Col du Soulor and the Col d'Aubisque. To get to the Aubisque from the east, you have to ride to the top of the Soulor and then traverse this 2km stretch: on one side it hugs a sheer cliff-face, on the other is a precipitous drop, with no road barriers to prevent you from falling. For someone who suffers from vertigo – that is to say, me – it is the stuff of nightmares. It is also one of the Tour's most iconic sections of road. Pick up a book about the race and there's a good chance that you'll find a photograph of the peloton gingerly picking its way across it. I simply have to do this.

The rational part of me says it'll be absolutely fine, that people travel along here without incident day after day. It is not steep. It just rises gently for a couple of kilometres and, as long as I manage to not ride off the edge, all will be well.

It's just that sometimes, when your mind is telling you in the strongest terms not do something, that's exactly what you go and do. Like when you're watching a horror film – you hide your eyes behind your hands but you always end up taking a look. Well, that's what I'm worried about – that my brain will be concentrating so hard on telling me not to ride off the edge that I'll go and do precisely that.

My climb to the top of the Soulor started in Argelès-Gazost, 21km from the summit. After a difficult opening couple of kilometres out of the town, the road levelled off and, for the next 8km or so, the riding was easy. Just a gentle slope through pretty villages and pasture land. It was all very pleasant.

ON ONE SIDE IT HUGS A SHEER CLIFF-FACE, ON THE OTHER IS A PRECIPITOUS DROP, WITH NO ROAD BARRIERS TO PREVENT YOU FROM FALLING. FOR SOMEONE WHO SUFFERS FROM VERTIGO – THAT IS TO SAY, ME – IT IS THE STUFF OF NIGHTMARES.

Things changed at Arrens, where the road suddenly ramped up. From this point it was still 8km to the top of the Soulor, at an average of 8%. It was tough-

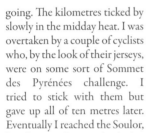

going. The kilometres ticked by slowly in the midday heat. I was overtaken by a couple of cyclists who, by the look of their jerseys, were on some sort of Sommet des Pyrénées challenge. I tried to stick with them but gave up all of ten metres later. Eventually I reached the Soulor, but for once this wasn't job-done. There's another 8km to go to the Aubisque.

DUBOC HAD BEEN POISONED. REMARKABLY HE RECOVERED SUFFICIENTLY TO COMPLETE THE STAGE, COMING IN 21ST, A LITTLE OVER THREE AND THREE-QUARTER HOURS DOWN.

● ● ●

The Aubisque was one of the original crop of Pyrenean peaks to be included in the Tour de France in 1910, when it was the final climb en route to Bayonne and the finish after the Tour's first trek through the Pyrenees. That day François Lafourcade led the way over the climb, although he didn't survive at the head of the race – he finished fifth in Bayonne, 10 minutes behind stage winner Octave Lapize. This was the stage made famous by Lapize's "assassins" outburst (see pp18–19). In 1911 the Aubisque was back, with stage 10 a carbon-copy of the 1910 stage, taking climbs of the Peyresourde, Aspin, Tourmalet and Aubisque.

Paul Duboc, a French rider from Rouen, had finished fourth overall at the 1909 Tour and was enjoying the 1911 edition as it entered stage 10, lying second overall having picked up back-to-back stage wins on stages 8 and 9. Duboc set off quickly from Luchon. He led over the Peyresourde and the Aspin and, by the time he soared over the Tourmalet, all was looking good for the stage win and a rise to the top of the overall classification.

At the Argelès-Gazost control station he grabbed a bottle and continued on his way towards the Aubisque. Suddenly Duboc collapsed. Bent double, he curled up and started to vomit violently. Weak and feverish, Duboc remained curled at the side of the road as riders that he had cruised by a few hours ago began to pass. Henri Desgranges wrote: "All the race cars stopped in front of the poor man, he was given a little mint alcohol in vain. I suspected a bidon he had by his side... it seemed not to smell of tea."

Duboc had been poisoned. Remarkably he recovered sufficiently to complete the stage, coming in 21st, a little over three and three-quarter hours down. Even more remarkably he won the next day's stage into La Rochelle. But who had poisoned him? Initially eyes fell on Gustave Garrigou who, as the leader of the race, was the man most threatened by Duboc's romp through the mountains. Although he was later cleared of any wrongdoing he had to be given a bodyguard and ride in disguise in order to make it through the rest of the Tour, particularly when it passed through Duboc's home town of Rouen.

Eventually fingers were pointed elsewhere, with Pierre Chany later writing: "It is stated that the culprit was none other than former rider François Lafourcade, who had become a *soigneur* on an opposing team... specialising in the preparation of suspect drinks: doping for some, poison for Duboc!"

● ● ●

I finish my *pain aux raisins* and take a moment to prepare myself. Then I slowly start to descend towards the corniche, taking my time, concentrating hard. Soon I am on the stretch of road that has so dominated my thoughts. Traffic is mercifully quiet so I decide to ride nearly in the middle of the road, preferring to take my chances with an oncoming car rather than slipping off the edge.

Eventually I start to enjoy the experience. Over to my right, where the cliff edge falls away, there are awesome views over the Ouzom valley. This has to be one of the most scenic routes through this mountain range. As if that wasn't enough, I am riding over a surface that is a huge part of the legend of the Tour. It is a humbling moment. Despite my nervousness, it is a real privilege to be here.

• • •

Whether Wim van Est considered it to be a privilege to be on the Aubisque in 1951 is another question. Van Est, a national pursuit champion on the track and winner of Bordeaux–Paris, was making his Tour debut in 1951. On stage 12 into Dax he was part of a ten-man escape that stayed away until the finish, all crossing the line over 18 minutes in front of the next rider. Van Est won the stage and also took the yellow jersey by 2 minutes 29 seconds. The next day the Tour entered the Pyrenees, with the climb of the Aubisque first on the agenda.

Now van Est was no specialist climber, but he was a strong and fiercely proud man. The yellow jersey is said to give its bearer extra strength, and so it proved for van Est. He climbed the Aubisque with the top riders of the day and was very much still in touch as they crested the summit and started the descent.

Unfortunately his descending skills that day did not quite match his climbing. The descent of the eastern side of the Aubisque is narrow and technical, and after a couple of wobbles and near-misses he hit a low wall, careered off the road and into the abyss. Riders who had been immediately behind the Dutchman stopped and raised the alarm. Team officials pulled up in their cars and peered down into the chasm. Far below they could make out the yellow jersey of van Est. Eventually the jersey began to twitch – miraculously, he had survived. Now the only problem was how to help him up. A rope fashioned out of spare tubulars was used to lower rescuers down onto a less steep section of the mountainside. From there they crawled down to the stricken rider and helped him back up to the rope of tyres and to the safety of the road.

Van Est was not allowed to continue, but his story captured the imagination of the public, particularly in the Netherlands. An advert for Pontiac, who supplied the Dutch team with watches, soon appeared in the press. It featured a photograph of van Est, perched on the side of a mountain, a pained expression on his face, and the following slogan: "Seventy metres I fell. My heart stood still. But my Pontiac never stopped! Indeed, a Pontiac can take a beating."

• • •

After the corniche the climbing remains steady until three kilometres to go. Here it ramps up and, once again, I find the going difficult. The accumulated affect of the 21km climb of the Soulor is beginning to take its toll and my energy levels are falling quickly. I pass the plaque documenting Wim van Est's crash and pause for a few moments of reflection.

● ● ●

Two Tour stages have finished at the top of the Aubisque, in 1985 and 2007. And both stages featured curious incidents.

There were two climbs of the Aubisque in 1985: the first, on the morning of July 17th, took the riders to a summit finish up the eastern slope from Luz-Saint-Saveur, while the afternoon stage took them from Laruns to Pau via the western ascent.

The morning's summit finish was noteworthy not only for being the first ever stage finish at the top of this famous mountain, but also for its short distance, just 52.5km. Ireland's Stephen Roche had his eyes on the stage and his team manager, Raphaël Géminiani, thought he had just the thing to help him get the win.

In his autobiography, *Born to Ride*, Roche writes: "On the morning of the stage he (Géminiani) presented me with a special silk skinsuit that he'd had handmade for me. My first reaction was to tell him that I wouldn't be turning up at the start wearing a kit like that, that I'd be a laughing stock. But he insisted 'The stage is only 40 kilometres [sic]. You don't need food, you're going to get clear on the Aubisque and they won't be able to catch you. You're going to ride it like a time trial.'"

And that's exactly what he did. Still disturbed by the skinsuit, Roche wore a jersey over it until they reached the Aubisque, then he threw the jersey away, caught the leading rider and powered away to win the stage by over a minute.

The second summit finish came in 2007 and was won by Danish rider Michael Rasmussen, who was wearing the yellow jersey. The stage itself was an intense battle between Rasmussen and Alberto Contador, with the Dane fending off attack after attack and finally

pulling away in the final kilometre. Unfortunately, Rasmussen came with some baggage. Just prior to the Aubisque stage it was revealed that he had missed three drugs tests and had lied to the authorities about his whereabouts. Rasmussen's explanations failed to satisfy anyone, and he was booed from the mountainside as he rode to his win on the Aubisque. That evening, under intense scrutiny, Rasmussen was thrown off the Tour by his Rabobank team. He later received a two-year ban.

●●●

Onwards, and the ride changes character again. Now I'm riding through rough scrubland, not dissimilar to what you might find on Dartmoor or Exmoor. At last the summit comes into sight – I can see the restaurant at the top.

The last kilometre up to the col is the hardest. It averages 8% and it is almost too much to bear. The end point is tantalisingly close but my legs want to stop turning now. Behind me another cyclist is gaining ground quickly. For some reason it suddenly becomes important to me to crest this beast alone, so I dig some energy up from somewhere and make it to the top ahead.

After taking a few moments to recover I take time to enjoy the views over to the west, wander around the oversized bicycles mounted there and generally soak up the feeling of being at the top of one of the Tour's greatest climbs. Then I spot a recognisable face.

Paddy Sweeney runs La Lanterne Rouge Cycling Lodge and Velo Peloton Cycling Tours in nearby Saint-Savin. We'd traded some emails about the possibility of getting together for a ride but our respective schedules, and some poor weather, had meant that it looked like I wouldn't get to meet him. Now here he is on top of the Aubisque with a group of cyclists who are staying at his lodge. A complete coincidence.

Paddy tells me that he's been in the Pyrenees for four years and that business is good. "After a difficult couple of years it's really picked up," he says. "I only have two days free for the next four months, and there's a good chance they'll get booked. Look at it," he continues throwing his arms wide-open and grinning, "it's paradise for a cyclist, isn't it?"

I look around me and have to agree – a cycling paradise it is.

Julio Jiménez was born in Ávila, in the province of Castile and León, on October 28th 1934. He discovered cycling early but didn't record his first significant win until he was 25 years old. Forced to find employment to fund the early part of his career, Jiménez found work in Ávila as a watch repairer, a move that was to earn him his unimaginative, if accurate, nickname: the Watchmaker of Ávila.

Jiménez eventually secured a move to the Bilbao-Goyoaga team in 1959 after finishing third in the previous year's Gran Premio de Torrelavega, but he couldn't record any wins for the team. A move to the bigger Lambretta-Mostajo team came in 1960, as did his first win, when he claimed the Gran Premio de Llodio.

It was in 1962, however, that Jiménez – now with the Faema squad – really began to make his name. In a prelude to what was to come, the Watchmaker won the national hill-climb championships, a feat he would repeat in 1965, as well as picking up stage wins in the Critérium du Dauphiné and Volta Ciclista a Catalunya.

The Spaniard was forging a reputation as a good climber, a reputation that would grow the following year, when he took the first of six Grand Tour mountains prizes by winning that classification at the Vuelta a España.

In 1964 he entered the Tour de France for the first time, riding for the KAS-Kaskol team, and picked up two stage wins. Predictably, they were on summit finishes, and one of them came on the infamous climb to the Puy-de-Dôme, when Jacques Anquetil and Raymond Poulidor went to head to head (see pp120–121).

His first win in the mountains classification at the Tour

JULIO JIMÉNEZ

came the following year. He dominated the competition, securing nearly double the points of the second-placed rider, Frans Brands. It was a win that was secured with two devastating performances: one in the Pyrenees, one in the Alps.

Stage 9 that year went from Dax to Bagnères-de-Bigorre, over the Aubisque and the Tourmalet. Jiménez got himself into the day's break, along with the favourites for the overall Tour, including Raymond Poulidor and eventual winner Felice Gimondi. The Spaniard led over the Aubisque and then attacked as the riders approached the top of the Tourmalet. Having lost a lot of time in the preceding stages, Jiménez was not really a threat to any of the favourites and so was allowed to fly the coop. He rose over the Tourmalet alone, one and a half minutes ahead of the next rider and picking up maximum points. Then he continued alone, down the Tourmalet's eastern slopes, along the valley road and into Bagnères-de-Bigorre. He won the stage by nearly three minutes.

After losing the Mont Ventoux stage to Poulidor, Jiménez secured the climber's prize on stage 16, to Aix-les-Bains. That stage took the peloton over four climbs: the Lautaret, Porte, Cucheron and Granier. Jiménez went over the last three in the lead and went on to win in Aix. His lead in the mountains classification was now unassailable and he rolled into Paris as the Tour's best climber. It was the first of three straight mountain prize wins in the Tour, to match the three he would win in the Vuelta (1963, 1964 and 1965).

In 1966 Jiménez would ride his first Giro d'Italia, going on to win two stages and wear the leader's pink jersey for eleven days. He would finish fourth overall. The following year he would record his best Grand Tour finish, taking second overall in the Tour, just 3 minutes and 40 seconds behind winner Roger Pingeon, despite not claiming a single stage.

It comes as little surprise that Jiménez's best overall result came on a Tour that had just 53km individual time-trialling kilometres. There can be little doubt that, if Jiménez had been just slightly better in the "race of truth", he would have been a Tour winner. As it is, the Watchmaker of Ávila is ranked as one of the best climbers the peloton has ever contained.

JULIO JIMÉNEZ SELECTED RESULTS:

1961: 1st Gran Premio de Llodio

1962: 1st national hill-climb championships
One stage win Critérium du Dauphiné
One stage win Volta Ciclista a Catalunya

1963: 1st mountains classification Vuelta a España
1st Mont Faron

1964: Two stage wins Tour de France
1st mountains classification and one stage win Vuelta a España
1st national championships

1965: 1st mountains classification and two stage wins Tour de France
1st mountains classification and one stage win Vuelta a España
1st national hill-climb championships

1966: 1st mountains classification and one stage win Tour de France
Two stage wins Giro d'Italia

1967: 1st mountains classification and 2nd overall Tour de France
One stage win Tour of Luxembourg

1968: Two stage wins Giro d'Italia

COL DE PORTET D'ASPET

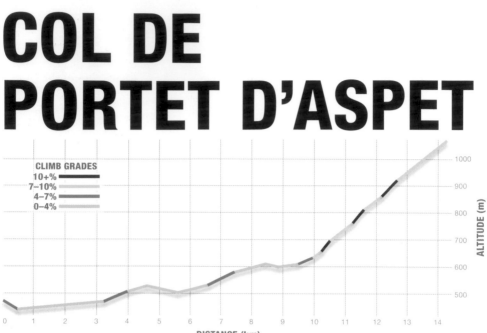

CLIMB GRADES
10+%
7–10%
4–7%
0–4%

ALTITUDE (m)
1000
900
800
700
600
500

DISTANCE (km)
0 1 2 3 4 5 6 7 8 9 10 11 12 13 14

The Portet d'Aspet, situated in the Haute-Garonne, has been visited by the Tour 52 times and some famous names have led the peloton over its summit. Gino Bartali, Charly Gaul, Federico Bahamontes and Julio Jiménez have all danced up its slopes at the head of the race, en route to crafting their own heroic stories. But I am here for one reason only: to pay my respects to a man who may never have led the peloton over the Portet d'Aspet, but one who made the ultimate sacrifice here: Fabio Casartelli.

I cycle out of Aspet just before 1pm. It is a dank, dark and miserable day, the sky clouded and the breeze brisk, with the threat of rain not far away. A sharp descent takes me out of the town. Already thinking of my return ride I take a mental note: in this case what goes down must come back up.

I follow the signs for the col. It is not immediately obvious that I am on an ascent of the Tour de France. The road gently rises and falls as I head towards the village of Sengouagnet. In truth it is easy going, like nothing more than a Sunday morning meander along the damp country lanes of England.

A sharp turn left and the road plunges into a wooded valley. Above me mist is enveloping the forested peaks. Rather than the sky-scraping summits of the Hautes-Pyrénées, here the mountains are covered in trees and regular in shape. They look like they have been cast in pudding bowls.

There are no signs telling me how far I have to go, or what the gradient is, but it is still relatively gentle. I remember from a profile of the climb that this easy riding won't last and I hold back my efforts accordingly. Through the tiny but ominously named Henne-Morte it suddenly occurs to me how quiet this road is. I've barely seen anyone else: a couple of cars and motorbikes have passed and a couple of walkers and I have exchanged cheery "bonjours", but other than that nothing. Cyclists have been conspicuous by their absence.

• • •

This climb has a fearsome reputation. Although difficult uphill, it is feared more for its technical and precipitous descent. A number of riders have crashed on their way off this mountain.

Raymond Poulidor was one rider to come to grief here. In 1973 the popular Frenchman was riding his 11th Tour, having already finished second twice and third three times. As the race started stage 13, from Bourg-Madame to Luchon via the climbs of the Puymorens, Portet d'Aspet, Col de Menté and the Portillon, Poulidor was lying in eighth place, nearly half an hour down on the leader, Luis Ocaña.

Poulidor never finished the stage. On the descent of the Portet d'Aspet he crashed, careering off the road and into the rocky scrub below. Some reports said he

START POINT / Aspet
START ELEVATION / 475m
FINISH ELEVATION / 1069m
LENGTH OF CLIMB / 14.3km
AVERAGE GRADIENT / 4.2%
MAXIMUM GRADIENT / 12.8%
FIRST TOUR / 1910
APPEARANCES / 52

collided with a police motorbike. Whatever the reason for his crash, he smashed his head badly, emerging battered and bloodied, with a broken nose. Although his race was over he had at least escaped with his life. Poulidor was always described as being unlucky for never winning the Tour, but on the Portet d'Aspet in 1973, luck was certainly on his side.

• • •

Shortly after Henne-Morte the road splits in two. To the right is the climb to the Col de Menté, another climb used often by the Tour, but I'm heading left. This is the road to the Col de Portet d'Aspet, the sign helpfully informing me that 4.4km of 9.7% pain lies ahead. Now the real climb begins.

• • •

Poulidor's lucky escape in 1973 was a precursor of what was to come 22 years later. Only this time, Fabio Casartelli would not share Poulidor's good fortune.

Casartelli was lying 87th overall going into stage 15 of the 1995 Tour. Three years previously he had won gold in the road race at the Barcelona Olympics. Recently married, and with a three-month-old child, Casartelli was steadily building a promising career in the professional ranks, having ridden his first Tour in 1994. He had been called up by his Motorola team to ride his second Tour just two days before the race started in Lille.

The peloton went over the summit of the Portet d'Aspet, the first big climb of the day, just before noon. As they descended the mountain, a group of six riders

fell on one of the last challenging corners. While most of the riders managed to pick themselves up or, in the case of French rider Dante Rezze, were rescued from the ravine below, Casartelli lay motionless in the road, blood pouring from his head. It was a desperate sight.

He was immediately attended by the race doctor but his head had hit a concrete block at the side of the road and he had suffered multiple cranial injuries as a result. He was airlifted to hospital in Tarbes with medics trying to revive him on the way. But it was no use. Fabio Casartelli was pronounced dead as his team-mates and colleagues were still riding to the stage finish.

The next day the peloton observed a minute's silence and neutralised the stage, riding slowly in respect, mourning their friend. At the finish in Pau the Motorola team went ahead, the other teams leaving Casartelli's team to cross the line first. *L'Équipe* said: "It was a day of mourning, and it was poignant and admirable," adding in conclusion, "Wherever he is now, Fabio Casartelli can say that he was a member of one of the finest professions in the world."

• • •

Immediately after the turn the gradient ramps up and I'm searching for my lower gears. It's not long before I come across the monument to Casartelli. I've arrived here much quicker than I'd expected, with a under a kilometre ridden since the turn-off, and I am unprepared for it. I'd always thought his fall had occurred much nearer the top of the climb, perhaps because on most mountains it is at the top where the turns are sharp. It is an added cruelty that he had so very nearly made it off the steep section of the mountain.

THIS CLIMB HAS A FEARSOME REPUTATION. ALTHOUGH DIFFICULT UPHILL, IT IS FEARED MORE FOR ITS TECHNICAL AND PRECIPITOUS DESCENT. A NUMBER OF RIDERS HAVE CRASHED ON THEIR WAY OFF THIS MOUNTAIN.

I stop and take a walk around the monument, reading the inscriptions and studying the intricate design work. It's an emotional experience. Here, today, in the overcast gloom, it is difficult to picture the hot and sunny day in 1995 that turned a family's life upside down and cast such a huge shadow over the Tour and bike racing. I sit on the wall in a reflective mood, gazing at the white marble that has been carved into a wheel with wings. The monument includes a sundial that has been designed to show the dates of the Italian's birth, death and Olympic gold medal performance. It's difficult to tear myself away and a large part of me doesn't want to carry on up the climb. I feel that I've done what I have come here for. But of course I remount and continue my journey to the top.

It is steep all the way, with at least a couple of stretches at 17% to deal with, but I gradually weave my way up. It's dark, damp and eerie. Moist air swirls around, leaving everything with a certain sheen. The last kilometre is shrouded in fog as I ride over names of Tour favourites painted in 2011 when the race last came this way. The summit comes quicker than I'd expected. There is absolutely no one here – my only company is a

dog wandering aimlessly around. Today the Portet d'Aspet is a forlorn place.

Almost immediately I turn to face the descent back to Aspet. I have no desire to remain here. With its precipitous drop, damp road and sorry history, the ride back down is somewhat of a daunting prospect and I want to get it over with.

As the bike builds up speed, I apply gentle pressure on the brakes, carefully slowing myself before entering corners. Through tight bend after tight bend, it's an exercise in total concentration. In some ways it is harder than the ride up.

At last I arrive back in Aspet. I sit in its tiny square and contemplate the effect that Casartelli's crash must have had on the people here and the mood in the town. That day had been eagerly anticipated for months. It was meant to be a celebration. A day when the residents of Aspet would have decamped excitedly to the climb to enjoy a picnic and wait for the country's greatest sporting event to pass by. A day when they were primed to roar on their heroes.

Instead it ended shattered on the descent of the Col de Portet d'Aspet as the Tour experienced one of its bleakest days.

LAURENT
FIGNON

WHEN, IN 1983, IT WAS SUGGESTED TO HIM THAT THE GREAT EDDY MERCKX HADN'T EXACTLY TAKEN THE NEW FRENCH SENSATION TO HIS HEART, FIGNON IS REPORTED TO HAVE REPLIED "MERCKX, YOU SAY? DON'T KNOW HIM."

Laurent Fignon won the Tour de France twice but he is more famous for a Tour he didn't win: the 1989 edition, which he lost by eight seconds to Greg LeMond, after an enthralling final-day time trial. It remains the narrowest ever margin of victory in the history of the Tour.

Fignon was born on August 12th 1960 in Montmartre, Paris, and his first love was football – his bike was principally young Laurent's mode of transport to the football pitch. But it was on these journeys that he first discovered that he could ride a good deal faster than any of his football-playing friends.

Intrigued, Fignon joined a local cycling club, La Pédale de Combs-la-Ville, where he was immediately informed he had started too late to ever amount to anything. Despite this discouragement and against his parents' wishes, Fignon continued to ride with the club and started to enter races, often without his family's knowledge. He won his very first event, a 50km road race, and went on to dominate the local cycling scene.

But cycling as a way of making a living was far from his thoughts and, aged 18, as his parents wanted, he enrolled to study Structural and Material Sciences at the Université Paris XIII in Villetaneuse. However, Fignon's studies were not to last. He dropped out to do his military service, joining the Bataillon de Joinville, where he continued cycling. Finally, having enjoyed continued success, he decided that the lure of the road was too great and that he should try to make the bike his future.

In 1981 Fignon was selected for the French amateur team to ride in the Tour of Corsica, a race in which amateur and professional riders competed against each other. Also present was a certain Bernard Hinault, already a multiple Tour de France winner.

Fignon impressed during the race, and his performance was good enough to earn him a professional contract for the 1982 season with Hinault's Renault team, managed by Cyrille Guimard. He promptly won the renowned Criterium International and, when the 1983 Tour de France rolled around, with Hinault unable to ride due to injury, Fignon entered the world's greatest race for the first time, as Renault's team-leader. He was just 22 years old.

Fignon's first yellow jersey in that 1983 Tour should have passed into legend, coming as it did at the top of the fabled Alpe d'Huez. But it arrived after the previous race leader, Pascal Simon, had finally abandoned the race after riding with a broken shoulder for an incredible six days. The power of yellow had given Simon almost superhuman strength, but even the yellow jersey has its limits and, on stage 17, from La Tour-du-Pin to Alpe d'Huez, he was forced to climb off his bike, thereby handing the jersey to Fignon. Some felt that Fignon's yellow jersey was therefore somewhat tainted, a feeling exacerbated by the fact that he had yet to win a stage. In Dijon, on the penultimate stage of the race, he rectified the latter objection, winning the time trial by fifty seconds and claiming the Tour overall by just over four minutes.

With his blond ponytail, rimless glasses and headband, Fignon cut an unorthodox figure in the peloton. He was disparagingly dubbed "Le Prof", partly because of his academic looks, partly because of his university background. And he was a charismatic and outspoken figure right from the start. When, in 1983, it was suggested

1984 Tour, which turned into something of a grudge match between Fignon and Hinault, who had left Renault and his mentor Guimard to join the new La Vie Claire team.

Although Hinault won the 1984 Tour's prologue, Renault took control of the race and, by stage 5, had Fignon's team-mate Vincent Barteau ensconced in yellow. There he stayed until Fignon was ready to take over custody on stage 17, again on the slopes of Alpe d'Huez. Hinault was two-and-a-half minutes behind Fignon going into the stage and relentlessly attacked on the climbs before the Alpe. But Fignon repelled each assault with ease and, as the race hit the Alpe, rode Hinault off his wheel. He didn't win the stage – that honour went to Luis Herrera – but by the end Fignon had put nearly three more minutes into Hinault. Although not taking yellow until the final week, Fignon was imperious throughout the whole race, which featured no fewer than five time trials. Aside from the opening prologue, Fignon won them all, with Renault winning the team time trial. He added to this impressive haul by claiming two mountain stages (La Plagne and Crans-Montana), and in the end he won the race by over ten minutes, ahead of Hinault. A period of Fignon dominance beckoned.

But it was not to be. Fignon became prone to injury and never won the Tour again. He came closest in 1989, when arguably he had his best season. He claimed his second win in Milan–San Remo and, in June, finally won the Giro d'Italia. Then came the Tour.

The 1989 Tour de France became a glorious battle between Fignon and Greg LeMond. In his book, *Blazing Saddles*, Matt Rendell likens the fight for yellow to a tennis match, with the race lead being batted back and forth as the race trailed around France. The hold on the jersey switched four times between the pair from stage

to him that the great Eddy Merckx hadn't exactly taken the new French sensation to his heart, Fignon is reported to have replied "Merckx, you say? Don't know him." .

The 1984 season brought more success. He took second place in the Giro d'Italia (only losing it on the final day), and won his first French national championships before dominating the

FIGNON WAS IMPERIOUS THROUGHOUT THE WHOLE RACE, WHICH FEATURED NO FEWER THAN FIVE TIME TRIALS. ASIDE FROM THE OPENING PROLOGUE, FIGNON WON THEM ALL.

5 to the end of the race. Fignon looked to have taken hold of the jersey definitively as the race exited the Alps, holding a fifty-second lead into the final stage, a 24.5km time trial from Versailles to the Champs-Élysées.

It was of course conceivable that LeMond would gain enough time, but few expected it. LeMond competed with aero bars and a streamlined helmet; Fignon, his blond hair flapping in the wind, looked decidedly old-school in comparison. The television pictures of the clock counting down as Fignon laboured to the line, while LeMond, surrounded by reporters, looked on, wide-eyed, are indelibly etched in any cycling fan's memory. A closer finish than the eight seconds of 1989 is all but unimaginable. Unfairly, it was to become Fignon's defining moment.

In a fitting piece of symmetry, Fignon's last major stage win was in the 1990 Critérium

International, the race that had given him his first professional title. Upon his retirement from cycling in 1993 he entered the business world, running a number of cycling ventures, including a brief tenure as owner of the Paris–Nice race. He also became a fixture on French television and, in 2010, published a typically forthright book, *Nous étions jeunes et insouciants* – We Were Young and Carefree. "Sometimes when I was physically at my best," he wrote, "I could sense moments of utter ecstasy, those rare fleeting times when you are in total harmony with yourself and the elements around you: nature, the noise of the wind, the smells." That year, he died from stomach cancer, aged only fifty.

LAURENT FIGNON SELECTED RESULTS:

1982: 1st Critérium International
1st Grand Prix de Cannes

1983: 1st overall and one stage win Tour de France
1st Grand Prix de Plumelec
1st Tour du Limousin

1984: 1st overall and six stage wins Tour de France
1st national championships
2nd overall and 1st mountains classification Giro d'Italia
1 stage win Tour de Romandie

1985: 1st overall and one stage win Semaine Internationale Coppi-Bartali

1986: 1st La Flèche Wallonne

1987: 2nd overall and one stage win Tour du Luxembourg

3rd overall and two stage wins Paris–Nice
3rd overall and one stage win Vuelta a España

1988: 1st Milan–San Remo
3rd Paris–Roubaix

1989: 1st overall and 1 stage win Giro d'Italia
1st Milan–San Remo
1st Grand Prix des Nations
2nd overall and two stage wins Tour de France

1990: 1st overall Critérium International

1991: One stage win Giro di Puglia

1992: One stage win Tour de France

1993: 1st overall and one stage win Ruta Mexico

MONT VENTOUX

START POINT / Bedoin
START ELEVATION / 296m
FINISH ELEVATION / 1912m
LENGTH OF CLIMB / 21.1km
AVERAGE GRADIENT / 7.6%
MAXIMUM GRADIENT / 10.8%
FIRST TOUR / 1951
APPEARANCES / 14

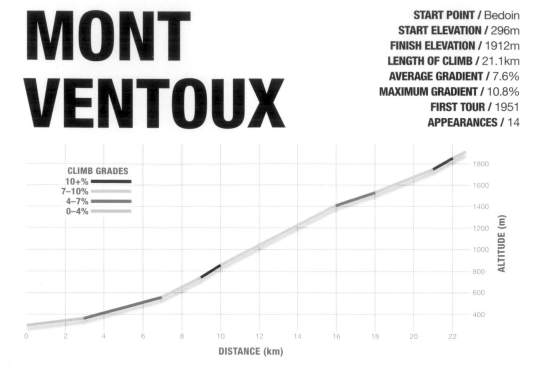

CLIMB GRADES
10+%
7–10%
4–7%
0–4%

ALTITUDE (m)

DISTANCE (km)

Monday May 28th, 7.30pm
The municipal campsite in Carpentras

I'm sitting outside my little caravan. The sun is getting lower in the sky and I'm nursing a beer. I can't stop thinking about Mont Ventoux. If you walk a short way up the road from here you can see the summit as plain as day. I did that earlier and stood and stared at the observatory that's perched atop the bald peak. There it was, looking down on me, taunting me, daring me.

"You? Ride up here? Tomorrow? We'll see about that. Come and have a go. We'll see if you're hard enough."

• • •

The first recorded ascent of Mont Ventoux was in the 1300s, when Francesco Petrarca, the Italian poet, embarked by foot on a quest to reach the top of the mountain for no reason "but the desire to see its conspicuous height". He recorded his exploration in a letter to Dionigi da Borgo San Sepolcro, a professor of theology, in which he told of meeting an elderly shepherd on the slopes, who claimed to have climbed to the summit of the Ventoux fifty years earlier, and who implored Petrarca not to continue, saying "[he]

had brought home nothing but regret and pains and his body as well as his clothes torn by rocks and thorny underbrush." According to his letter, when Petrarca made it to the top he stood "almost benumbed, overwhelmed by a gale such as I had never felt before and by the unusually open and wide view."

More than six centuries later, in 1951, the Tour de France made its inaugural visit to the mountain. French rider Lucien Lazarides crested the summit in the lead, having broken away from the pack as the Ventoux cast its spell on the peloton for the first time.

• • •

Tuesday May 29th, 6.30am
The municipal campsite in Carpentras

The alarm sounds but I don't need it. I've barely slept a wink thinking about what today might bring. I need an early start because I want to beat the heat. I don't want to be riding through the lunar landscape at the top of Ventoux with the midday sun beaming down and bouncing off the pale rock into my face. I slowly and methodically gather all my gear and, with the church bells of Carpentras ringing out their 7am call, I set off for Bédoin and the start of the climb.

Tuesday May 29th, 7.45am
A car park in Bédoin

Bédoin gets more than its fair share of cyclists. It even has car parks set aside for them. I park up and assemble my bike in front of a gaggle of school children. They take little notice of me as I check the wheels, fumble about in various bags, check camera and recorder batteries, scrutinise the contents of my pockets and generally do anything to put off the inevitable.

So why does the Ventoux hold me in such a grip of fear? Well, I've been here before, in 2009, to watch the Tour pass. That day was one of the hardest I have ever experienced on a bike. Despite the many and varied distractions of the Tour circus, the company of thousands of other cyclists and the cheering of those walking or standing by the roadside, I struggled like never before. Or since. My most vivid memory of that day is of sitting on a rock, in the shade of the trees, looking at the road ahead with a growing sense of how ridiculous it was to think that I could ride up here. On that rock I realised I was not going to make it to the top. I got as far as Chalet Reynard, the legendary café two-thirds of the way up the mountain, and stopped. Completely drained. Totally dejected.

Ventoux had defeated me in 2009. Today I was back and with no choice but to make the summit.

•••

After its debut in 1951, the Tour returned the following year and again in 1955, when the first real indications came of the pain and suffering that this mountain could impose.

Going into the Ventoux stage in 1955, eventual winner Louison Bobet was trailing the race leader by more than eleven minutes. As the race entered the lower slopes of the Ventoux in intense heat, Bobet sensed that this was the moment to try to retrieve some of that lost time. He timed his attack perfectly, distancing his great rival Charly Gaul, who was just twenty seconds behind him overall but hated the heat. Bobet went over the summit alone before embarking on a headlong descent to the stage finish in Avignon, where he crossed the line 49 seconds ahead of Jean Brankart but, more crucially, well over five minutes ahead of all the other favourites, thus setting the foundation for his third Tour win.

But behind Bobet there was carnage. Ferdi Kübler, winner of the 1950 Tour, set off up the Ventoux like a rocket, to the alarm of Raphaël Géminiani, who shouted out a warning: "Careful Ferdi, the Ventoux is a climb like no other." In response Kübler shouted back: "And Ferdi is a champion like no other." But Kübler

KÜBLER HAD SERIOUSLY UNDERESTIMATED THE VENTOUX. HE WAS SOON WEAVING ALL OVER THE ROAD, IN A STATE OF DELIRIUM, SWEAT DRIPPING FROM HIS BROW, EYES HAUNTED.

had seriously underestimated the Ventoux. He was soon weaving all over the road, in a state of delirium, sweat dripping, eyes haunted. He stopped to rest, then promptly tried to set off in the wrong direction before a spectator endured his wrath to put him right. "Ferdi going to explode!" he yelled. Amazingly, given his state, he fell into Avignon just 26 minutes down on Bobet, but he had paid a heavy price. He abandoned that night and never rode again at the Tour. "Ferdi killed himself on the Ventoux," he said later.

And there were others. Jean Malléjac collapsed 10km from the top. The following day's race report read: "Malléjac was inanimate, his eyes rolled back, his skinny physique accentuated by a waxy pallor and drawn features." The Frenchman could only be given a drink after his teeth had been forced apart by the race doctor. Once he came round in the ambulance he had to be restrained as he demanded he be given back his bike. Malléjac survived – just – but the Ventoux had shown the peloton who was the boss.

• • •

The opening kilometres have run their course without difficulty. I've passed vineyards and cycled through pretty hamlets, all the time with the summit of Ventoux over my left shoulder. Now I'm in Saint-Estève, where I know the serious business begins.

The road pitches up as I head into the forested section of the climb. For the next 8km or so the gradient won't fall below 9%, with stretches much tougher. The road goes straight up the mountain, with barely any hairpins to break down the ascent into segments.

The forest I'm now riding through once wasn't here. For a time Mont Ventoux was completely bald, having been stripped bare of its trees for use in shipbuilding. A programme of reforestation was embarked upon in the 1800s, when the forest of cedar and oak was replanted. Today trees crowd the road, ensuring that, for the first time in nearly 24 hours, I can no longer see the summit. The forest also provides welcome shelter from the sun, which is already strong – every time I pass through a section where the trees are thinner, I can feel the heat burning my skin.

The section between 10km and 12km is particularly tough. My legs are beginning to feel heavy and my

lungs are burning. I take a short rest and try to take some photographs but my hands are shaking too much. As I rest a German couple in their late fifties stop on their bikes, both with a wobble. They nod a greeting and start talking to each other. I can't understand what they're saying but I'd bet my house it isn't: "Well that last bit was nice and easy, wasn't it?"

• • •

Three years after Bobet's win in Avignon the race returned to the Ventoux. This time the mountain was to host its first time trial, 21.5km from Bédoin to the summit. Going into the stage Luxembourg's Charly Gaul was in ninth position, more than ten minutes behind race leader Vito Favero. Gaul was a great climber and a terrific time triallist but, once again, Ventoux was a cauldron of heat and Gaul hated the heat.

Nevertheless the Luxembourger destroyed all but fellow climbing specialist Federico Bahamontes. Setting off two minutes after Bobet, with less than half of the time trial gone, Gaul blew by the Frenchman to finish in 1 hour 2 minutes and 9 seconds. Only Bahamontes was able to come anywhere close, crossing the line 31 seconds down. All the others were minutes behind. Géminiani said Gaul was "beyond human".

The result catapulted Gaul into the top three and with three days in the Alps to come it appeared that an assault on yellow was but a formality. But the following day he lost nearly eleven minutes on the race leaders and it seemed his chances were over. It took a dramatic day in the Chartreuse Massif to saved the race for him (see pp244–245).

• • •

Tuesday May 29th, 9.45am
Chalet Reynard

Approaching Chalet Reynard the road flattens and then falls briefly. Up to this point the famous café has been my initial target. Psychologically I've broken the Ventoux into two parts: pre and post Chalet Reynard. For the entire climb so far I've been working out how far it is to here, deducting 6km from every kilometre marker to calculate how much further I have to go to reach my first goal. My plan was to rest here for the second section but, to my surprise, I actually don't feel too bad so, keen to continue while the legs are still willing, I opt to press on immediately.

• • •

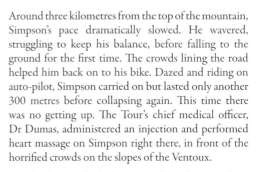

For all the exploits of Bobet and Gaul, Mont Ventoux is famous for one terrible incident above all others. This mountain has blood on its slopes.

In 1967 Britain's Tom Simpson was one of the best riders in the world. At the end of the 1950s the Doncaster-born rider had moved to France to try to crack the big time. He succeeded, going on to win the Tour of Flanders, Bordeaux–Paris and Milan–San Remo over the next four years. He had even grabbed the Tour's race lead for one day in 1962, the first British rider to do so, prompting a flurry of photographs of him in the yellow jersey, sipping tea, carrying an umbrella and wearing a bowler hat. His lead lasted just one day, and eventually he finished sixth. Five years later, having won the world championships in 1965, Simpson had his eyes on a stronger Tour showing.

Simpson was lying in seventh position, 8 minutes and 20 seconds behind race leader Roger Pingeon, as the peloton started stage 13, 211.5km from Marseilles to Carpentras. Again, it was a day of formidable heat. On the initial slopes of the Ventoux Simpson fell in with a group containing Pingeon that was chasing Julio Jiménez and Raymond Poulidor. So far, so good. But as the chasing group reached Chalet Reynard, Simpson started to fall behind.

Around three kilometres from the top of the mountain, Simpson's pace dramatically slowed. He wavered, struggling to keep his balance, before falling to the ground for the first time. The crowds lining the road helped him back on to his bike. Dazed and riding on auto-pilot, Simpson carried on but lasted only another 300 metres before collapsing again. This time there was no getting up. The Tour's chief medical officer, Dr Dumas, administered an injection and performed heart massage on Simpson right there, in front of the horrified crowds on the slopes of the Ventoux.

But the doctor who had saved the life of Jean Malléjac twelve years earlier on the Ventoux could not perform the same trick twice. Dumas tried to revive the British rider for more than an hour. Eventually Simpson was helicoptered off the mountain to hospital. He was pronounced dead upon arrival. Simpson had died of cardiac arrest. Traces of amphetamines were found in his blood and drugs were found in his jersey pockets.

"Hardly a day goes by without the press denouncing the damaging effects of drugs, which attack not just a person's health but his very personality... But today let us weep for Tom Simpson, a decent chap who probably simply feared defeat," wrote Jacques Goddet, the Tour director.

•••

Tuesday May 29th, 10.25am
1km to go

Beyond Chalet Reynard the vegetation retreats. I am cycling amid a desolate, barren and sorry place. The gradient has relented slightly for the last four or five kilometres and, after the difficult forest section, it feels markedly easier on the legs. But I am lucky today. Often, on this part of the climb, the strong wind that gives the mountain its name blows straight into the faces of the hardy souls who are brave enough to ride here. Gusts over 274km/h have been recorded. Not today. Today there is just a brisk breeze. Today the Ventoux is being as kind as it ever deigns to be.

The mountain still plays tricks with me, though. Through the hairpins of the top section I often lose sight of the observatory for a few minutes, only for it to reappear seemingly as far away as it was when it escaped my gaze. For the final three or four kilometres it feels as if I am riding towards an ever-moving target.

I'm tired now, and just when I need the gradient to shallow, it kicks up – one final test thrown at me to ensure I'm worthy. The last section of this climb, past the memorial erected to Tom Simpson, is at 8% and it's a real grind to get to the top. When it comes, the end is up on me in a flash. One moment the observatory still seems far away, the next I round a corner and there it is: the summit of the Ventoux. I have arrived.

As I sit recovering under the summit sign I meet Charlie, who has cycled up here on an old, steel-framed bike that stands out among all the expensive carbon. It turns out that Charlie lives about fifty miles from me in south-west England. He's here on a cycling holiday and arrived in Bédoin last night. I ask him how he found the climb.

"Not as bad as I feared," he says. "I'd read all the horror stories and rode well within myself. It took me two-and-a-half hours, so I won't be winning any speed records. But I don't care. I got here."

Charlie tells me he is packing up his tent tomorrow, loading his camping gear on to his bike and heading for the Alps. I leave him looking at a map for a circular route back to Bédoin.

I spend a long time at the top, soaking up the atmosphere of this unique place. There is a constant stream of cyclists, all realising their dream to climb this giant of cycling. Eventually I make my way down to the Simpson memorial. I want to spend some time there to pay my respects to Mr Tom.

DUMAS DESPERATELY TRIED TO REVIVE THE BRITISH RIDER FOR MORE THAN AN HOUR. EVENTUALLY SIMPSON WAS HELICOPTERED OFF THE MOUNTAIN TO HOSPITAL. HE WAS PRONOUNCED DEAD UPON ARRIVAL.

As I reach the memorial, an Australian coming up, obviously in some trouble and veering all over the road, suddenly stops. A car immediately pulls up.

"You alright mate?" says the driver.

The cyclist is obviously on a supported ride. He could stop the madness and get into the car at any time.

"Yeah... just need rest," the cyclist gasps.

"Good on ya. You've under 1km to go."

"I'm so tired... going so slow. I'm sorry."

The driver stares into the eyes of the struggling rider and says something that I will always remember.

"It's not about the speed or the time or keeping up with the others. It's about your own journey."

BERNARD THÉVENET

It is July 13th 1975. It's a Sunday and the Tour is heading into the Alps for its final-week shakedown. Thousands have lined the route from Nice, over climbs of the Saint-Martin, Couillole, Champs and Allos, on the way to the summit finish at Pra-Loup. Millions more are watching on television at home and in bars up and down the country.

After seven hours of racing the riders are on the final climb. Out front is Eddy Merckx, in the yellow jersey, as usual. He had been punched in the stomach two days earlier by a spectator (see p122) but at the moment he is not showing any signs of discomfort. More than a minute behind Merckx is Felice Gimondi, winner of the Tour in 1965 and lying fifth overall. He is in no-man's-land. Further down the road is a chasing group of three: Lucien Van Impe, Joop Zoetemelk and Bernard Thévenet, who's riding his sixth Tour.

Thévenet is doing all the work in this group. Rocking from side to side, head nodding like a pull-along toy dog, the Frenchman is towing his rivals up this last ascent. He looks behind, slowly reaches down and changes gear. He takes a bottle from a spectator, takes a swig and throws it to the ground. His team car pulls up and he shares some words with his director, Maurice de Muer. Then he pushes harder on the pedals and storms away. Van Impe is dropped immediately. Zoetemelk is a little tougher to shake off, at least at first. He scampers across the gap like a lamb seeking a feed from its mother. But he can't hold the pace for long. Soon Thévenet is alone.

The cameraman on the motorcycle that has been following Thévenet's attack suddenly zooms up the road, keen to find out how far the Frenchman has to go before catching Gimondi. The camera fixes on the rider in front. "Non, non,

c'est Merckx!" comes the astonished cry from the commentary booth. The next rider on the road is the yellow jersey. Merckx has cracked. Gimondi is now the leader of the stage and Thévenet, just 58 seconds behind the Belgian colossus at the beginning of the day, is closing in on the race leader.

Gimondi keeps looking back. It's like he can't quite believe what is happening. Nor can anyone else. Thévenet passes Merckx and then, a few minutes later, powers past Gimondi and takes the stage win and the yellow jersey. He leads Merckx, who now looks human, by 58 seconds.

But more is to come. The next day is Bastille Day and, to the delight of France, Thévenet storms the Izoard. He rises over the legendary peak all alone, over two minutes in front. He wins his second stage in a row. The country is in raptures. What panache! A fan holds a sign: "Merckx is beaten – the Bastille has fallen!" Louison Bobet is jubilant, saluting Thévenet's ride over the Izoard as the display of a true champion and predicting that the Frenchman would go on to win the Tour.

And win the Tour he did. It was the first year that the race finished on the Champs-Élysées and Bernard Thévenet became the first man to ride around the famous avenue wearing the yellow jersey.

Born in Saint-Julien-de-Civry in 1948, Thévenet had enjoyed a successful spell as an amateur, winning a stage at the Tour de l'Avenir and winning the amateur national championships before the call came from Peugeot. After that win at La Mongie, more stage wins at the Tour and Vuelta, and overall victories at the Tour de Romandie and Volta Ciclista a Catalunya came before his 1975 Tour success.

Thévenet followed that 1975 win with another in 1977, when he had to turn himself inside out on another legendary Tour climb to salvage his win. Going into stage 17, from Chamonix to l'Alpe d'Huez, Thévenet was in yellow but only just. He had 11 seconds on Dietrich Thurau, 33 seconds on Van Impe and 49 seconds on Hennie Kuiper.

Van Impe attacked on the Glandon and arrived at the foot of the Alpe alone, with a two-minute advantage on Thévenet, who was being shadowed by Kuiper and Zoetemelk. With 5km to go and with Van Impe still up the road, seemingly riding to the stage win and into yellow, Thévenet looked on the limit. Then Kuiper launched an attack. Thévenet, head down, staring at the road right beneath his wheels, didn't even glance up. Either he didn't realise what was happening, or he couldn't do anything about it. Kuiper sprinted off up the road, never to be seen again by his former companion.

Ahead, while Thévenet rode himself ragged in defence of his jersey, Van Impe was in a bad way. Beginning to suffer after his earlier exertions on the Glandon, his face was a picture of pure pain.

THÉVENET COLLAPSED, HIS ARMS THROWN AROUND TEAM HELPERS. IT HAD BEEN ONE OF THE MOST ASTONISHING DEFENCES OF THE YELLOW JERSEY THAT THE TOUR HAD SEEN FOR YEARS.

The difference in the respective speeds of Van Impe and Kuiper was marked. A two-minute lead quickly became a one-minute advantage.

Then things got worse for Van Impe. He was knocked off his bike and on to the rocky verge by a car following the race. The Belgian ace remounted and carried on for a few metres but his rear wheel had been damaged and he needed a replacement. As he put his hand up to summon his team car, Kuiper powered past. Van Impe's chance of the stage and yellow had gone.

Thévenet, trying desperately to salvage yellow, then passed Van Impe. Just as Kuiper crossed the finish line, Thévenet rounded the corner into the final, long straight. The clock ticked on. Thévenet, head bowed, drove for the line, summoning every last ounce of energy. Had Kuiper done enough to take yellow or had Thévenet saved the day?

Thévenet crossed the line 41 seconds after Kuiper. Incredibly, he was still in yellow by eight seconds. Thévenet collapsed, his arms thrown around team helpers. It had been one of the most astonishing defences of the yellow jersey that the Tour had seen for years. Six days later he stood on top of the Paris podium for the second time.

Thévenet retired from racing in 1981 at the age of 33. He spent some time as a team manager before working as a journalist, television commentator and for ASO, organisers of the Tour. In 2001 he was made a Chevalier de la Légion d'Honneur.

BERNARD THÉVENET SELECTED RESULTS:

1966: 1st amateur Tour du Roussillon

1968: 1st Grand Prix de France

1969: 1st Mont Faron
One stage win Tour de l'Avenir

1970: One stage win Tour de France

1971: One stage win Tour de France

1972: Two stage wins Tour de France
1st overall and one stage win Tour de Romandie

1973: 2nd overall and two stage wins Tour de France
1st national championships
One stage win Vuelta a España
2nd overall and one stage win Critérium du Dauphiné

1974: 1st overall and one stage win Volta Ciclista a Catalunya
One stage win Paris–Nice
1st Critérium International

1975: 1st overall and two stage wins Tour de France
1st overall and one stage win Critérium du Dauphiné
2nd Liège–Bastogne–Liège

1976: 1st overall and two stage wins Critérium du Dauphiné
2nd overall Giro di Lombardia

1977: 1st overall and one stage win Tour de France

1981: One stage win Circuit Cycliste Sarthe

PUY-DE-DÔME

CLIMB GRADES
10+%
7–10%
4–7%
0–4%

ALTITUDE (m)

DISTANCE (km)

The Puy-de-Dôme is a legendary climb. Up to 1988 the precipitous road that wraps itself around this extinct Massif Central volcano was regularly used by the Tour, and its imposing hulk has played host to many a memorable moment. So the Puy-de-Dôme simply had to be included in this book. But I knew before I left that getting to the summit on a bike was not going to be easy.

• • •

Fausto Coppi won the very first stage here, just two days before the end of the 1952 race. Coppi had dominated the three weeks, winning four stages, including the first ever summit finish at Alpe d'Huez. The Tour was won, but Coppi wanted the Puy-de-Dôme as well. In the leading group on the climb, Coppi kept his powder dry, coming to the front with less than 2km to go, when Dutchman Jan Nolten made his bid for the stage. Coppi gave chase, overhauling him just before the line to win by ten seconds.

It took seven years for the race to return. On that occasion Federico Bahamontes won the short time trial to the volcano's peak, on his way to the race win (see p157). Two summit finishes, and both times the winner had gone on to win in Paris. The Puy-de-Dôme was getting a reputation.

• • •

Until relatively recently it was possible to cycle to the top of the climb using the road that the Tour used to take. Access was restricted – cyclists were allowed on the last, narrow five kilometres of the climb, the section that constitutes the proper part of the ascent, only on a couple of days a week – but it was possible. That changed in 2010, when all access was stopped to allow work to protect the volcano from erosion. The works were scheduled for completion in 2012 and I had understood that cyclists would then be granted access.

But I discovered that it had been decided that the road would not be reopened. Members of the public would no longer be able to drive, ride or walk up the road that the Tour used to use. It was going to be impossible to follow directly in the tracks of the peloton, but this peak's tale had to be told. I had to get to the summit. I had to find an alternative, and one that didn't involve taking the train that now runs to the top.

After a bit of research it looked like it might be possible to reach the summit using a mountain bike and taking an off-road route. I've only once mountain-biked properly, so riding to the top of a 1400m volcano was going to be difficult, but it was worth a go. I don't own a mountain bike, so step forward my friend James. James is a mad-keen club cyclist – the type of guy who isn't truly happy unless he's racing around a disused

START POINT / Clermont-Ferrand
START ELEVATION / 368m
FINISH ELEVATION / 1415m
LENGTH OF CLIMB / 14km
AVERAGE GRADIENT / 7.5%
MAXIMUM GRADIENT / 12.7%
FIRST TOUR / 1952
APPEARANCES / 13

airfield at seven in the morning. He is also partial to haring about in woods on his mountain bike. James was joining me for my last few days in France to shame me by speeding up mountains far faster than I could, and he agreed that, in compensation for inflicting that humiliation on me, he'd bring a couple of bikes out. Sorted. The Puy-de-Dôme by mountain bike it was.

● ● ●

The race came back to the volcano in 1964. Not only was it to be the most famous stage that ever took place on the slopes of the Puy-de-Dôme but it was to provide the backdrop for one of the most iconic photographs the race has ever produced.

By 1964 the rivalry between Jacques Anquetil and Raymond Poulidor was at its most intense, and the French nation was split into two camps. Stage 20, just three days before the end of the race, was 237.5km from Brive to Puy-de-Dôme. Going into the stage, just 56 seconds separated Anquetil from Poulidor, in second. As the race entered the final five kilometres, four riders were leading: Jiménez, Anquetil, Poulidor and Bahamontes. Then Jiménez accelerated and Bahamontes followed, after a hesitation that perhaps cost him the stage. That left the two Frenchman engaged in a personal battle lower down the slopes.

For more than three kilometres they rode the murderous slopes of the Puy-de-Dôme together. Not one behind the other. Together. Anquetil on the inside, Poulidor on the outside. First and second overall. Shoulder to shoulder. Head to head. They banged into each other. Heads bowed, arms clashing, bikes leaning, eyes fixed. Flashbulbs fired. The Tour's most famous photograph had been captured.

With less than one kilometre to go Poulidor pulled away. Anquetil could no longer maintain the pace and fell behind. Dramatically so. The destiny of the yellow jersey was about to be decided with less than 900m left. Poulidor rode as fast as he could, gaining time with every revolution of his pedals. He crossed the line 57 seconds behind Jiménez. Now all eyes turned down the road. How far away was Anquetil?

To the crowd's surprise the next rider to arrive was not the Frenchman but Vittorio Adorni. Then, nine seconds later, Anquetil appeared, crouched over his

FOR MORE THAN THREE KILOMETRES THEY RODE THE MURDEROUS SLOPES OF THE PUY-DE-DÔME TOGETHER. NOT ONE BEHIND THE OTHER. TOGETHER. ANQUETIL ON THE INSIDE, POULIDOR ON THE OUTSIDE.

handlebars, occasionally glancing up to see when he could end the hell of turning the pedals. He had lost 1 minute 39 seconds to Jiménez but, crucially, only 42 seconds to Poulidor. Paul Howard's biography of Anquetil, *Sex, Lies and Handlebar Tape*, describes Anquetil collapsing in a heap on the car of his team director Raphaël Géminiani.

"How much?" he asked

"Fourteen seconds."

"That's thirteen more than I need."

They were talking about the gap that Anquetil had managed to keep over Poulidor in the overall standings. Poulidor would later learn just how close he had come to winning the Tour. "If he had taken the jersey from me," Anquetil said after the race had entered Paris, "I would have gone home."

As it was Anquetil didn't go home. Instead he won the final time trial and took his fifth Tour by 55 seconds over his great rival.

•••

After weeks of riding a slender machine built for speed, it feels odd to be perched on top of a robust mountain bike designed to stay in one piece no matter what terrain you throw at it. As we slowly ride the climbing road away from Clermont-Ferrand, the town at the foot of the Puy-de-Dôme, the volcano stands stately in front of us. Set against a sky uncluttered by cloud and pointing towards a still visible moon, the television transmitter on the Puy's peak towers skyward like a rocket standing primed for take-off.

We're looking for the start of the off-road route that we've been told we should be able to ride to the summit. Sure enough we soon pass a sign inviting us into the woods and on to a dirt path. The path winds its way through the pine forest, rising gradually. There are protruding roots to jump over, sudden dips to navigate, the odd rock to negotiate. It's a complete contrast to all the other riding I've done on this trip and I'm enjoying it very much. Then the path shoots up dramatically and suddenly I'm struggling for breath. I find the lowest gear but my technique is lacking. If I stand the back wheel slips, if I sit I strain to turn the pedals and the front wheel lifts. I am forced to remain in the saddle, hunched over the front handlebars. It is uncomfortable and draining. I stop for breath. Big mistake. There's

no way I can get going again on this slope and I have to walk a little way to a flatter section. Eventually I emerge panting from the forest, to find James waiting for me, smiling. "A bit tough, that last bit," he says jauntily. "We have a section on our regular route back home like that, probably steeper though." I can't answer. I'm still trying to breathe and stand up at the same time. For the first time in my life I feel like I might need an inhaler. James looks puzzled, "You okay?"

• • •

In 1975 Eddy Merckx was going for a record sixth Tour title. With over two weeks of the race gone he was in the yellow jersey, and had been for ten days.

Going into the Puy-de-Dôme stage, Merckx's advantage was 1 minute 32 seconds over Bernard Thévenet. During the course of the stage the race's main protagonists – Merckx, Thévenet, Van Impe and Joop Zoetemelk – had pretty much stayed together. Then, with a little over 5km to go, Thévenet and Van Impe attacked.

For once Merckx couldn't answer. Zoetemelk was either unwilling or unable to respond as well and so Thévenet and Van Impe pulled away. The pair quickly built a lead, with Van Impe eventually going on to win the stage by fifteen seconds.

In his pursuit Merckx had managed to put a little distance between himself and Zoetemelk but, with just over 100m to go, Merckx was struck twice. First a woman slapped him on his back, an apparent expression of frustration at his continued dominance,

FIRST A WOMAN SLAPPED HIM ON HIS BACK, AN APPARENT EXPRESSION OF FRUSTRATION AT HIS CONTINUED DOMINANCE, THEN, A SECOND LATER, A MAN PUNCHED HIM. MERCKX IMMEDIATELY GRABBED HIS SIDE IN PAIN.

then, a second later, a man punched him. Merckx immediately grabbed his side in pain. He was badly winded, his rhythm interrupted. Zoetemelk came back up to the Belgian, who was now in agony, and the two crossed the line together, 49 seconds behind Van Impe.

The punch would cost Merckx far more than a few seconds on the Puy-de-Dôme. He was still feeling the effects of the attack two days later. On the stage from Nice to Pra Loup he cracked, losing the yellow jersey to Thévenet (see p115). He would never wear the jersey of the leader of the Tour again.

• • •

We cross a road to the Chemin des Muletiers footpath. We'd been told we'd be able to ride up this path but we're dismayed to find signs everywhere telling us it is forbidden to do so. We push our bikes up until no one else is around, and then we ride. But the gradient and the heavily gravelled surface make it very difficult going. We pass a few people. No one tells us to stop, so we keep going. Eventually we come to the road that the Tour used to take.

We discuss our options. We seriously consider just riding up the road and seeing what happens. Then

a Frenchman appears walking his dog. He reads our minds and tells us that the road is regularly patrolled and that we won't make it far before the police are called. It seems criminal to us to have this legendary road right in front of us, wide and empty and off-limits. We want to cycle it in homage to our heroes. This road is begging to be cycled up. It is unbelievably frustrating, but we cross over and continue with the footpath.

It immediately becomes apparent that continuing with the bikes on the footpath is no longer possible either. We grudgingly admit defeat and decide to hide the bikes among the trees and proceed on foot. So the last thirty minutes of our adventure to the top of the Puy-de-Dôme is undertaken on foot. The path is difficult going. It climbs sharply as it hairpins up the side of the volcano. Soon our calves are burning and our backs are aching. This climb is hurting. And that's the one saving grace to this episode: our trip up to the top of this peak is making us suffer, as it should do. It wouldn't feel right to just cruise to the summit feeling fresh and rested. I want it to be hard, I want to feel a little of what the Tour's riders experienced as they rode up here with heaving lungs and heavy limbs.

Eventually we reach the top. The views are far-reaching but it all feels a bit underwhelming. Maybe it's the presence of all the buildings: the large restaurant, the gift shop, the train terminal and the television transmitter. Maybe it's because we can't see the road so we don't know where the top of the climb used to be. Maybe it's because there's no sign of its importance to the Tour. Of course, the race only came here thirteen times, so there's no reason to expect this place to be any sort of shrine for cyclists. It's unreasonable for me to want to see only cyclists and walkers here, people who have earned the right to stand on this summit. Unreasonable it may be, but that is exactly how I feel.

We return to the bikes happy to have been here, content that we respected the history of the Tour and the Puy-de-Dôme. It's a real pity that cyclists are no longer allowed to cycle here. Apparently from 2013 there will be two or three days set aside each year for organised rides to the top. At least that's something, I suppose.

JACQUES ANQUETIL

Jacques Anquetil emerged into the French public's consciousness in 1953 when he won the first of his nine Grand Prix des Nations titles. The race was an individual time trial that took place from 1932 until 2004, when the introduction of the discipline to the UCI World Championships resulted in the removal of the Grand Prix des Nations from the calendar. Anquetil, an absolute master of racing alone against the clock, was its dominant force throughout the 1950s and into the 1960s.

Anquetil had come to the attention of Francis Pélissier, the sports director of the La Perle bike team, thanks to his performances in 1952 and 1953. Pélissier had received a bundle of race reports featuring the young rider's exploits, including a 1952 Olympic bronze medal in the team time trial, which he rode alongside Alfred Tonello and Claude Rouer. The great Louison Bobet had captured the hearts of the nation, and Pélissier was keen to find a rider for his team who could match him. In Anquetil, a young, good-looking and – most of all – talented rider, he thought he'd found what he was looking for.

In August 1953 Anquetil destroyed the field during the Paris–Normandie race, winning by over nine minutes. The press lapped up the performance, writing: "Who can resist the young Anquetil?" One person who couldn't resist was Pélissier and, one month later, Anquetil lined up at the start of the Grand Prix des Nations in a La Perle jersey, ready to take on the sport's established stars.

What followed was nothing short of remarkable. Anquetil, aged just 19 and not yet a professional, wiped out the opposition. He was nearly one minute up after only 20km of the 140.3km race and never looked back, extending his lead all the way to the finish. He won by nearly seven minutes. Pierre Chany wrote that, until that day, "we truly did not know Jacques Anquetil." The young amateur's performance had been nothing short of a revelation. As for his director Pélissier, Chany describes him looking on with a cigarette at the corner of his lips as his new protégé was surrounded by admirers. "Now, we will make some cry," he said. "You have not seen anything yet."

Anquetil was born in 1934, in Mont-Saint-Aignan near Rouen, to parents who worked a strawberry plantation. While studying at the local technical college, he joined his first cycling club, the Association Cycliste de Sotteville, which was directed by André Boucher, a local bike shop owner. It was at Boucher's behest that he entered his first race, aged 18. Naturally, he won.

Wins in the amateur road championships and the Grand Prix de France followed in 1952, a year topped off with that Olympic bronze medal. Five more victories followed in 1953, including one stage and the overall at the Tour de la Manche, before the call from Pélissier and Anquetil's move to La Perle.

Anquetil was often described as a cold and calculating rider. Imperious in time trials, he would win races by gaining handfuls of time during solo rides against the clock and then ride conservatively to ensure that he stayed with his rivals when the route headed into the mountains. More than once Anquetil was described as being a rider who could not distance anyone on the slopes of the Alps and Pyrenees, but equally one who could not be distanced. The insinuation was that he was not a true climber. But Anquetil rode in the era of Charly Gaul and Federico Bahamontes, and no one could have won what Anquetil won against those men without having been a real climber.

His first Tour win came in 1957, following his move from La Perle to Helyet-Potin the previous year. There is a picture of him in the Parc des Princes at the end of the race, wearing the yellow jersey, perched on his saddle, holding up a bouquet of flowers, surrounded by his team manager Daniel Dousset and a clutch of youngsters. Anquetil's hair is swept back neatly, his cheekbones chiselled. He looks every bit the star he has just become. There is a coolness about him in this, his finest moment. He looks detached, his eyes gazing into the distance. Yes, his lips are curled into a smile, but his eyes appear emotionless, the epitome of calm.

His win came as more established Tour riders fell by the wayside. To the horror of France, Louison Bobet didn't even start the 1957 race, deciding instead to concentrate on the Giro d'Italia. Charly Gaul lasted only two days, abandoning in infernal heat during the stage to Caen. One week later it was the turn of Federico Bahamontes, fourth the year before, to climb off his bike, leaving it lying in the road. He was described by *Sport et Vie* as being "deaf to the exhortations of his entourage" as they desperately tried to convince him to remount.

Anquetil continued riding his own race. Appropriately enough, he won his first Tour stage in Rouen, his home town, before taking his first yellow jersey two days later. He briefly lost the race lead in Colmar but won it back on stage 10 and held it until Paris, despite difficulties in the Pyrenees, where he came under ferocious attack. Things looked particularly precarious for Anquetil on the stage to Pau, when he paid for a misjudged attack on the Tourmalet, dropping back dangerously on the slopes of the next climb, the Soulor. The Belgian rider Marcel Janssens looked to capitalise and exploded up the road in pursuit of the race lead, despite being nearly twelve minutes down on Anquetil at the start of the stage. The Frenchman dug into his deep reserves of energy and, in enormous pain, managed to arrive in Pau having ceded only two-and-a-half minutes to Janssens. He was still in yellow and he cemented the win in the last time trial, which he won by more than two minutes. In Paris Jacques Anquetil stood as the winner of the Tour de France for the first time. He had won by nearly fifteen minutes.

The man from Normandy would have to wait another four years to win another Tour, but his 1961 win would start a run of victories that would make him the first rider to win four Tours on the trot, and the first to win five overall.

In 1961 Anquetil stated his intention to take custody of the yellow jersey on day one and wear it all the way into Paris. Such a feat is something no rider would ever attempt today, such are the demands placed on the leader of the race, but Anquetil duly lived up to his promise, securing his place at the top of the classification on the first day, after a time trial in Versailles. There he stayed for three weeks, impervious to attacks, efficiently snuffing out any attempt to make inroads into his lead. The public and media didn't take well to his domination. Jacques Goddet wrote a scathing article called the "Yellow Dwarves", which accused the other riders of being submissive and impotent, "satisfied in their mediocrity". Anquetil may have been winning, but he was not capturing the hearts of the nation.

THE INSINUATION WAS THAT HE WAS NOT A TRUE CLIMBER. BUT ANQUETIL RODE IN THE ERA OF CHARLY GAUL AND FEDERICO BAHAMONTES, AND NO ONE COULD HAVE WON WHAT ANQUETIL WON AGAINST THOSE MEN WITHOUT HAVING BEEN A REAL CLIMBER.

In 1962, he was booed in Paris as the public tired of his calculating ways, but in 1963 Anquetil went some way to getting the recognition he deserved. The Tour organisers reduced the amount of time trialling in 1963, anxious to introduce a different dynamic to the race. So Anquetil was forced on to the offensive in the mountains for the first time. He won stage 10 from Pau to Bagnères-de-Bigorre, over the Aubisque and Tourmalet, to ensure he remained ahead of his principal rival, the terrific climber Federico Bahamontes, but it was on stage 17 in the Alps that he took the yellow jersey. Then, for the first time, the public began to warm to him.

By the time the peloton started stage 17, from Val d'Isère to Chamonix, Bahamontes was leading the race from Anquetil, if only by three seconds. But the Alps were Bahamontes country, and the stage was set for the Spanish climber to rise. On the third climb of the day, the unpaved Col de la Forclaz, Bahamontes attacked. He distanced everyone other than Anquetil, who stuck by him. What Bahamontes didn't know was that Anquetil had an advantage.

In 1963 the swapping of equipment mid-stage was forbidden unless required because of mechanical failure. Faced with the unforgiving ascent of the Forclaz, Anquetil's director, Raphaël Géminiani, hatched a plan for Anquetil to switch, at the foot of the mountain, to a bike that was set up specifically for climbing, then to switch back for the descent to the finish. "It's forbidden," said Anquetil. "That's my business," replied Géminiani.

Sure enough, just before the climb of the Forclaz, Anquetil threw his hands up in mock horror exclaiming, "My derailleur!" The commissaires confirmed that a wire had inexplicably snapped and, in ignorance of the assistance given to said snapping by a mechanic and a pair of wire cutters, permitted the bike change.

The change of equipment enabled Anquetil to stay with Bahamontes as the Spaniard tried in vain to gain enough time to secure a firmer hold on the yellow jersey. As they descended into Chamonix alone, Anquetil outsprinted Bahamontes to take the win by a single second. More crucial was the thirty-second time bonus that came with a stage win, propelling Anquetil into yellow.

Throughout the second part of his career Anquetil endured an engrossing rivalry with fellow Frenchman Raymond Poulidor. In stark contrast to the public's opinion of Anquetil, France unreservedly loved Poulidor, despite, or maybe because of, the fact that he never wore the yellow jersey. Anquetil's greatest showdown with Poulidor came in 1964 on the slopes of the Puy-de-Dôme when, as Anquetil rode to his fifth Tour win, they went head to head and wheel to wheel in one of the greatest battles the Tour has ever witnessed (see pp120–121).

Nicknamed *Maître Jacques,* Anquetil dominated the sport throughout the first part of the 1960s. Not only did he become the first rider to win five Tours but he also became the first to win all three Grand Tours, winning the Giro in 1960 and 1964 and the Vuelta in 1963.

ONE OF HIS MOST STAGGERING ACHIEVEMENTS CAME IN 1965, WITH BACK-TO-BACK WINS IN THE WEEK-LONG DAUPHINÉ LIBÉRÉ AND THE 556KM BORDEAUX–PARIS RACE, JUST 24 HOURS APART.

One of his most staggering achievements came in 1965, with back-to-back wins in the week-long Dauphiné Libéré and the 556km Bordeaux–Paris race, just 24 hours apart. It was Géminiani's idea to tackle the two races, and he said he would bet on Anquetil's chances. He was to be proved right, but the stunt presented all sorts of logistical challenges, not least how to get Anquetil from Avignon, where the Dauphiné Libéré finished in the late afternoon, to Bordeaux, where the second race started just seven hours later – and how to get him there in a fit state to compete.

Having won the Dauphiné by a slender margin, Anquetil hot-footed it to the airport, having had a shower and massage, followed by steak, cheese, strawberry tart and two beers. Having arrived in Bordeaux, he grabbed a brief sleep and was on the start line at midnight. Bordeaux–Paris was a mad hotch-potch of a race. The initial section was raced alone, normally with an agreement to keep the pace light, but then, just under halfway, the racers collected pacemakers on Derny motorcycles, who would then lead them to Paris.

Anquetil, suffering the effects of his rapid transit, came under constant attack from all quarters. "They rode like bees," writes Les Woodland in his book *Cycling Heroes*, "swarming, dispersing, stinging and generally making life hell." Anquetil came close to abandoning, even getting into the team car at one point, but Géminiani convinced him to continue. In the end, Maître Jacques rode into the Parc des Princes alone, winning by 57 seconds, ahead of Jean Stablinski and Tom Simpson, to complete a quite remarkable double.

Anquetil stopped racing in 1969, retiring to his farm and occasionally commentating for French radio. He was a single-minded man who said what he thought. On drug-taking he was unrepentant. "What, you think I win my races on sugar alone?" he said. He would shock onlookers by drinking with friends, feasting on sea-food and staying up late, and still winning the following day. Tom Simpson was once prompted to remark, "I don't know what Jacques has been eating but I've never seen him so strong." He was unaware that just hours previously Anquetil had been drunk on Champagne and whisky after gorging on pasta and cheese.

His private life was equally startling. In his biography of Anquetil, *Sex, Lies and Handlebar Tape*, Paul Howard writes of Anquetil seducing the wife of his doctor (and friend) before marrying her, having a child with a stepdaughter who was acting as a surrogate mother because his wife could no longer bear children, and finally having an affair with the former wife of his stepson. It was, writes Howard, "a series of events at which even Casanova might have baulked."

Jacques Anquetil died in 1987 of stomach cancer, aged 53. He was visited on his deathbed by his great rival Poulidor, whom he had beaten on so many occasions. "Sorry Raymond," Anquetil said, "you'll come second again."

ON DRUG-TAKING HE WAS UNREPENTANT. "WHAT, YOU THINK I WIN MY RACES ON SUGAR ALONE?" HE SAID.

JACQUES ANQUETIL SELECTED RESULTS:

1952: 3rd Olympic Games, Helsinki, Team Time Trial

1953: 1st Grand Prix des Nations
1st Gran Premio di Lugano
1st Tour de la Manche

1954: 1st Grand Prix des Nations
1st Gran Premio di Lugano

1955: 1st Grand Prix des Nations
1st Grand Prix de Genève

1956: 1st Grand Prix des Nations
1st Grand Prix de Genève
Hour record

1957: 1st Grand Prix des Nations
1st Grand Prix de Genève
1st overall and four stage wins Tour de France
1st overall and one stage win Paris–Nice

1958: 1st Grand Prix des Nations
1st Grand Prix de Genève
1st overall and one stage win Four days Dunkirk

1959: 1st Grand Prix de Genève
1st overall and one stage win Four days Dunkirk
2nd overall and two stage wins Giro d'Italia

1960: 1st overall two stage wins Giro d'Italia

1961: 1st Grand Prix des Nations
1st overall and two stage wins Tour de France

1st overall and one stage win Paris–Nice

1962: 1st overall and two stage wins Tour de France
1st Trofeo Baracchi

1963: 1st overall and four stage wins Tour de France
1st overall and one stage win Vuelta a España
1st overall and one stage win Dauphiné Libéré
1st overall and two stage wins Paris–Nice

1964: 1st overall and four stage wins Tour de France
1st overall and one stage win Giro d'Italia
1st Gent–Wevelgem

1965: 1st Grand Prix des Nations
1st overall and two stage wins Dauphiné Libéré
1st Bordeaux–Paris
1st overall and one stage win Paris–Nice

1966: 1st Grand Prix des Nations
1st overall and one stage win Paris–Nice
1st Liège–Bastogne–Liège

1967: 1st overall Criterium International
1st overall and one stage win Volta Ciclista a Catalunya

1968: 1st Trofeo Baracchi

1969: 1st overall Vuelta Ciclista al País Vasco

COL DE LA RÉPUBLIQUE

START POINT / Saint-Étienne
START ELEVATION / 577m
FINISH ELEVATION / 1161m
LENGTH OF CLIMB / 17km
AVERAGE GRADIENT / 3.5%
MAXIMUM GRADIENT / 6.3%
FIRST TOUR / 1903
APPEARANCES / 13

CLIMB GRADES
4–7%
0–4%

ALTITUDE (m)
1100
1000
900
800
700
600

DISTANCE (km)
0 2 4 6 8 10 12 14 16

And so to the thorny issue of the first mountain pass to be visited by the Tour. I wanted to ride it. I felt that to fully recognise the huge part that the mountains of France have played in shaping the Tour, I should scale the climb that kicked the whole thing off.

Until I started researching this book I had shared the common misconception that the first mountain climb ever tackled by the Tour was the Ballon d'Alsace in 1905, five years before the high peaks of the Pyrenees were introduced. Why had I thought that? Mainly because over the years I had read it in many books and articles. In fact there was a time when the Tour's own historical section on its website had stage 2 of the 1905 Tour, from Nancy to Besançon, over the Ballon d'Alsace, listed as the race's first mountain stage.

Then I discovered that in 1903, on the very first Tour, the peloton had ridden at least two climbs that could be classified as mountain passes. The Col du Pin-Bouchain, at 760m, was tackled on the very first stage, while the Col de la République, also known as the Col du Grand Bois, standing at 1161m, was ridden on stage 2, from Lyon to Marseille.

So which one to ride? Now, what constitutes a mountain is a tricky subject. By some definitions, any sudden rise over 610m in height is a mountain; others settle for 300m. Both of the 1903 climbs would meet

these altitude criteria, but what of their respective gradients? Were they sudden enough? Again, there was no agreement as to how steep a hill had to be before it could be considered a mountain. I found one authority that defined a mountain simply as "a large, steep hill". It's surely within the bounds of possibility that the Tour had already gone over "a large, steep hill" before the Pin-Bouchain was crested in 1903.

With no definitive definition available, I decided to change my target. I would make it something not open to interpretation. Instead of riding the first "mountain" of the Tour I would ride the first pass that went over 1000m. That was objective and easy to quantify. So that's why my friend James and I find ourselves in Saint-Étienne, at the foot of the Col de la République, early one Saturday morning.

The first man over the République in 1903 was the splendidly named Hippolyte Aucouturier. If his name conjures up an image of a circus strongman, his actual appearance only strengthens it. Aucouturier possessed a large, handle-bar moustache and invariably wore a thickly striped jersey and a flat-cap. And he was a big chap. He looked like someone who should be lifting a

barbell one-handed. But a racing cyclist is what he was and in an eight-year professional career he won his fair share of races, including Paris–Roubaix twice and five stages of the Tour. The first of those five Tour stages was stage two of the 1903 Tour into Marseille, the one that he led over this very climb.

The climb has featured 13 times in the race but only one man has been first over its summit on more than one occasion – Federico Bahamontes, who led the way in 1959 and 1963. In 1959 he was part of a two-man escape with Charly Gaul: Bahamontes led over the République and the ensuing Col de la Romeyère, but Gaul caught him on the way to Grenoble and took the stage, with Bahamontes a whisker behind, gaining enough to claim the yellow jersey, which he would keep until Paris. Four years later, on the same stage from Saint-Étienne to Grenoble, Bahamontes again rose over the summit of the République first, and again led over the following climb (this time it was the Col de Porte). But, unlike four years previously, in 1963 he was not caught. Bahamontes won the stage by over a minute from Henri Anglade. Although he could only finish second

THE CLIMB HAS FEATURED 13 TIMES IN THE RACE BUT ONLY ONE MAN HAS BEEN FIRST OVER ITS SUMMIT ON MORE THAN ONE OCCASION – FEDERICO BAHAMONTES.

in Paris, the stage had helped him claim the fifth of his six King of the Mountains titles.

While the République helped set Bahamontes on his way to two of his seven Tour titles (one overall, six mountain prizes), the climb is more famous for what happened on its slopes on only the second edition of the race.

As in 1903, the 1904 Tour's second stage set out from Lyon on its way to Marseille. Once again on the route was a ride through Saint-Étienne and then over the République. In an echo of the previous year, Maurice Garin was again leading the race after the opening stage.

But local residents had other ideas. Antoine Fauré, a 21-year-old from Gerzat, a couple of hours away, had strong ties to the area, unlike Garin, who had taken French nationality but had been born in Italy. Fauré was the favourite of the people that lived around the République, and they decided to try to help him win. Their method? Simple: battering the other riders.

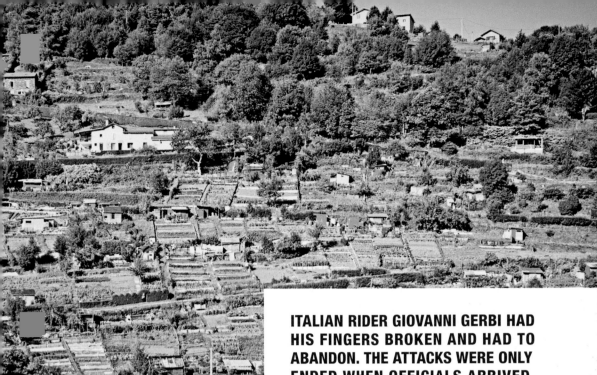

ITALIAN RIDER GIOVANNI GERBI HAD HIS FINGERS BROKEN AND HAD TO ABANDON. THE ATTACKS WERE ONLY ENDED WHEN OFFICIALS ARRIVED, FIRING PISTOLS INTO THE AIR.

On the climb of the République, locals armed with sticks and rocks formed a barrier. They let Fauré pass and then set upon the other riders, raining stones down on them and beating them about the head. Pierre Chany described the events as "a swarm of fanatics, sticks raised, screaming insults from their lips, falling on the other riders." Garin was specifically targeted, as was his younger brother César. According to Chany the mob screamed "Vive Fauré! Down with Garin! Kill them!" as they set about their work.

The Garin brothers weren't the only ones attacked: Italian rider Giovanni Gerbi had his fingers broken and had to abandon. The attacks were only ended when officials arrived, firing pistols into the air. Fauré didn't win the stage, Aucouturier did. But then, months after the race, Aucouturier was disqualified, along with many others (see p29). And who was then awarded the stage 2 win? None other than Antoine Fauré.

• • •

The sun is still low in the sky as we start the climb. The road rises from the southern side of Saint-Étienne and breaks us in gently. That's good – the previous day had been spent cooped up in a van on the long drive here and this morning my legs are stiff and unwilling. A couple of kilometres go by fairly easily as we make our way up the climb. To our right are views over trees and vegetable allotments. with sheds painted in various shades of green. Back home I have an allotment and so other people's are of interest to me. I'm keenly perusing the various plots when I spot a road sign: Rue Paul de Vivie, dit 'Velocio' 1853–1930.

• • •

Paul de Vivie was the man who did more than almost anyone else to publicise the benefits and attractions of cycle-touring in the latter 1800s. More than that, he designed the mechanism that made it possible for the masses to drag themselves and their machines up the hills of France – the derailleur.

De Vivie owned a silk business but sold it when he discovered the joys of cycling. Convinced that a life in cycling was for him he moved his family to Saint-Étienne, started a magazine called *Le Cycliste* and opened a bike shop.

He started importing bicycles from Britain and, writing under the name *Velocio*, published articles on his cycling tours, equipment and nutrition. De Vivie started to design his own bikes and, in 1906, devised the first derailleur. With the République on his doorstep he was a regular sight on its slopes, demonstrating the effectiveness of his newfangled gear mechanisms. In

1922 he was joined on its slopes by cyclists from all over the local area, for a ride that became known as the first Velocio Day.

His writings included many evocative descriptions of his adventures on the mountain passes of France and Switzerland, as well as his Seven Commandments for the cyclist, including the wonderful: "Never ride just for the sake of riding."

De Vivie died in 1930, hit by a tram while was pushing his bicycle.

● ● ●

The gradient picks up as we continue on our way. Seven kilometres follow of 5 or 6% percent, before the road relaxes again at the village of La République, around five kilometres from the top of the pass.

From this point to the top everything is most pleasant. We are riding through dappled shade, the early morning September sun is piercing the pine trees, releasing their heady scent. The air is still deliciously

cool and the riding is easy. Just a gentle rise all the way to the summit. Before we know it we are at the top. There, alongside a memorial to Paul de Vivie, is a sign that announces that this is indeed the first pass over 1000m to be conquered by the Tour. We stop and take photographs. In truth there isn't much to see. The summit is hemmed in by the forest. There are no wide-ranging views. In fact, despite being 1161m above sea level, this mountain feels distinctly un-mountainlike.

Compared to the huge climbs of the Alps and Pyrenees, the République is no great challenge. At 17km, its distance is comparable with first and *hors* category ascents, but it is simply nowhere near as tough. When it was last used, in 1997, it was listed as a category three climb. But it was the first road to take the riders over 1000m and, once the riders had proved that they could cope with this climb, the organisers sought out others that offered greater tests. The République was the first, tentative step on the road that would ultimately lead us to the Tourmalet, the Galibier and the Ventoux. And for that, we should all be grateful to the Col de la République.

GREG
LEMOND

IT WAS THE FIRST TIME AN AMERICAN HAD WON THE WORLD CHAMPION'S RAINBOW JERSEY. HE WAS JUST 22 YEARS OF AGE.

When Greg LeMond rode his maiden Tour in 1984, aged 23, he was one of only two Americans in the race, the other being Jonathan Boyer who, three years earlier, had become the first rider from the States to take to the Tour's start line. LeMond was an instant hit, finishing third overall and taking the white jersey as the best young rider, and his achievements opened the door for the Americans. Just two years later there were no fewer than ten US riders in the Tour, the majority of them for 7-Eleven, the first American team invited to the race.

As he grew up in California, and later Nevada, LeMond wasn't interested in cycling. He was a skier. More accurately, he was a freestyle skier. Not for him the smoothed pistes of the slalom or the downhill. No, LeMond was a moguls man. And cruising over the lumps and bumps of a snowbound mountain, rather than flying over the tarmac perched on a bicycle, was where he saw his future.

That changed when he was advised to take up cycling as a way of maintaining fitness when the mountains lost their coat of snow. On rides with his father he quickly identified an affinity with the bike. At age 14 he joined his first club, the Reno Wheelmen, and rode their weekend race against men more than twice his age. He finished second. The bicycle beckoned.

By 1979 LeMond had grown from a promising junior, dominating the local and regional scene, into a world champion. Two junior national titles (1977 and 1979), and a host of impressive wins in Europe during the summer of 1978, were followed by the junior world championships in 1979. Entering the final moments of that race in Buenos Aires, LeMond was away with Belgian rider Kenny De Marteleire. De Marteleire didn't like it much when LeMond tried to spring out

of his slipstream with just 250m or so to go, so he swerved off his line forcing the American wide, not once but twice, pushing him into the wall of tyres that flanked the finish straight. Amazingly LeMond managed to avoid coming off his bike, trailing in second. But De Marteleire was disqualified for his actions and LeMond was awarded the win. It was the first time an American had won the title.

LeMond turned professional in 1981, settling in France and joining the Renault-Elf team of Bernard Hinault. Although wins came in his first two years as a professional, most notably in the Tour de l'Avenir and Tirreno–Adriatico, 1983 was his breakthrough year, when he followed a June win in the Critérium du Dauphiné with the world champion's title in September.

LeMond was part of a three-man breakaway that escaped with around 30km of the 270km world championship race still to go. He was joined in the break by Faustino Rupérez of Spain but then, as the race entered its decisive phase, Rupérez, a former winner of the Vuelta a España, fell away as LeMond upped his pace on the final climb. LeMond was now locked into a punishing solo ride to the finish, pursued by Rupérez, Ireland's Stephen Roche, Belgium's Claude Criquielion and Holland's Adri Van Der Poel.

But the American held on to his advantage and, after more than seven hours in the saddle, he crossed the line over one minute ahead of the four pursuers. It was the first time an American had won the world champion's rainbow jersey. He was just 22 years of age.

In the following season, his third place in the Tour showed a glimpse of what was to come. For the

1985 season he followed Bernard Hinault to La Vie Claire. It was a decision that perhaps cost him a fair crack at the Tour. He spent the 1985 race in the service of Hinault when arguably he was the stronger rider, eventually finishing second behind the French hero, who claimed his fifth title. In 1986 those roles were reversed when Hinault eventually helped LeMond to his, and America's, first Tour title (see p58 and p144 for more on the 1985 and 1986 Tours).

After the 1986 Tour, all looked set for a period of American dominance, but a hunting accident cost LeMond nearly two years of his career. Accidentally shot by one of his hunting party, he lost pints of blood, suffered a collapsed lung and broken ribs, and had lead pellets peppered all over his insides. To this day he still has more than thirty pieces of lead trapped in his chest.

After a hard-fought recovery, LeMond returned to cycling. In 1989 he returned to the top of the sport, first of all finishing the Giro d'Italia and placing second in the final time trial, and then, six weeks later, winning the Tour for a second time. That 1989 win over former team-mate Laurent Fignon remains the closest race in Tour history, with LeMond's winning gap a mere eight seconds (see p103–105).

It had been an incredible comeback but LeMond wasn't done yet. He followed his second Tour win with a second world championships, when he triumphed at a rain-sodden Chambéry. LeMond remains the only American to have won the title twice; Lance Armstrong, with one title, is the other US world champion.

THAT 1989 WIN OVER FORMER TEAM-MATE LAURENT FIGNON REMAINS THE CLOSEST RACE IN TOUR HISTORY, WITH LEMOND'S WINNING GAP A MERE EIGHT SECONDS.

LeMond's great form continued into the following season, when he took his third Tour title. This time he had to battle against that Tour's surprise package, Claudio Chiappucci. The Italian was in yellow, leading LeMond by two-and-a-half minutes heading into stage 16, 215km from Blagnac, over the Aspin and Tourmalet to a mountain-top finish at Luz-Ardiden. This was the last big day in the mountains and everyone expected LeMond to emerge from it draped in yellow.

But Chiappucci took the fight to the American. On the Aspin he followed an attack by Jörg Müller and led LeMond over the climb by 34 seconds. The American seemed unperturbed, but on the descent to Sainte-Marie-de-Campan and then up the Tourmalet, the Italian's lead grew as he chased the lone leader, Miguel Martinez.

With 4km to the top of the Tourmalet, LeMond finally roused himself. He upped the pace, dragging himself and four others, including Miguel Indurain, clear of the pack as they started to chase the yellow jersey. By the time they topped the Tourmalet they had reduced Chiappucci's lead to just over a minute. They finally caught him at the foot of the climb to Luz-Ardiden. Normally when a lone rider is caught in this situation he immediately falls away, but not Chiappucci. He stuck with LeMond, Indurain and the rest of the group, even trying to raise the pace on the early slopes until, just 8km from the finish, he could hold on no more.

Such was the pace that LeMond was setting that eventually only Indurain could match him. The two caught Martinez with a little more than 2km to go and powered right past. Indurain, who had done nothing to contribute to the break, finally came round to take the lead with 400m to go. The Spaniard held on to take the stage win, LeMond, wearing his trademark yellow-rimmed Oakleys, coming in six seconds down, to be mobbed by the press and towelled down by his team. Then, all eyes turned to the clock. Where was Chiappucci?

The answer: not quite as far away as LeMond had hoped. Inspired by the yellow jersey, the Italian had found reserves of energy he didn't know he possessed. As he rounded the final corner he sprinted for the line with just seconds to spare. That night Chiappucci still had custody of the yellow jersey, but LeMond had cut his lead to a mere five seconds.

And that was the way it stayed until the penultimate stage, a 45.5km time trial on the shores of Lac de Vassivière. LeMond finished fifth, 57 seconds behind Erik Breukink but, more importantly, 2 minutes 21 seconds ahead of Chiappucci. The American's third Tour de France was in the bag.

It was his last major win. He finished seventh at the Tour the following year and then, having abandoned the race in 1993 and 1994, and been diagnosed with mitochondrial myopathy, he retired from racing. He returned to live in the States, switching his attention to the business world.

GREG LEMOND SELECTED RESULTS:

1977: 1st junior national championships

1978: 1st overall Vuelta de Bisbee

1979: 1st junior world championships
1st junior national championships

1980: 1st overall Circuit Cycliste Sarthe

1981: 1st overall and two stage wins Coors Classic
Two stage wins Tour de Picardie

1982: 1st overall and three stage wins Tour de l'Avenir
One stage win Tirreno–Adriatico

1983: 1st world championships
1st overall and two stage wins Critérium du Dauphiné

1984: One stage win and 1st young rider classification Tour de France
One stage win Critérium du Dauphiné

1985: Two stage wins Tour de France
1st overall and one stage win Coors Classic

1986: 1st overall and one stage win Tour de France
One stage win Giro d'Italia
2nd Milan–San Remo

1989: 1st overall and three stage wins Tour de France
1st world championships

1990: 1st overall Tour de France

1992: 1st overall and one stage win Tour du Pont

ALPE D'HUEZ

START POINT / Bourg d'Oisans
START ELEVATION / 723m
FINISH ELEVATION / 1850m
LENGTH OF CLIMB / 13.8km
AVERAGE GRADIENT / 7.9%
MAXIMUM GRADIENT / 14%
FIRST TOUR / 1952
APPEARANCES / 27

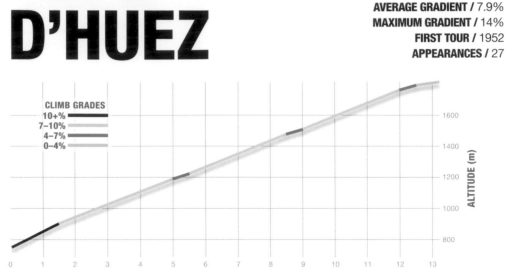

CLIMB GRADES
10+%
7–10%
4–7%
0–4%

ALTITUDE (m)

DISTANCE (km)

Bourg d'Oisans is primed for a party: the Tour de France is in town and celebrations are in full swing. I've ridden here, to the foot of Alpe d'Huez, from Allemont, 10km away along the valley road. Flanked by other cyclists all heading the same way, I had time to relish the prospect of what's to come. The author Tim Moore once described the Tour on Alpe d'Huez as "the Glastonbury Festival for cycling fans". I can't wait to sample that festival spirit for myself.

Cyclists weave their way in and out of the people who are heading to the mountain on foot carrying picnic hampers, rugs and bottles of wine. It's crowded and manic and loud. Excited chatter fills the air as the day's impending action, still six or seven hours away, is keenly discussed. As well as French, I catch traces of German, Spanish, Italian and Norwegian among the English, American, Australian and Irish accents. And Dutch. Oh yes, there are plenty of Dutch here. More on them later.

I round a left-hand bend and a wall of tarmac abruptly announces itself: unmistakably the start of the climb. Dark, with the sunlight suddenly shut out by a high wall and trees, it's an eerie and claustrophobic gateway. The Alpe gives an aura of the ominous right from start, a grim foreboding of what lies ahead, daring you to continue. Instantly I hear the clicking of gears as the

gradient kicks in at around 15% and everyone around me searches for a comfortable cog. I know that this early stretch is one of the toughest on the entire climb so I relax, select my lowest gear and slowly turn the legs.

Ahead of me a cyclist, clad head to toe in the kit of Lance Armstrong's old Discovery Channel team, has already dismounted. He is standing with his head in his hands, propped against the wall. I recognise him as a rider who had sped past me on my ride in from Allemont, legs spinning like a hamster in a wheel. Now he is stationary. "I can't do it," I hear him wail as I inch my way past. This guy is a flat track bully. The Alpe demands more respect.

I reach the first bend and glance up to read the names on the sign. Every Tour stage winner on the Alpe gets his name on one of the 21 signs that count down the hairpins all the way to the top. This one belongs to Fausto Coppi and Lance Armstrong, two legends of the sport.

• • •

Since its first appearance in 1952, when it became the race's first ever summit finish, the Alpe has hosted some of the Tour's most famous moments, giving the mountain its place at the top table of Tour climbs.

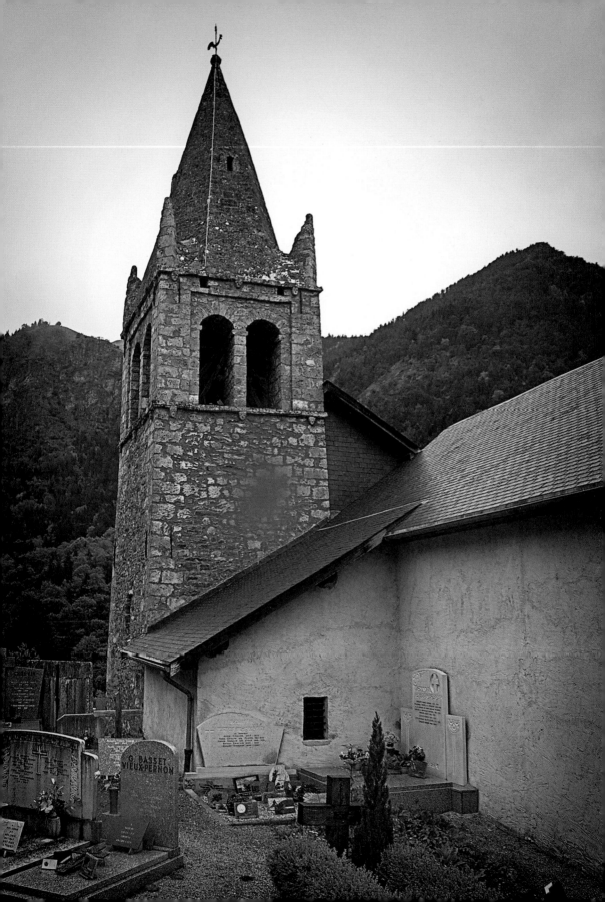

The climb couldn't have asked for a worthier inaugural winner, for the stage ended in triumph for the *Campionissimo*, Italian superstar Fausto Coppi.

On that day, approaching the first of the Alpe's hairpins, Coppi and France's Jean Robic were locked together. On the early slopes Robic suddenly attacked and opened a gap. Coppi responded and dragged himself back up to the Frenchman's wheel. Then, six kilometres from the finish, Coppi accelerated. But even the Italian master, who always rode with flair and panache, couldn't shake Robic with one decisive attack. Robic was too strong for that. Instead Coppi maintained his pace, steadily but gracefully building an advantage.

There was nothing Robic could do. In six kilometres Coppi gained 1 minute and 20 seconds and climbed into a yellow jersey he would never relinquish, going on to win the 1952 Tour by almost half an hour. Robic would finish fifth in Paris. It was the first piece of sporting drama to be played out on the slopes of Alpe d'Huez. But the spectacle wasn't universally popular. This was nothing to do with Alpe d'Huez itself but rather the principle of finishing the stage on top of a mountain, which was considered by some to have eliminated the possibility of any attacks early in the stage.

• • •

THERE WAS NOTHING ROBIC COULD DO. IN SIX KILOMETRES COPPI GAINED 1 MINUTE AND 20 SECONDS AND CLIMBED INTO A YELLOW JERSEY HE WOULD NEVER RELINQUISH, GOING ON TO WIN THE 1952 TOUR BY ALMOST HALF AN HOUR.

I ride on steadily, trying to conserve energy. After the first couple of kilometres the gradient eases and I settle into a rhythm, falling in with groups who are riding at my pace. Ahead an American woman becomes

frustrated with a slow-moving bunch and yells out, "C'mon guys, let's go! C'mon!!" She needs to relax and just soak up the experience, I think to myself.

I pass through the village of La Garde, with its small, attractive church. Here the road is still hemmed in by high walls but occasionally I get a glimpse of the mountain rising above me. Campervans, parked days ago in anticipation of the race, are packed on the high horizon. It seems unfathomable that I will ride past them later.

The day's heat is taking its toll, so I pause to catch my breath and fill my bottle from a delicious torrent of water that's pouring from the mountainside. Beside me a Spanish couple are posing for photographs, happily documenting their day. A young boy stops and starts to get off his bike to walk. His father detains him. "No," he says gently. "We can rest for as long as you need, as often as you need, but we will not walk up the Alpe."

And so onwards towards the Dutch. Their slice of this mountain is fast approaching. I can't see it yet but I can certainly hear it. The Dutch love Alpe d'Huez and bathe hairpin seven in a sea of orange every time the Tour visits, blasting euro-pop across the Alps from huge speakers. Other countries may try to imitate them (I notice pockets of Luxembourgers and Norwegians on my ride) but no one really compares. The Dutch take partying on the Alpe to a whole different level. I round the corner to be greeted by more than a hundred of them sitting in the middle of the road, pretending to row a boat up the mountain. To the side,

hundreds more are dancing, perfectly in sync, with chairs raised above their heads. I get a loud cheer and some welcome water over the head. It's no coincidence that I chose to wear an orange jersey today.

● ● ●

The Dutch association with this mountain began in the 1970s. After Coppi's win in 1952, Alpe d'Huez didn't host a stage finish again until 1976, when Dutchman Joop Zoetemelk won the 258km stage from Divonne-les-Bains, with the 10km Col du Luitel thrown in en route. The Luitel posed little problem, but once the peloton reached the foot of the Alpe two of the best climbers in the world started to systematically attack each other.

At the first turn on to the climb, Belgium's Lucien Van Impe accelerated and left everyone standing – apart from Zoetemelk. The Dutchman followed and the two went toe to toe, pedal to pedal, all the way up the mountain. Neither rider could shake the other. They were described the next day in the *Dauphiné Libéré* as riding in tandem. Zoetemelk managed to take the win on the line, in one of the closest battles the Alpe has ever hosted. But it was Van Impe who would have the last laugh – he took the yellow jersey and went on to win the race in Paris.

Zoetemelk's success on the Alpe started a run of three consecutive wins for the Dutch. They would go on to claim eight victories in thirteen finishes between 1976 and 1989, cementing the country's love affair with the mountain. Although they haven't had a win since, the Dutch still hold the record for most victories here.

• • •

Through the village of Huez the gradient kicks up again. It's tough going. My legs are aching, my lungs feel like they are on fire, my heart is splitting. I peer upwards. I'm past the 4km-to-go mark and the climb has at last opened up. I'm riding through lush Alpine meadows, with a backdrop of the sharp peaks that surround the Romanche valley. Desperate for another breather, I stop and reach for more water. Above, my destination looms large.

• • •

In 1986 Alpe d'Huez hosted a stage finish for the eleventh time. The French team La Vie Claire was in the unique position of boasting two of the overwhelming Tour favourites. Bernard Hinault had won five of the previous eight races, including the 1985 edition, which many felt would have been won by the team's young American rider, Greg LeMond, had he not been so dutiful in his support of Hinault.

After LeMond had helped Hinault win the previous year's Tour, 1986 was supposed to be the turn of the

American, with Hinault pledging that he would work for his team-mate. The Frenchman demonstrated his "support" by launching a ferocious attack in the Pyrenees, gaining over four minutes on his team-mate and taking yellow. LeMond fought back and, by the time the race got to the final big day in the mountains, from Briançon to the top of the Alpe, he was leading the race by 2 minutes and 24 seconds over Swiss rider Urs Zimmerman, with Hinault a further 23 seconds back.

But LeMond was ill at ease, and with good reason. On the descent of the Galibier Hinault attacked again, forcing the leader of the Tour to set off in a risky pursuit. LeMond caught Hinault in the town of Saint-Jean-de-Maurienne, at which point the Frenchman finally became the faithful team-mate. He towed LeMond up the Croix de Fer, building their lead over Zimmerman. Over the climb the pair were over two minutes ahead, a lead they continued to build in the valley.

Once they reached the Alpe they were untouchable, putting yet more time into their nearest rivals as they tackled the 21 hairpins. As they approached the finish they had more than five minutes on Zimmerman. In the last few metres the two team-mates, who had battled each other relentlessly over the previous two weeks, finally joined hands. LeMond, recognising the work that Hinault had done, then ushered Hinault through to take the win. It was described by commentator Phil Liggett as "the most emotional thing I can ever recall during the Tour de France".

• • •

Two more hairpins and I arrive in the town of Alpe d'Huez. Here the slope relents at last and I am left to soak up the feeling of having ridden up to this mythical place. All around me cyclists are stopping for photographs underneath the banner that denotes the end of the climb. Others desperately search for friends so that they can recount the story of their ride.

• • •

The rivalry with Jan Ullrich defined Lance Armstrong's early Tour victories and, in 2001, the pair played out a piece of pure theatre on the Alpe's slopes. The 209km stage from Aix-les-Bains also took in climbs of the Madeleine and Glandon. Early on Armstrong appeared to be in trouble, just about hanging on to the back of the bunch, frowning and grimacing. Ullrich, sensing an opportunity, sent his team to the front to ratchet up the pace, seeking to distance the American.

But Armstrong was faking, and on the Alpe he came back up to a tired and now isolated Ullrich. Armstrong

IN THE LAST FEW METRES THE TWO TEAM-MATES, WHO HAD BATTLED EACH OTHER RELENTLESSLY OVER THE PREVIOUS TWO WEEKS, FINALLY JOINED HANDS. LEMOND, RECOGNISING THE WORK THAT HINAULT HAD DONE, THEN USHERED HINAULT THROUGH TO TAKE THE WIN.

pulled level, edged in front and then turned round to stare at length straight into Ullrich's eyes, gauging his condition. He liked what he saw. Standing on his pedals, spinning a low gear, Armstrong blasted away from Ullrich, who stayed steadfastly in the saddle, churning a massive gear. In the blink of an eye, Armstrong was gone. He would win the stage and gain almost two minutes on the German.

• • •

Riding Alpe d'Huez you really get a sense of the history that has been written here: the duels of Coppi and Robic; Zoetemelk and Van Impe; Armstrong and Ullrich; and of the (eventual) teamwork of LeMond and Hinault. This isn't the hardest of climbs. Nor is it the highest or the longest. But legends have been born and reputations sealed on these very slopes. It is, quite simply, the most iconic of mountains.

No rider in the history of the Tour has been more successful, or more divisive, than Lance Armstrong. Having recovered from life-threatening cancer, the Texan dominated the Tour for seven straight years, surpassing the five wins of Anquetil, Merckx, Hinault and Indurain. He became a household name, the one cyclist of whom nearly everyone had heard. He appeared on late-night chat shows, hung out with presidents and Hollywood stars, wrote best-selling books. Nothing short of a superhero to many, he transcended the sport. But there were others, at first a minority, who simply didn't believe in him. They didn't believe in what was billed as the greatest comeback in sporting history.

Born in 1971, Armstrong was raised in Plano, Texas, by his mother, Linda. He started out as a triathlete but an invitation from the US Cycling Federation to ride in the 1990 junior world championships in Moscow led Armstrong onto a path that would eventually take him to Europe, where he joined the young cyclists of the US national team.

His first win of note came in the 1991 Settimana Ciclistica Lombarda. Still an amateur at the time, Armstrong won the prestigious race ahead of many professionals. No American had won it before. In August 1992 Armstrong turned professional with the Motorola team. His first race was the Clásica de San Sebastián, and he finished last. On a day of torrential rain, Armstrong trailed in more than thirty minutes down. But the telling fact was that he had finished, when nearly half the field had abandoned. It was a demonstration of the fighting spirit that would later become his saviour.

LANCE ARMSTRONG

I KNOW WHO WON THOSE SEVEN TOURS, MY TEAM-MATES KNOW WHO WON THOSE SEVEN TOURS, AND EVERYONE I COMPETED AGAINST KNOWS WHO WON THOSE SEVEN TOURS.

Armstrong's breakthrough year was 1993. First he won the US national championships; then he claimed a million-dollar prize for winning three US races dubbed the Triple Crown of Cycling; and then started his first Tour de France, becoming the race's youngest stage winner when he took stage 8. Then came the world championships in Oslo.

On another day of cold and heavy rain, Armstrong found himself in the lead group on the final lap. He attacked. No one went with him, and soon Armstrong had a gap of twenty seconds. In the treacherous conditions, Armstrong cautiously plotted his way through the remaining kilometres. Behind him the chasing group remained in a state of disarray, with no rider willing to tow the others up to the American. The result: little more than a year after turning professional, the 21-year-old Armstrong was world champion.

Second-place finishes in the 1994 Clásica de San Sebastián and Liège–Bastogne–Liège were the stand-out results during Armstrong's year in the rainbow jersey. He started the Tour again that year, but abandoned the race. He'd have to wait until 1995 for his second stage win, when he triumphed in Limoges. The victory was dedicated to his friend and team-mate Fabio Casartelli, who had been killed on the Col de Portet d'Aspet (see pp98–100). Two days after Limoges, Armstrong would roll onto the Champs-Élysées for the first time in his career, finishing in the 36th spot, 1 hour and 28 minutes behind winner Miguel Indurain.

Later, in his 2001 book, *It's Not About the Bike*, Armstrong would write that the 1995 Tour taught him much. "It poses every conceivable element to the rider," he wrote, "and more: cold, heat, mountains, plains, ruts, flat tires, high winds, unspeakably bad luck, unthinkable beauty, yawning senselessness and above all a great, deep self-questioning... The Tour is not just a bike race, not at all. It is a test. It tests you physically, it tests you mentally, and it even tests you morally." But far greater challenges lay ahead.

In October 1996 Armstrong was diagnosed with cancer. His chances of survival were given as less than 50%. After brain surgery and aggressive chemotherapy, Armstrong spent 1997 recovering and setting up his foundation to help other cancer sufferers. Remarkably, towards the end of the year, just twelve months after first being diagnosed, Armstrong was planning a return to the peloton.

But no one wanted him – no one believed he could return to professional cycling. Cofidis, the team he had signed with just before his diagnosis, had to be persuaded to make even a low offer to continue the arrangement. Eventually, he signed an incentive-laden deal with the newly established US Postal Services team.

At first his comeback went poorly: he abandoned the Paris–Nice race on the very first day, and subsequently told his family and friends that he was going to quit cycling. Thanks largely to the persistence of those close to him, however, he began to train again, and rediscovered a love for the sport he had seemed to have lost.

His form picked up. Fourth place at the US Pro Championships was followed by a stage win and overall victory at the Tour of Luxembourg. Then, as the season drew to a close, he took on his biggest challenge yet – the Vuelta a España. He rode well, finishing fourth, just a handful of seconds off a podium spot. It was only the second time Armstrong had completed a three-week race.

He turned his focus to the Tour and, nine months after his Vuelta ride, stunned the cycling world by riding into Paris in yellow. In less than three years he had gone from a world-class one-day rider to a cancer patient; from a cancer patient to a cancer survivor; from a cancer survivor to an unwanted rider; from an unwanted rider to a Grand Tour rider of promise; and from a Grand Tour rider of promise to a Tour champion, a time-trial demon who could also climb with the best.

Armstrong's approach to the Tour was revolutionary. He was focused on one thing, and one thing only: wearing yellow in July. Everything else, every other race, was just preparation for the big event.

147

And the approach of his team was the same. All other ambitions were sacrificed. US Postal weren't interested in stage wins, the green jersey, the climber's jersey or the team prize. It was all about Lance.

And they were highly effective. For seven years on the trot Armstrong stood on the top of the podium in Paris, holding aloft the Tour trophy, waving the sponsor's cuddly toys and bouquets. And in the process he won some of the Tour's greatest mountain stages, in crushing style. He climbed to victory at Sestriere, at Alpe d'Huez, at Pla d'Adet, at La Mongie, at Luz-Ardiden, at Plateau de Beille and at Le Grand-Bornand. He wore the yellow jersey for a total of 83 days, second only to Eddy Merckx. As Hinault had been, he was the undisputed boss of the peloton, the *patron*. It was an inspiring story: the cancer survivor who had become the greatest winner of the sporting world's biggest and most arduous annual event.

However, from early in his reign, doubts surfaced. Armstrong was dominating in an era when the use of performance-enhancing drugs in the peloton was rife, and some found it inconceivable that a clean rider could be so commanding at such a dirty time. Rumours of Armstrong's drug use were widespread, but he fought all allegations fiercely. Legal action was taken against publications and individuals who talked of doping within the US Postal team. Riders who were perceived to be in the enemy camp were ostracised, sometimes even humiliated during races.

In 2005, standing on the podium after his final Tour win, knowing he was about retire, Armstrong made an impassioned speech against those who had questioned his achievements. "The people who don't believe in cycling, the cynics, the sceptics; [I feel] sorry for you," he said. "You need to believe in these riders. I'm sorry you can't dream big and I'm sorry you don't believe in miracles."

He returned in 2009 and rode two more Tours, finishing 3rd in 2009 and 23rd in 2010, before retiring again. Still the doping stories circulated, gaining momentum. A US federal investigation was launched but came to nothing. Then, in the summer of 2012, the US Anti Doping Agency (USADA), following a two-year investigation, brought a series of charges against Armstrong, his former team manager Johan Bruyneel, doctors Pedro Celaya, Luis Garcia del Moral and Michele Ferrari, and team trainer Jose "Pepe" Marti. The charge sheet was long and damning, with Armstrong being accused of, among other things, the use and possession of prohibited substances; trafficking EPO, testosterone, and/or corticosteroids; and the administration and/or attempted administration to others of prohibited substances.

After failing in a legal challenge to USADA's jurisdiction, Armstrong issued a statement saying he would not contest the allegations. "There comes a point in every man's life when he has to say, 'Enough is enough,'" said Armstrong. "Over the past three years, I have been subjected to a two-year federal criminal investigation followed by Travis Tygart's [USADA CEO] unconstitutional witch hunt. The toll this has taken on my family, and my work for our foundation and on me leads me to where I am today – finished with this nonsense... I know who won those seven Tours, my team-mates know who won those seven Tours, and everyone I competed against knows who won those seven Tours. We all raced together. For three weeks over the same roads, the same mountains, and against all the weather and elements that we had to confront. There were no shortcuts, there was no special treatment. The same courses, the same rules. The toughest event in the world where the strongest man wins. Nobody can ever change that."

With Armstrong refusing to go to arbitration, on August 24th 2012 USADA imposed a lifetime ban from competition and "disqualification of competitive results achieved since August 1, 1998." In one swoop Armstrong had been stripped of his Tour titles. Six weeks later USADA published its reasoned decision, setting out the evidence it had gathered. The thousand-page document included sworn statements from eleven former team-mates of Armstrong and team employees as well as financial records, email traffic and laboratory results. It made for startling reading. Though many had long suspected Armstrong and US Postal, the scale of the alleged misdemeanours was shocking. In USADA's words, Armstrong had been at the centre of "a massive team doping scheme, more extensive than any previously revealed in professional sports history."

The UCI soon ratified USADA's decision, and then the fallout gathered pace. All of Armstrong's major backers announced they were ending their sponsorship arrangements with him. He soon quit the board of the Livestrong foundation as well. Yet still he was continuing to insist that he was innocent. Then, on the night of January 17th 2013, Armstrong's interview with Oprah Winfrey was broadcast, and at last the truth was acknowledged.

In the opening exchanges Winfrey asked: "In all seven of your Tour de France victories, did you ever take banned substances or blood dope?" Armstrong's simple answer finally unravelled a decade of Tour history. "Yes," he replied. "This is too late" he continued. "And that's my fault. [This was] one big lie, that I repeated a lot of times... this story was so perfect for so long... you overcome the disease, you win the Tour de France seven times. You have a happy marriage, you have children... it's just this mythic perfect story, and it wasn't true."

LANCE ARMSTRONG SELECTED RESULTS:

1991: 1st amateur national championships
1st overall Settimana Ciclistica Lombarda

1992: One stage win Settimana Ciclistica Lombarda
1st overall Vuelta a Ribera

1993: One stage win Tour de France
1st world championships
1st US Pro championships

1994: One stage win West Virginia Classic
2nd Liège–Bastogne–Liège

1995: One stage win Tour de France
One stage win Paris–Nice
1st Clásica de San Sebastián

1996: 1st La Flèche Wallonne
1st overall and five stage wins Tour du Pont
2nd Liège–Bastogne–Liège

1998: 1st overall and one stage win Tour de Luxembourg*

1999: 1st overall and four stage wins Tour de France*

One stage win Critérium du Dauphiné*

2000: 1st overall and one stage win Tour de France*
One stage win Critérium du Dauphiné*

2001: 1st overall and four stage wins Tour de France*
1st overall and two stage wins Tour de Suisse*

2002: 1st overall and three stage wins Tour de France*
1st overall and one stage win Critérium du Dauphiné*

2003: 1st overall and two stage wins Tour de France*
1st overall and one stage win Critérium du Dauphiné*

2004: 1st overall and six stage wins Tour de France*

2005: 1st overall and two stage wins Tour de France*

2009: 3rd overall and one stage win Tour de France*

*Result annulled

COL DE LA BONETTE

START POINT / Jausiers
START ELEVATION / 1213m
FINISH ELEVATION / 2802m
LENGTH OF CLIMB / 24km
AVERAGE GRADIENT / 6.6%
MAXIMUM GRADIENT / 9%
FIRST TOUR / 1962
APPEARANCES / 4

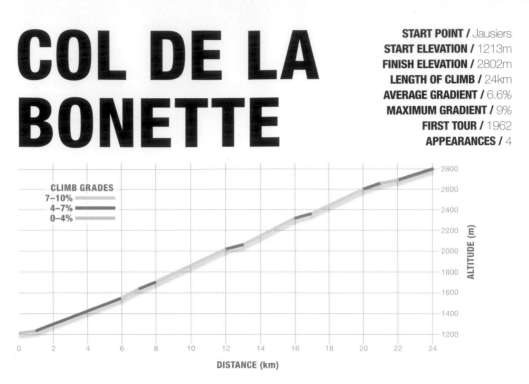

CLIMB GRADES
7–10%
4–7%
0–4%

This chapter was going to be called the Cime de la Bonette, after the highest paved road in France and the highest point that the Tour has ever been to. But, for reasons that will become clear, it isn't. It's called the Col de la Bonette instead, in reference to the natural pass just 87m lower down the mountain than the Cime.

It's a peculiar beast, not least because the section of road that enables the Bonette to call itself the highest paved road in France isn't strictly necessary. The lower, natural pass had been used for hundreds of years and there was nothing wrong with it. Apart from one thing: it wasn't high enough.

Locals wanted their road to be the highest, and with the Col de l'Iseran nearly 50m higher, the Col de la Bonette didn't cut the mustard. So they made an application to build a loop extending from the pass, up around the conical summit of the Bonette, before coming back down to rejoin the pass. Absolutely no point to it at all, other than to raise the height of the road. Incredibly the application was accepted, and in 1960 the new highest paved road in France was built.

The Bonette was hard work for me. First of all, the other big-name passes and summit finishes are clustered some distance north and west of the Bonette,

and it was amid them that I was staying. To ride up the Bonette meant a drive of more than three hours before I could even swing a leg over my saddle. But it is the highest climb so, although it may only have featured in four Tours, I had to attempt it.

It is not until just after 10.30am that I pull into a deserted car park in Jausiers, the pleasant town at the foot of the Bonette. I change into my cycling clobber, assemble the bike, eat a banana, do some stretching, have a slurp of energy drink and then decide that I can't put things off any longer.

Immediately on leaving the car park I'm greeted by a sign: "23[km], Route de la Bonette: La plus haute d'Europe, Alt. 2802m". That's when what I'm doing really hits home. I'm going to try to tame a monster. However, its claim to be the highest road in Europe would seem to be wide of the mark, with at least the Pico de Veleta in Spain nearly 500m higher. You can spin the argument whichever way you want though – the road to Veleta is an access road only, so some discount it. But does that really matter? It still leads somewhere. It's still a road. Then some say that the Bonette is the highest *through* road in Europe. But isn't the genuine through road the natural pass, the one that pre-dates the loop that was built in 1960, and is

lower than several others – the Iseran and Agnel, to name but two? Frankly it's a right road riddle. What is indisputable, though, is that it is very, very high.

• • •

Two years after the construction of the loop around the summit, the Tour de France paid its first visit. The Bonette was an unknown quantity. It was, in the words of the monthly magazine *Sport et Vie*, "a col no peloton, no rider has ever crossed before."

That publication was so fascinated by the inclusion of this new giant that it invited a man who had worked on its construction, a Monsieur Guichard, and Spanish climbing ace Federico Bahamontes, on an expedition to reconnoitre the climb a few weeks before the Tour. The trip was brought to a halt by a wall of snow, two kilometres after the Camp des Fourches, a collection of dwellings once used by soldiers stationed to protect the strategic route, and six kilometres from the summit.

As the trip ended, the article recounts, Guichard turned to Bahamontes and helpfully offered tactical advice: "At Camp des Fourches there will be serious damage [to the peloton]. You should do it alone." Bahamontes disagreed. He thought it too early on the stage, with the Vars and Izoard still to be tackled.

One month later, riding its southern ascent, Bahamontes crested the Bonette for the first time. He was at the front of the race. And he was alone.

Following Guichard's well-meant advice, Bahamontes had soared up the Bonette, nearly two minutes ahead of Eddy Pauwels. The peloton, nervous of what was to come, had maintained a modest pace on the climb itself. The Spaniard had flown. He was caught on the descent and trailed on the Vars. But then he rose again over the final climb of the Izoard and, although he couldn't hang on for the stage win in Briançon, his performance was enough to further cement his position at the top of the King of the Mountains classification. A title he would win in Paris for the fourth time.

Two years later the Tour paid another visit to the Bonette. This time the race ascended from the north.

TWO YEARS LATER THE TOUR PAID ANOTHER VISIT TO THE BONETTE. THIS TIME THE RACE ASCENDED FROM THE NORTH. IT MADE NO ODDS TO BAHAMONTES. AGAIN HE CROSSED THE SUMMIT AT THE HEAD OF THE RACE. AGAIN HE WAS THE TOUR'S KING OF THE MOUNTAINS.

It made no odds to Bahamontes. Again he crossed the summit at the head of the race. Again he was the Tour's King of the Mountains.

• • •

The early slopes of the climb are pretty easy. My legs feel good despite the drive, and the kilometres fly by. In what feels like no time at all I've ridden 6km. The sun is out, the scenery is interesting, the road surface is great. I've seen some long-horned goats with a big white Pyrenean mountain dog dolefully looking after them, and I've even overtaken another cyclist – which for me is a real rarity. Life on the Bonette is good. Seventeen kilometres more of this will suit me just fine. I pass a sign telling me I am on a high mountain route and can't expect to be rescued should anything happen; even that can't dampen my spirits.

Then the real Bonette starts.

• • •

After two visits from the Tour in three years, the Bonette had to wait another 29 years before the race returned. In 1993 it featured on stage 11, from Serre-Chevalier to Isola 2000. It was the penultimate climb of the day, but it was to be the final climb of a rider who was a real French champion and who had won the race twice: Laurent Fignon.

Fignon (see pp102–105) had won the Tour in 1983 and 1984. He'd been a national champion and had won the Giro d'Italia and Milan–San Remo, but by 1993 his career was on the slide. He was only 32 years old but his best years were well and truly behind him. A fact that came crushingly obvious to the Frenchman during the 1993 Tour.

The stage, which was lit up by Scotland's Robert Millar when he attacked and led over the Bonette, was ultimately won by Tony Rominger, who would go on to finish second in Paris behind Miguel Indurain. As Millar danced away over the summit of the Bonette, much further down the mountain Fignon was struggling.

The previous day Fignon had launched an attack on the climb of the Télégraphe. In years past such a move would have launched him towards a stage win.

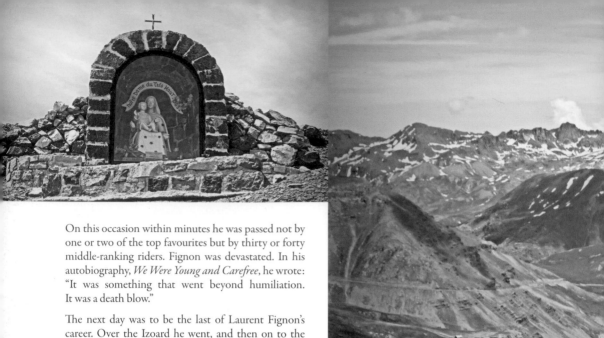

On this occasion within minutes he was passed not by one or two of the top favourites but by thirty or forty middle-ranking riders. Fignon was devastated. In his autobiography, *We Were Young and Carefree*, he wrote: "It was something that went beyond humiliation. It was a death blow."

The next day was to be the last of Laurent Fignon's career. Over the Izoard he went, and then on to the Bonette. "I rode up the whole climb in last place," he wrote. "Because I wanted to... This col was all mine and I didn't want anyone to intrude... It was total harmony."

Fignon completed the descent and then got off his bike for the last time. The Bonette had brought the curtain down on a great career.

• • •

From about 16km to go the road rears up, hovering around 8 or 9%. It stays like this for the best part of 12km. Suddenly I am in a very different mood. The scale of this climb is immense. It is a long, long way to the top. It just goes on and on, corner after corner, getting higher and higher. The Bonette has quickly become very daunting.

I plough on and try to forget just how far there is to go, but my brain won't switch off. All of sudden my legs don't feel so good. I'm constantly looking for the next number daubed on the road, signifying another kilometre gone. They are taking longer and longer to appear. Sometimes I think I must have missed one, so long has it felt since the last, only for it to appear further up the road. It's hugely demoralising.

With just over 7km to go I'm overtaken by another cyclist. He pulls up alongside me. I'd first noticed him when he was a 100m behind, and its taken a kilometre or so for him to get to me. He isn't going that much faster but he is in far better spirits than me.

"C'est belle non?" he says.

"Oui," I lie. "Et loin."

"Oui, c'est loin," he grins back. He goes on his way and points to the road, "Sept kilometres!"

I carry on, willing the legs to turn but, in truth, I feel like I could give up. The wind is picking up, blowing straight into my face, the gradient remains punishing and there is no sign of any let-up. I've been on the bike now for more than two hours and still have over 6km of the Bonette to go. I could end the madness now and turn around.

Except, of course, I don't. That's not what cyclists who ride among these giants do. We suffer, we dig deep, we want to be able to look at ourselves in the mirror tomorrow, when the pain has gone, and know that we did all that we could to achieve what we set out to do. I get out of the saddle with renewed commitment. I will get to the top of this brute.

With just over 3km to go I swing left and the gradient at last eases. Over to my right I can now see the conical peak and the road that lassoes it. All the descriptions that I've ever read of this giant, slagheap-like summit ring true. As I near the top I am reminded of my ride to Mont Ventoux, heading towards my final destination across a barren landscape, on a road flanked by snow poles. After all I have been through on this climb, the pain, the doubts, the overwhelming desire to give in,

it feels incredible to have finally have got here, to the top of France's highest road.

At the top of the natural pass the loop starts. There are two choices as to which way to tackle the final ascent. First of all I choose the anti-clockwise way. I get less than 50m up it before the road is completely covered in snow. No matter, I think. A minor inconvenience, I'll go the other way up.

I ride through the natural pass, ignore the turning to my left that heads down the other side of the mountain towards Nice, and turn right to start the clockwise way up. I ride past three or four bemused looking cyclists as I do so, including my friend who pointed out the 7km marking.

I get another 100m before I grind to a halt. This side is snowed in as well. I can't quite believe it, neither side is passable. Over two hours of riding, the last hour in agony, all for nothing. I can't complete my journey. It's impossible to fathom. I sit on the snow and put my head in my hands, distraught. This can't be it. I try to shoulder my bike and start to climb through the snow but it's no good. I'm nearly 2800m up a mountain, 23km from my car, with a cold wind blowing strongly.

FIGNON WAS DEVASTATED. IN HIS AUTOBIOGRAPHY, HE WROTE: "IT WAS SOMETHING THAT WENT BEYOND HUMILIATION. IT WAS A DEATH BLOW."

I stay there thinking for another five minutes, unwilling to turn my back on my goal, trying to figure out a way. In the end, though, there's nothing else to do. Dejected, I return to the pass and the other cyclists. They look a little relieved that I thought better of it.

And so I failed to get to the top of the highest road in France. That's why this chapter is called the Col de la Bonette, not the Cime de la Bonette. I tried my damnedest, got within a few hundred metres and had to plough new furrows of effort to get as close as that, but ultimately fail I did. Some might say it was at least an heroic failure. All I know is that the following morning, when I rose wearily from my bed, I was at least able to look at myself in the mirror.

FEDERICO BAHAMONTES

ONE MOMENT HE COULD BE SOARING UP THE MOUNTAINS, THE NEXT HE COULD BE SITTING BY THE ROADSIDE IN DESPAIR, THREATENING TO ABANDON THE RACE.

Federico Bahamontes, the Eagle of Toledo, became the first Spanish winner of the Tour de France in 1959. An exceptional climber, he won the Tour's mountain prize six times, a record later equalled by Lucien Van Impe and only surpassed by the controversial Richard Virenque in 2004. He was also a temperamental figure: one moment he could be soaring up the mountains, the next he could be sitting by the roadside in despair, threatening to abandon the race.

His 1959 Tour win was his sole major stage race victory. Until that year he had been content with mountain classification prizes but, with encouragement from the great Fausto Coppi, Bahamontes entered the 1959 Tour believing that the overall win was possible.

Despite his belief, the opening two weeks did not go well. With flat roads not to his liking, he was unsurprisingly trailing when the race hit the Pyrenees. Then, unusually for the great climber, he was unable to make inroads during the first two days in the mountains. In fact he went backwards and, as the race entered stage 13, Bahamontes was nearly fifteen minutes behind the race leader Michel Vermeulin.

Slowly the Spaniard began to recover. He put in a terrific performance during the time trial to the summit of the Puy-de-Dôme, winning the 12.5km stage by nearly one-and-a-half minutes from fellow climbing specialist Charly Gaul and catapulting himself up to second overall, just 24 seconds behind the new yellow jersey, Jose Hoevenaers.

Two days later, on stage 17, Bahamontes tore towards the Alps with Gaul. There were just a couple of mountains to tackle, neither of them monsters (they would come later), but Bahamontes and Gaul crushed the rest of the peloton. They gained three-and-a-half minutes

on the rest of the favourites, with Gaul winning the stage and Bahamontes satisfying himself with the yellow jersey – the first time he had worn it. Just five stages remained.

But as the race entered its final week a sub-plot was developing. The top-placed Frenchman was a rider called Henri Anglade but, in an era when the Tour was contested by national and regional teams, as opposed to the trade teams with which riders rode for the rest of the year, all sorts of chicanery was brewing. Also on the French national team were Jacques Anquetil and Roger Rivière, both of whom were leaders on their trade teams and thought they should be leader of the French team at the Tour. Neither was prepared to work for the other and, as the race progressed, they were united only in one aim – that Anglade, who was riding for a regional team, should not be permitted to win.

Stage 18 took the riders over the alpine giants: the Galibier, Iseran and Petit-Saint-Bernard passes were on the menu before a finish into Saint-Vincent d'Aoste. Going into the stage, Bahamontes had a lead of just under five minutes over Anglade, who was in fourth place overall.

During the stage Anquetil and Rivière found themselves in an escape along with Anglade that, at one point, had over four minutes on the yellow jersey. But Anquetil and Rivière refused to work to maintain the gap, allowing the Spaniard to get back to the break. Suspicions grew that the pair didn't want the break to succeed, as it would have helped the position of Anglade. In the end Bahamontes lost just 47 seconds to Anglade and the pair finished as one and two in Paris, with Anquetil taking the final podium spot.

157

The affair left a bitter taste in the mouths of the French media and public. The weekly sports paper *Miroir-Sprint* asked whether Bahamontes had won a "*Tour-bidon*", roughly translated as a "tinpot Tour". They called it the "most curious and disappointing Tour since the war." Not that Bahamontes or Spain was particularly bothered. The Eagle of Toledo returned a hero, complete with Spain's first yellow jersey.

Bahamontes was born in Val de Santo Domingo in 1928, before moving to Toledo with his family when he was eight. One of four children, he entered his first race aged 17, winning despite wearing normal trousers and a baseball shirt. In 1950 he won the national amateur championships and, three years later, turned professional for the Splendid trade team before a run of good results led to him being selected by the Spanish national team for the 1954 Tour.

NEARLY SIXTY YEARS AFTER HIS FIRST KING OF THE MOUNTAINS TITLE HE IS STILL REGARDED AS ONE OF THE FINEST CLIMBERS EVER TO GRACE THE TOUR, IF NOT THE FINEST.

His exploits in the mountains during the 1954 Tour have passed into legend and not just because he won the mountains classification at the first time of asking. Despite his awkward, upright position when riding, Bahamontes had only one equal when the race went uphill – Charly Gaul. But Bahamontes was poor at descending. During his first Tour, at the top of the Galibier, which he crested alone at the head of the race, Bahamontes pulled over and, much to the bemusement of the crowd, bought an ice-cream and sat on the wall.

It was widely believed that Bahamontes had been scared of descending alone since crashing into a cactus in his youth, and had stopped to allow the other riders to catch up. But in an article for the *Independent* in 2009 he told Alasdair Fotheringham that one of his spokes had broken and he was only waiting for the arrival of his mechanics. Whatever the real reason for his ice-cream break, Bahamontes and his cornet are now part of Tour history. As are the tales of his temper. Bikes and shoes were variously thrown off the mountain when the going got too tough and he'd decided enough was enough.

Although race wins were relatively rare for him, Bahamontes dominated the mountains classifications. As well as picking six King of the Mountains titles at the Tour, he also won the mountain prizes at the 1956 Giro d'Italia and the 1957 and 1958 Vuelta a España.

Bahamontes retired from racing in 1965, going on to run a bike shop in Toledo. Nearly sixty years after his first King of the Mountains title he is still regarded as one of the finest climbers ever to grace the Tour, if not the finest.

FEDERICO BAHAMONTES SELECTED RESULTS:

1950: Amateur national championship

1954: 1st mountains classification Tour de France

1955: 1st Mont Faron
Two stage wins Volta Ciclista a Catalunya

1956: 1st mountains classification Giro d'Italia
2nd mountains classification Tour de France

1957: 1st mountains classification and one stage win Vuelta a España
1st Mont Faron
1st Vuelta Ciclista Asturias

1958: 1st mountains classification and three stage wins Tour de France
National champion
1st mountains classification Vuelta a España
One stage win Giro d'Italia

1959: 1st overall and one stage win Tour de France
One stage win Vuelta a España

1960: One stage win Vuelta a España

1961: 1st Monaco–Mont Agel
1st Nice–Mont Agel

1962: 1st mountains classification and one stage win Tour de France
One stage win Tour de Romandie

1963: 1st mountains classification, 2nd overall and one stage win Tour de France
1st Mont Faron

1964: 1st mountains classification and two stage wins Tour de France
1st Mont Faron

1965: 1st Tour du Sud-Est

COL DE L'ISERAN

START POINT / Bonneval-sur-Arc
START ELEVATION / 1787m
FINISH ELEVATION / 2770m
LENGTH OF CLIMB / 13.5km
AVERAGE GRADIENT / 7.3%
MAXIMUM GRADIENT / 10.5%
FIRST TOUR / 1938
APPEARANCES / 8

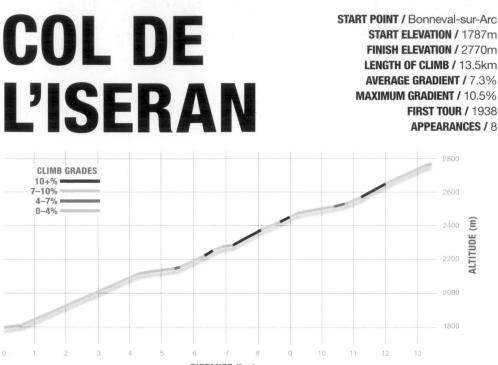

CLIMB GRADES
10+%
7–10%
4–7%
0–4%

ALTITUDE (m)

DISTANCE (km)

I'm standing at the top of the Col de l'Iseran, a 2770m monster of a mountain, and I am not alone. Despite the Iseran having a reputation as a desolate and untamed place, today it is busy. There's even a queue at the col sign, with people waiting patiently for the obligatory photographs to be taken. The pass only opened yesterday after being closed for nearly six months and everybody wants to come and visit the highest paved pass in France. Yes, the Tour de France has been higher (see pp150–155), but as genuine, natural passes go, the Iseran is the queen.

At last my turn at the col sign comes and I ask a German woman if she'll take a photo for me. She gets me to lift the bike up in celebration. "I'm surprised he's got the strength left to do that," an Australian voice pipes up from the back of the queue.

A fleet of Ferraris arrives. It's a Dutch club on a rally. The occupants float out, all looking rather pleased with themselves. Many are wearing Ferrari baseball caps. A woman gets out of the lead car, spots me in my cycling gear and proudly shows me her rally tee-shirt. It's yellow, has Ferrari written all over it and is emblazoned with the logo of the Tour de France. I can barely disguise my disgust. Such a thing is nothing short of heresy in my view. To wear that logo, one that is

synonymous with toil and pain, effort and endeavour, sacrifice and suffering, on a jolly jaunt around the mountains in an open-topped sports car, reveals that the person wearing it knows nothing of the history of the event. Either that or they don't care. I walk away. Some of the motorbikers here are none too happy either. "Look at this lot," I hear one say. "No better way to say 'look at us, for we have more money than thou.'"

And then with a roar the Ferraris are gone. Apart from one, which gets stuck behind a van. Then a couple of guys start playing table tennis. Oh yes, it was all happening the day I rode the Col de l'Iseran.

• • •

In 1938, on the eve of the Tour's first visit to the Iseran, Italy's Gino Bartali was in yellow, following a ride over the Izoard and into Briançon that had destroyed the field (see p170). But that night he was tired and nervous. The mighty Galibier and the unknown Iseran lay ahead. Bartali could not stop his mind racing. There were still ten stages to go, during which he would have to defend his race lead.

On the start line he felt bad. He already knew he was in trouble without turning a pedal. Later he would write: "… the truth is that I felt I was in inferior condition

compared to the stage start at Digne [the previous day]." Sure enough, on the Galibier he was dropped and by the time the race reached the upper slopes of the Iseran, Félicien Vervaecke, the third-placed rider overall, was leading the stage.

But then Bartali fought back. He threw himself into a madcap descent of the Iseran, diving into dangerous corners on the long drop into Bourg-Saint-Maurice. He caught the leading group before the valley and then managed to stick with them to the finish in Aix-les-Bains. He finished just 12 seconds behind the stage winner. Bartali had salvaged his maiden Tour win.

Eleven years and a world war later, Bartali would return to the mountain to help the new idol of Italy win his first Tour.

● ● ●

The top of the Iseran had arrived sooner than I had expected. I rode the southern ascent, from the pretty village of Bonneval-sur-Arc. Out of the village the road had weaved its way up the mountain, with a constant view of Bonneval and the valley. Around me, towering peaks grazed the sky. Already I was higher than every other climb in this book other than the Galibier and the Bonette, and I still had nearly 10km to go. To borrow a line from Spinal Tap, this one goes up to 11.

● ● ●

Having returned to the mountain for a second time in 1939 for a time trial, the Tour included the Iseran on its route for the third time in 1949. Bartali was there riding for the Italian national team, as was Fausto Coppi, his rival for the affections of the Italian public. A truce of sorts had been called between them for the Tour, facilitated by Italian team director Alfredo Binda, himself a multiple winner of the Giro d'Italia.

It appeared that history was repeating itself. Going into the stage Bartali was again in yellow, again courtesy of a fantastic ride over the Izoard. This time, however, he'd had company – Coppi had been with him all the way. The stage had been run on July 18th, Bartali's 35th birthday, and the birthday boy had asked his younger compatriot to let him win in Briançon. In return Bartali promised to help Coppi take the following stage and the yellow jersey, and thus effectively finish the Tour. Coppi let Bartali take the stage in Briançon.

The next day the Tour left Briançon for Aosta. On the route were climbs of Montgenèvre, Mont Cenis, Iseran and the Petit Saint-Bernard. As the race approached the Iseran, Pierre Tacca of the Île de France team was up the road. On the slopes of the climb Bartali started the chase. Coppi, and a handful of others, including Tacca's team-mate Jacques Marinelli, who would finish third in Paris, followed. By the time the pursuing group had crested Iseran and reached Val d'Isère they had caught Tacca. The leaders were all together.

ALREADY I WAS HIGHER THAN EVERY OTHER CLIMB IN THIS BOOK OTHER THAN THE GALIBIER AND THE BONETTE, AND I STILL HAD NEARLY 10KM TO GO. TO BORROW A LINE FROM SPINAL TAP, THIS ONE GOES UP TO 11.

Then, on the climb of the Petit Saint-Bernard, Bartali launched an attack with Coppi on his wheel. Robic and Marinelli tried to respond but they were unable to get up to the Italian duo. Bartali towed his team-mate up the climb and they crested the summit together with a healthy lead. Then, on the descent, disaster struck Bartali – he punctured and crashed. Coppi sat up and looked back, then Binda, following in the team car, came alongside and told him to go on. Coppi flew down the rest of the descent. In the final 42km he gained nearly five minutes. That night Coppi slipped on the yellow jersey for the first time in his career, and he held it all the way to Paris. Bartali would finish second overall, nearly 11 minutes back, completing an Italian one-two for the first time. (The feat has so far been repeated just once, in 1960, when Gastone Nencini and Graziano Battistini finished first and second.)

• • •

Bonneval disappeared from view as I started the second phase of the climb, having entered the Vanoise National Park, a protected area. This took me on to a high plateau where the road eased for a short time. I had seen little traffic but then a big red van approached with orange

lights flashing. As it got closer it became clear that it was an old fire engine. In the cab were three men. They waved and gave me a thumbs up. The fillip came just at the right time, as the gradient again picked up, forcing me out of the saddle.

I found the mid-section of the climb more difficult than I thought I would. For long stretches the gradient didn't look particularly harsh but I was crawling along. At times it felt ridiculous how slowly I was going in relation to the amount of effort I was expending. Then I realised that no other cyclist had yet come past me, though I had spotted some lower down the mountain. Maybe the sheer scale of this climb makes it harder than the bare statistics would suggest.

• • •

The Iseran's link with Italy continued in 1992. That year the Tour returned after a 29-year absence and, for the first time, the race used the longer, northern ascent from Bourg-Saint-Maurice. Stage 13 was a 254.5km slog from Saint-Gervais over the Saisies, Cormet de Roselend, Iseran and Mont-Cenis passes, and up to the Italian ski station of Sestriere.

Over the Saisies and Cormet de Roselend, Italy's Claudio Chiappucci set a ferocious pace, forcing a selection of ten riders. Then, on the northern slopes of the Iseran, some 48km in length, he went alone. Over the top of the climb he had well over three minutes on the peloton. On to the next mountain, Mont Cenis,

163

and Chiappucci maintained his advantage. Behind, a flurry of activity left just two riders in pursuit of the Italian: Miguel Indurain and Chiappucci's compatriot Gianni Bugno.

But Chiappucci would not be caught. While the chasing riders gradually whittled down the Italian's lead on the final climb to Sestriere, the advantage that he had built over Iseran meant that he held on to a memorable stage win. In one of the most incredible days in the Alps that the Tour has witnessed, Chiappucci rode alone for more than 125km. The next day's headlines marvelled at the Italian's exploits, heralding him as "magnificent".

● ● ●

I passed through a short tunnel and suddenly, ahead of me, people were skiing on the last of the winter snow. It was an odd juxtaposition: me on a bike sweating in short sleeves and cycling shorts, them skidding down a piste not one hundred metres away in full winter gear. As I rode by I heard a cry of "allez!" from one of the skiers. I waved. It's always great to get an "allez". Especially from someone wearing salopettes.

It was a tiring drag up to the next corner. I could see it, a left-hand bend by some ski lifts, but it was a long time in coming. I tried to take my mind off the pain by watching the skiers hurtle down the slopes. I drove on, told my legs that it would soon be over and that they were not to let me down. There had been no official markings since the start of the climb but my calculations told me that I still had more than two kilometres to go as I finally rounded the corner by the ski lifts.

IN ONE OF THE MOST INCREDIBLE DAYS IN THE ALPS THAT THE TOUR HAS WITNESSED, CHIAPPUCCI RODE ALONE FOR MORE THAN 125KM. THE NEXT DAY THE HEADLINE ON THE FRONT OF THE DAUPHINÉ LIBÉRÉ NEWSPAPER SUCCINCTLY SUMMED THINGS UP: "CHIAPPUCCI, THE MAGNIFICENT."

On to a steep ramp, the snow piled high to my right, I stood on the pedals in a bid for more power. I branched right and there, suddenly, incredibly, amazingly, and most of all, surprisingly, was the summit sign in all its glory. Two kilometres sooner than I'd expected, I had made it.

It's a strange feeling, arriving at your target well before you expect to. Mentally, I was prepared for another two kilometres of agony, so to suddenly stop threw me a little. My brain was telling me that I should still be suffering, that I hadn't yet earned the right to stop, despite all the physical evidence to the contrary. I was of course happy to get there, but also strangely deflated that it was all over. I couldn't escape the feeling that perhaps I would have enjoyed the final moments a bit more had I known how close I was to the end, maybe savoured more the sensation of a last push for the line.

But I suppose there was at least one advantage. Another two kilometres and, as my Aussie friend had helpfully suggested, I probably wouldn't have had the strength to lift my bike for that photo.

GINO BARTALI

DE GASPERI SAID THAT THE COUNTRY NEEDED BARTALI TO WIN. "IT COULD MAKE A DIFFERENCE," HE SAID. BARTALI ANSWERED THAT HE WOULD DO HIS BEST.

There's a photograph, taken on July 16th 1948 and published the next day in the *Miroir-Sprint*, that captures in a single frame the very essence of cycle racing. Louison Bobet of France (see pp198–201) and Italy's Gino Bartali are pictured battling their way up the Col de la Croix de Fer during stage 14 of that year's Tour de France. The road surface is so poor it's not really a road: it's a mud-laden, gravel-strewn track, hacked into the side of a murderously steep mountain. It's more suited to mules than to athletes.

In the photograph Bobet is in the lead: goggles crookedly perched atop his head, spare tyre draped across his shoulders in a figure of eight, white socks miraculously still gleaming, brow creased, eyes closed, hands held high on the handle bars uncomfortably close to the cages that house his metal water bottles. Bartali is just behind. Grim-faced, he is hunched lower than Bobet, shoulders broad and rounded, with a nose that has been likened to that of a boxer's and ears protruding unflatteringly, thanks to a tight-fitting cap. His eyes are locked in a downward stare, his hands grip the handlebars behind the brake levers. It's a portrait of contradiction: a man of colossal strength, calmly plotting his next move in this toughest of sports.

It's a picture that freezes in time the true story of any cycle race. That moment when riders are not just pedalling against each other but are also riding against the worst that nature can throw at them. The effort, the agony – all suffered for the ultimate glory of crossing the finish line first.

In 1948 Gino Bartali was part of a rivalry that had Italy transfixed and divided. Born in 1914, Bartali had recorded his first notable victory at the age of 21 when he took the Italian national championships in 1935, going on to win the Giro d'Italia in successive years (1936 and 1937) and again in 1946. He'd captured his first Tour de France in 1938, becoming only the second Italian to win the yellow jersey in Paris after Ottavio Bottecchia (1924 and 1925). He was the undisputed darling of Italy... until the arrival of Fausto Coppi (see pp186–191).

By 1948 Bartali's battle with Coppi was at its most intense. (In August of that year, as team-mates on the Italian national team, they would both climb off their bikes at the world championships rather than help the other.) In the Tour, Bartali was the undisputed leader of the Italian team, if only because Coppi wasn't riding. However, the early days of the Tour did not go completely to plan for the 34 year old. Despite three stage wins, poor displays in a couple of other stages meant that going into stage 13, a 274km slog from Cannes to Briançon over the Col d'Allos, Col de Vars and Col d'Izoard, he stood more than twenty minutes behind the yellow jersey and home favourite, Louison Bobet. Bartali was now considered to be completely out of contention. Meanwhile, back in Italy, a dire situation was unfolding.

In 1946, the Italian people had voted in favour of a republic, a decision that resulted in the drafting of a new constitution, which took effect in January 1948. Elections were held in April 1948 and Alcide De Gasperi's Christian Democrats swept the board, taking over 48% of the popular vote and well over half of the available seats. Italy appeared to have taken its first steps towards political stability. But a little over two months later, the well-liked Palmiro Togliatti, the chairman of the Italian Communist Party, was shot outside the parliament building. Togliatti's condition was critical and Italy descended into chaos. Strikes and demonstrations were called,

and Communist supporters soon occupied key facilities. The atmosphere was anarchic. Civil war seemed a real possibility.

De Gasperi was desperate. Seeking a diversion for his country he called Bartali in Cannes and told him of the crisis in his homeland. De Gasperi said that the country needed Bartali to win. "It could make a difference," he said. Bartali answered that he would do his best.

The next day, Bartali, with Bobet on his wheel, launched an almighty attack on the Allos. He accelerated away from the Frenchman and

AS THEY STARTED THE COL DE PORTE, AN 8KM CLIMB IN THE CHARTREUSE MASSIF, BOBET'S WILL SNAPPED AND HIS LEGS FAILED HIM. BARTALI, THE SEASONED CHAMPION, SIMPLY RODE AWAY.

rode over the Allos, the Vars and the Izoard in glorious isolation, through freezing rain. Stage 13 was a one-man show. He stopped the clock in Briançon in a time of 10 hours 9 minutes and 28 seconds, to win the stage. Bobet crossed the line in 12th place, over 18 minutes down. That night Bartali lay second, just 51 seconds behind Bobet, who was still in yellow. Over the border, Italy paused to take notice.

The next day Bobet fought back. During the 263km stage from Briançon to Aix-les-Bains, the two riders were locked in combat. Over the Lautaret, the Galibier and the Croix de Fer they matched each other, attack for attack, pedal stroke for pedal stroke, putting the rest of the peloton to the sword. Finally Bobet, the darling of France, cracked. As they started the Col de Porte, an 8km climb in the Chartreuse Massif, Bobet's will snapped and his legs failed him. Bartali, the seasoned champion, simply rode away. Over the Porte, Cucheron and Granier, Bartali ruthlessly increased his lead in a mighty display of power. That night, as night fell in Aix-les-Bains, the yellow jersey was hanging in the wardrobe of the Italian master. He now had a lead of over eight minutes. Gino Bartali had fought back to gain nearly thirty minutes in two simply astonishing days in the Alps.

The next day France's sports writers described Bartali's ride lavishly, with the tale of the titanic battle between the two great riders splashed all over the front pages. But there was another story to be told as well, a story from across the border, a story of peace descending in Italy.

De Gasperi had been right. As Bartali had risen over the passes of the Alps, Italy had been glued to its radios. As Bartali slipped the yellow jersey over his shoulders that night in Aix-les-Bains, the country rejoiced. Italy had for one day stood still and listened while their hero took a vice-like grip on the world's greatest bike race. And then it had stepped back from the edge. Seven days later Bartali stood wearing yellow in Paris. His winning margin? A quite incredible 26 minutes and 16 seconds.

Born to a hard-working and deeply religious family, Bartali was nicknamed Gino the Pious. He used to attend Mass during races and even had his first yellow jersey blessed by a priest. He famously said that for him the weather was never too hot nor too cold, an attitude that gained him another nickname, bestowed upon him by fellow Italian riders: The Iron Man.

His national championship title in 1935 was followed the next year with his first Giro win. Riding for the Legnano team, Bartali took the race lead on stage 9, which he won by over six minutes. Though his margin was gradually eroded, not least by Giuseppe Olmo, who won no fewer than ten stages, Bartali managed to hold on to take his first major win by just over two minutes.

After successfully defending his title in 1937 he was sent straight to the Tour. Despite being fatigued by his efforts in the Giro he took the yellow jersey during the stage over the Galibier. The next day, however, he crashed into a river and injured himself badly. He limped to the finish, still in the lead overall, but he lost the jersey the next day and abandoned two days later.

Despite his misfortune, the 1937 Tour had proved that Bartali was a force to be reckoned with outside of his native Italy. The next year he

showed just what a force he was. In the lead-up to the race's decisive stage 14, 219km from Digne to Briançon, over the Allos, Vars and Izoard, Bartali and Belgian Félicien Vervaecke had been engaged in a game of cat and mouse: Vervaecke had held the race lead since stage 8, but on the eve of stage 14 was 1 minute 35 seconds up.

Riding in the lead group from the start, Bartali made sure he was leading over the first climb of the day, the Allos, picking up the time bonus at the top. Again, towards the top of the Vars he upped the pace, going over the top alone. It was then that he launched his serious bid for the win. Dropping dramatically off the Vars, Bartali put a huge amount of time into his rivals: at the top of

HE FAMOUSLY SAID THAT FOR HIM THE WEATHER WAS NEVER TOO HOT NOR TOO COLD, AN ATTITUDE THAT GAINED HIM ANOTHER NICKNAME, BESTOWED UPON HIM BY FELLOW ITALIAN RIDERS: THE IRON MAN.

the Vars he had a gap of under two minutes on Vervaecke; at the bottom it was over seven. No wonder that Bartali would later write: "It was on the descent from the Vars that I won the Tour de France." By the time he arrived in Briançon he had taken more than seventeen minutes out of Vervaecke and had secured his first Tour win.

The gap of ten years between that first Tour win and his second in 1948 remains a record to this day. Of course, the gap is explained by the war. During the conflict Bartali worked as a military bike messenger but was secretly helping Jewish families, harbouring them in his house and running fake papers and money that he hid in his bike during "training rides".

His actions only came to light after his death from a heart attack in 2000. In January 2012 the International Cycling Union (UCI) marked Holocaust Memorial Day by releasing a short article on Bartali's war efforts. According to the article, Bartali never really spoke of what he did, saying only: "Good is something you do, not something you talk about. Some medals are pinned to your soul, not to your jacket."

GINO BARTALI SELECTED RESULTS:

1935: 1st national championships
1st mountains classification and one stage win Giro d'Italia
1st overall and three stage wins Vuelta Ciclista al País Vasco

1936: 1st overall and three stage wins Giro d'Italia
1st Giro di Lombardia

1937: One stage win Tour de France
1st overall and four stage wins Giro d'Italia
1st national championships

1938: 1st overall and two stage wins Tour de France

1939: 1st mountains classification and four stage wins Giro d'Italia
1st Milan–San Remo
1st Giro di Lombardia

1940: 1st mountains classification and two stage wins Giro d'Italia
1st Milan–San Remo
1st Giro di Lombardia
1st national championships

1946: 1st overall Giro d'Italia
1st overall and four stage wins Tour de Suisse

1947: 1st mountains classification and three stage wins Giro d'Italia
1st Milan–San Remo
1st overall and two stage wins Tour de Suisse

1948: 1st overall and seven stage wins Tour de France

1949: One stage win Tour de France
1st overall and two stage wins Tour de Romandie

1950: One stage win Tour de France
One stage win Giro d'Italia
1st Milan–San Remo

1951: 1st Giro del Piemonte

1952: 1st national championships
1st Giro dell'Emilia

1953: 1st Giro dell'Emilia

COL DE LA MADELEINE

START POINT / Feissons-sur-Isère
START ELEVATION / 415m
FINISH ELEVATION / 2000m
LENGTH OF CLIMB / 25km
AVERAGE GRADIENT / 6.2%
MAXIMUM GRADIENT / 11%
FIRST TOUR / 1969
APPEARANCES / 24

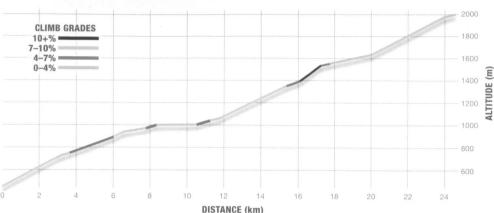

It is a perfect day for cycling on the Col de la Madeleine. There is a gentle breeze behind me, the sky is blue with occasional fair-weather cloud to filter the sun's rays, and the air carries the scent of wild flowers and pine trees as I wind my way up the sinuous road that is the early section of the Madeleine.

I've been riding for about an hour. After a tricky opening series of hairpins the road relented and for six or seven kilometres now I've been merrily making my way through the little villages that are dotted along this road. In the small cluster of homes that is Bonneval I bid a cheery "Bonjour" to an elderly local man who's tending to the verges outside his house. In La Thuile, where the buildings crowd the road, it's a woman checking her post that I greet. Then a crew from the French cycling magazine *Vélo* overtake, filming a group of four riders who are making their way up to the top. They wave and shout encouragement as they speed by with apparent ease. It's all very friendly and jolly. Everyone is happy today on the Madeleine. But then the Madeleine is a long climb. There's plenty of time for the going to get tough.

•••

The Madeleine was first used by the Tour in 1969 when Andrès Gandarias, a Spanish rider whose best result would come some years later when he picked up a Giro d'Italia stage win, was first over the summit. Since then the race has been over the Madeleine on another 23 occasions. Two riders share the record for being first over the climb: six-time King of the Mountains winner Lucien Van Impe (1979, 1981 and 1983) and the man who beat his polka-dot record by winning the jersey seven times, Richard Virenque (1995, 1996 and 1997).

While Van Impe never went on to win a stage that he had led over the Madeleine, four riders have, including Virenque in 1997. Although his performances in this period of his career would later need to be reassessed in light of the 1998 Festina affair (see p179), the Frenchman's exploits on stage 14 during the 1997 Tour would lead to headlines proclaiming his heroism as he took the fight to eventual winner, Jan Ullrich.

Stage 14 took the riders from Bourg d'Oisans to Courchevel. It was a relatively short stage, just 148km, but took in climbs of the Glandon and Madeleine on the way to the final ascent to Courchevel, the ski resort of the rich. It was a stage ripe for attacking from the off.

Virenque was in second place overall, more than six minutes down on Ullrich, who was in the yellow jersey. As soon as the flag went down Virenque and his team were aggressive, riding at such a fierce pace on the Glandon that only a handful of riders

could stay with them. By the time the race went over the summit, led by Virenque and four team-mates with him, Ullrich was isolated.

The descent of the Glandon's northern side is particularly technical, especially the first few kilometres. Virenque, a vastly superior descender, flew down the mountain. Trying to follow the fast-disappearing Frenchman, Ullrich nearly crashed before resigning himself to the realisation that to lose a few minutes was better than careering off the road.

On to the Madeleine and Virenque was still ahead, although he had dropped his squad. Behind, having sat up on the early slopes of the Madeleine, it was Ullrich who now had his team-mates alongside him. Crucially he had Bjarne Riis, the man Ullrich had helped win the 1996 Tour. The time had come for Riis to repay the German. Sure enough the Dane paced his leader up the climb, clawing back time with every metre that he covered. By the time they reached the summit of the Col de la Madeleine they were less than twenty seconds behind.

On the way down the Madeleine, Riis and Ullrich, joined by Fernando Escartin and Laurent Dufaux, a team-mate of Virenque's, launched a pursuit of the lone leader.

By the time the race was on the lower slopes of Courchevel, Virenque had been reeled back. Then Ullrich and Virenque went head to head for the right to claim the Tour.

Ullrich, wearing the yellow jersey, didn't have to make a move: he just followed Virenque's wheel all the way up the final climb. With huge crowds roaring Virenque on, the Frenchman tried to shake the German, but Ullrich sat there, grinding a huge gear, backside planted firmly on his saddle, in complete contrast to Virenque's dancing style. Virenque, who had been on the front of the race right from the start, and had led over both the Glandon and the Madeleine, crossed the line first. Still there, right on his wheel, was Ullrich.

DESPITE THE BEST EFFORTS OF VIRENQUE AND THE FESTINA TEAM, THE GERMAN HAD KEPT HIS YELLOW JERSEY. IT HAD BEEN ANOTHER DAY OF HEROICS ON THE TOUR – ALBEIT ONE THAT WOULD SOON BE SEEN THROUGH THE FILTER OF THE FESTINA AFFAIR.

Despite the best efforts of Virenque and the Festina team, the German had kept his yellow jersey. It had been another day of heroics on the Tour – albeit one that would soon be seen through the filter of the Festina affair.

•••

I approach the village of Celliers-Dessus, about 9km from the top, and sense a rider approaching from behind. Eventually he pulls up alongside.

"Bonjour," he says.

"Bonjour," I reply. A long pause. He's still beside me.

"You English?"

And that's how I meet Phil. As we huff and puff our way through the village, Phil tells me he is here on an organised cycling holiday with friends from his local club. I ask him what mountains they have already ridden but he can't remember their names (maybe he's wiped them from his memory); he says that Alpe d'Huez is next on the list tomorrow.

"How are you finding the climbs?" I enquire.

"They're hard aren't they?" he says. "It's just so different to back home. I mean where I'm from, Goodwood is our local hill. It's not quite the same is it?"

As we exit Celliers-Dessus the road kicks up abruptly. "I don't think I can talk much more, I think it gets harder from here," puffs Phil. Secretly I'm glad, as I'm beginning to struggle to keep up with him. "Okay, have a good holiday," I splutter as he goes on up the road.

• • •

The Madeleine was the scene of another day of heroism in 2010. This time, though, the heroics were believable. This time the hero was Maltese rider David Millar. And he was last up the climb.

Millar had served his own ban for EPO usage but had returned determined to play his part in cleaning up the sport. By 2010 he was riding for Garmin, as transparent a team as there has ever been, a team that had instigated its own, independent anti-doping test programme, a team that even cynical and hardened journalists had come to trust. Millar was (and remains) its figurehead, its leader, its talisman.

But on stage 9 he was struggling. He had crashed on the second stage and was in real pain. The Madeleine was the last of five climbs on the route from Morzine-Avoriaz to Saint-Jean-de-Maurienne. The Châtillon, Colombière, Aravis and Saisies all had to be tackled before the Madeleine could even be thought about. And Millar was in trouble right from the start.

Over the four preceding mountains he battled. He fell back on the Châtillon, just 18km into the 204km stage and, in truth, a small hill in comparison to the others. He just managed to hang on over the gentle rise but then, on the Colombière, he lost contact. He never saw the peloton again.

He rode alone, at the back of the race, for the next 180km. In his terrific autobiography, *Racing Through the Dark*, he writes of riding past crowds that were packing up their picnic lunches and of riding with the broom wagon hovering "a few metres off my shoulder, reminding me that quitting was an option."

But quit he did not. He rode on. Spectators on the mountainside, now aware of what was happening, shouted his name, cheered him on, implored him not to abandon. Millar was going through his own private hell. Tens of minutes behind the peloton by the time he was on the Madeleine, he continued dragging himself up the interminable mountain, unwilling to yield to it. Eventually, painfully, he made it to the top. Now he had to ride the descent of his life in order to get to the finish inside the time limit.

After a breakneck ride off the mountain and a head-down, knees-pumping drive along the valley, David Millar crossed the finish line 42 minutes and 45 seconds after stage winner Sandy Casar. He had just made it in time. He may have lost over 42 minutes but, after one of the most courageous rides in recent Tour history, he had won far more. He'd won the respect of every true cycling fan.

• • •

From Celliers-Dessus the character of the Madeleine changes rapidly. Gone are the woods lining the road as the climb finally opens up. Above me craggy peaks start to appear. The sharp, rocky outcrops are shrouded in cloud, giving them an air of mystery. It's a tough kilometre or so out of the village and I can feel myself beginning to tire. I probably

SPECTATORS ON THE MOUNTAINSIDE, NOW AWARE OF WHAT WAS HAPPENING, SHOUTED HIS NAME, CHEERED HIM ON, IMPLORED HIM NOT TO ABANDON. MILLAR WAS GOING THROUGH HIS OWN PRIVATE HELL.

rode too long outside of my comfort zone chatting to Phil, so I slow down, mindful that there is still a very long way to go.

Then, as the road flattens, I glance over to my left and spy a road rising straight up the mountainside. It looks nightmarish. That can't be where I'm going, I think to myself, but it is difficult to see where else this road will take me. There's simply no way I'll be able to cycle that – it's so steep, mountain goats would probably need to hitch a lift up it. I strain my eyes, peering up and down the ribbon of road, trying to see if there are any cyclists or motorbikes or cars negotiating it. I'm grateful to see that there aren't. As I get gradually nearer it becomes apparent that it is nothing more than a service track for the ski slope that I can now see runs alongside it. Panic over.

I can see the approach to the pass now, but it still seems impossibly high. Again the road ramps up for this final push and it is now that I really start to suffer. It's a steep climax to the climb and, at the moment, the fantastic views over Mont Blanc, resplendent in a coat of freshly fallen snow, will have to wait as I haul myself through this last section. I'm in and out of the saddle, searching for a comfortable position. Slowly I drag my bike up through the interminable hairpins until finally the road relaxes for the last 500m or so to the top. Satisfied that you have now earned the right to be here, the Col de la Madeleine allows an easy final flourish.

The pass is busy with cyclists and motorbikers. The *Vélo* crew are here, still filming. As I get off my bike I hear a familiar voice: "Made it then," says Phil. "Knew you would." We recover by gazing out over the magnificent 180-degree view that the Madeleine offers. Another cyclist joins us, keenly surveying the horizon. I've never met him before but he looks me in the eye.

"Makes it all worth it, doesn't it?" he says.

Richard Virenque holds the record for the most King of the Mountains titles in the Tour de France, claiming seven polka-dot jerseys between 1994 and 2004. But he remains a divisive figure both in France and across the world of cycling.

Born in Casablanca in November 1969, Virenque moved to France with his family when he was nine years old. He soon discovered cycling, joining a series of local clubs as he started to pursue a career in the sport. As he later said: "Very early in life, I realised that I did not have good intellectual prospects, so I therefore worked very hard on the bicycle."

In 1991 Virenque turned professional with the RMO team, taking his first win in 1992 at the Bol d'Or des Monédières-Chaumeil. He also lined up at the Tour for the first time in 1992. A late call-up to the team, Virenque rewarded his managers' faith with a long escapade on stage 3 over the climbs of the Ispeguy and the Marie-Blanque. Virenque was accompanied on his breakaway by Javier Murguialday, who outwitted him in the sprint into Pau for the stage win, but Virenque took not only the yellow jersey but also the green jersey in the points competition and the polka-dot jersey as well.

Though he would not hold on to any of those jerseys for long, that 1992 stage taught Virenque the value of long-distance breakaways in the fight for the mountains classification, the one competition in which he truly stood a chance.

Although he would go on to win several big mountain stages with summit finishes, most notably at Luz-Ardiden in 1994, Courchevel in 1997 and Mont Ventoux in 2002, he would secure the majority of his polka-dot wins by escaping early on mountain stages, mopping up the points on the day's initial

THE SHOT OF A WATERY-EYED VIRENQUE BEING DRIVEN AWAY FROM THE TOUR REMAINS ONE OF THAT RACE'S ENDURING IMAGES.

climbs, when the big guns were safely in the pack preparing for the skirmishes on the final ascent, before dropping back when the racing got frenetic in the closing kilometres. This tactic brought with it accusations that, though the record books may say otherwise, he was not the best climber in the peloton, a criticism that has dogged many King of the Mountains winners in recent years.

By 1998 Virenque had picked up four straight King of the Mountains titles as well as two podium positions in the overall classification (2nd in 1997 and 3rd in 1996). Just before the start of the 1998 Tour the car of Willy Voet, a *soigneur* on Virenque's Festina team, was stopped. It was found to be full of banned drugs of almost every sort. Voet was arrested but the Festina team still took to the start line.

Six days later, with new rumours and scandals erupting daily at the race, the team's manager Bruno Roussel admitted to a managed doping programme within the team. Virenque and the rest of the team refused to leave, so the Tour organisers said they were throwing them off the race. Virenque then announced that they refused to recognise the expulsion. A meeting with the race organisers took place, from which a tearful Virenque eventually emerged, protesting his innocence before getting into a car to be whisked away. The shot of a watery-eyed Virenque being driven away from the Tour remains one of that race's enduring images.

Virenque maintained his innocence, claiming that he knew nothing of any doping programme. He rode at the 1999 Tour for the Italian Polti team, again picking up the polka-dot jersey. Finally, towards the end of 2000, with former team-mates and managers singing like canaries, Virenque admitted the truth. He was banned for nine months.

He came back in late 2001, riding for the Domo-Farm Frites team, then moving to Quick Step-Davitamon in 2003. He recorded two more King of the Mountains titles and three more Tour stage wins before his retirement in 2004, including one on Mont Ventoux. There he rocked and rolled his way up the slopes of the Giant of Provence, face etched in pain, roared on by a huge crowd. It was his finest stage win.

RICHARD VIRENQUE SELECTED RESULTS:

1992: 1st Bol d'Or des Monédières-Chaumeil

1993: One stage win Tour du Limousin

1994: 1st mountains classification and one stage win Tour de France
1st Trophée des Grimpeurs

1995: 1st mountains classification and one stage win Tour de France
Two stage wins Critérium du Dauphiné

1996: 1st mountains classification
One stage win Critérium du Dauphiné

1997: 1st mountains classification and one stage win Tour de France

1998: One stage win Critérium du Dauphiné

1999: 1st mountains classification Tour de France
One stage win Tour de France

2000: One stage win Tour de France

2001: 1st Paris–Tours

2002: One stage win Tour de France

2003: 1st mountains classification and one stage win Tour de France

2004: 1st mountains classification and one stage win Tour de France

COL DU GLANDON
AND CROIX DE FER

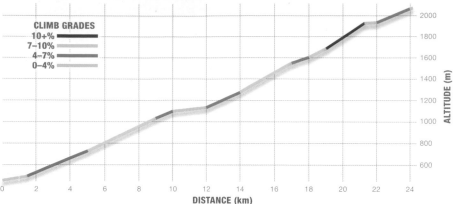

CLIMB GRADES
10+%
7–10%
4–7%
0–4%

ALTITUDE (m)

2000
1800
1600
1400
1200
1000
800
600

DISTANCE (km)

0 2 4 6 8 10 12 14 16 18 20 22 24

The Col du Glandon is notorious for making the men of the Tour suffer, and in 1977 it played a major part in bringing the curtain down on the career of the finest of them all: Eddy Merckx.

In truth Merckx's career had been on the wane for a few years, although, of course, all things are relative. He was still picking up plenty of victories, including Milan–San Remo in 1976, but his last Grand Tour win had been in 1974, when he'd completed his third Giro/Tour double. But Merckx was still hopeful of winning his sixth Tour when the 1977 edition rolled out of Fleurance.

He remained in touch with the leaders for nearly three weeks. Before stage 17, to Alpe d'Huez via the Madeleine and Glandon, the Belgian legend was only just over three minutes off the pace, nothing that the Merckx of old couldn't claw back.

AS THE NEW GENERATION SLIPPED AWAY, MERCKX WAS LEFT TO RIDE IN HIS OWN PRIVATE PURGATORY. THE CROWDS CHEERED HIM, OFFERED HIM "BON COURAGE", BUT HE PEDALLED OVER THE GLANDON MORE THAN TEN MINUTES BEHIND.

Except this wasn't the Merckx of old. Age was catching up with him. He'd been ill since the start of the race and this was the day it was all to come crashing down. Struggling on the Madeleine, he barely managed to remain in contact with the leaders but then, on the Glandon, as Lucien Van Impe ratcheted up the pace, Merckx fell away.

He simply had nothing left to give. As the new generation slipped away, Merckx was left to ride in his own private purgatory. The crowds cheered him, offered him "bon courage", but he pedalled over the Glandon more than ten minutes behind. Though he recovered slightly on the descent and rode a decent final climb to Alpe d'Huez, he still crossed the line 13 minutes 51 seconds down on Hennie Kuiper, who won the stage. All chances of winning the overall were gone – he was now 16 minutes behind the yellow jersey and eventual winner Bernard Thévenet.

Merckx would recover some time in the coming days, even winning the next stage and finishing sixth overall in Paris. But the Glandon had taken the Cannibal as its victim on his last Tour.

• • •

The evening before I'm about to tackle any climb I like to check the website climbbybike.com.

START POINT / Saint-Étienne-de-Cuines
START ELEVATION / 505m
FINISH ELEVATION / 2067m
LENGTH OF CLIMB / 22.4km
AVERAGE GRADIENT / 6.9%
MAXIMUM GRADIENT / 11%
FIRST TOUR / 1947
APPEARANCES / 30
(14 Glandon; 16 Croix de Fer)

Climbbybike.com has a page for many climbs the world over. Each contains a profile and a collection of brief stories from cyclists who have tackled the route. It's these stories that I look for, as they often reveal far more than any statistics can. So every night I go to the site to find out what the next day holds in store. Then I go to sleep either worried or relaxed. Nine times out of ten I'm worried.

The Col de la Croix de Fer is my final destination today, but I'm riding from the north and so I need to conquer the Col du Glandon first. The Glandon is a Tour giant in its own right and will constitute the majority of the ride. Depending on which way the Tour is heading, the Glandon sometimes features in the race by itself and sometimes as part of the Croix de Fer. Sometimes the race just goes up the Croix de Fer from the other side and ignores the summit of the Glandon completely.

Anyway, last night I looked up both the Col du Glandon and the Col de la Croix de Fer on climbybike. com. My favourite story came from "Teeside Clarion": "The mighty Glandon. Over the years we've broken it into 3 sections. Section 1 to the village is steady, a canopy of trees keep the sun at bay... Section 2 cow alley the gradient alters slightly, it gets warmer, lots of flys [sic] from the cows... keep a bit in reserve for the last 2k. 'POW-WOW' Very steep!"

I'm now two kilometres from the top of the Glandon and it's "Pow-Wow" indeed. Like Teeside Clarion, I can't think of a better way of describing the last part of this climb. When, after 18km or so of climbing, you round a corner and see the ribbon of tarmac that wriggles up the final slopes, kicking up to over 10% in places, it really does feel like a 1970's knockout blow delivered by Gotham City's finest.

Until this point the Glandon had been difficult but manageable. The opening kilometres had taken me out of Saint-Etienne-de-Cuines via a long, straight road with a noticeable but moderate pitch. I was in and out of tree-shade, accompanied only by the sound of rushing water and birdsong. At the 15km-to-go marker the road suddenly lurched round to the right, the first hairpin on the climb forcing me out of the saddle for the first time.

●●●

The Glandon and the Croix de Fer were first used in 1947, on stage 8 from Grenoble to Briançon. Edouard Klabinsky was the first rider to crest the Glandon, while Fermo Camellini led the way over the Croix de Fer on his way to the stage win. The race returned to the Croix de Fer in 1948 (the year of Gino Bartali's incredible Tour win – see pp167–171). Then in 1952 Bartali's great Italian rival, Fausto Coppi, used the climb as his launch pad to tighten his grip on the race.

By the time the Tour had reached the foot of the Croix de Fer, Coppi had already made history by winning the previous stage to Alpe d'Huez – the first time the race had finished at the top of the now legendary climb. That win had put him in yellow. His overall lead was just five seconds, but in second place was Andréa Carrea, a team-mate who was a loyal *domestique*. Stan Ockers of Belgium, Spain's Bernardo Ruiz and France's Jean Robic were Coppi's biggest rivals, and after Alpe d'Huez they were all more than thirteen minutes behind.

Coppi was in the driving seat, comfortably on his way to his second Tour win. He had only to defend his position. But that was not his way. Coppi rode on instinct and, as the race hit the Croix de Fer, he felt good. The rest of the field, anxious to make inroads

into his seemingly unassailable lead, kept attacking him, but Coppi was not to be distanced. Instead he responded with attacks of his own, forcing his rivals to dig deep to stay with him, softening them up for later. As they went over the summit of the pass, Coppi was at the head of the race, closely pursued by the rest of a fast-tiring group of favourites.

And at the front was where he would stay. Coppi let Frenchman Jean le Guilly take them over the Col du Télégraphe, but on the Galibier the Italian roared into action. He launched his own definitive offensive, to which no one had an answer. Over the Galibier he rode alone, and by the time he crossed the finish line in Sestriere his lead was over seven minutes. As he pulled on the yellow jersey again that evening his margin had ballooned to nearly twenty minutes. But even that wasn't enough. It would be 28 minutes 17 seconds in Paris.

• • •

I steadily make my way up to the village of Saint-Colomban-des-Villards. It's an unassuming and pleasant enough place, which owes its existence to winter sports. It's also one of the few places I've ridden through that understands that visitors might be interested in the names of the surrounding peaks. So I take a break from my ride and spend a happy few minutes peering at the village's panoramic viewing maps.

The road flattens through the village but as I exit it soon ramps up again. Other cyclists start to catch me: some pass as if I were standing still, others tail me for a while before edging by, leaving me to follow their wheels for as long as I can. The one consistent thing is a nod of the head and a "Bonjour" as they pass.

Mindful of what is to come, I try to ride within myself, but it doesn't really work out that way. I have to expend a lot of effort all the way up this mountain. At last, here I am: two kilometres to go. "Pow-Wow". More cyclists go by as I approach the final section. I'm already tired but now the Glandon rears up before me, throwing down its toughest challenge.

It is so steep it seems impossible that I will get myself up there. I resist the urge to look up at the summit and concentrate only on what is directly in front of me. It is slow and painful going. With my legs screaming, I finally let myself glance up and see thankfully that I've got less than 100m left. To my right a man applauds. To my left, directly facing me, another answers the call of nature.

But, of course, I'm not finished. The Col de la Croix de Fer, visible away to the east, beckons.

● ● ●

Four years after Coppi's ride over the Croix de Fer to Sestriere on his way to one of the most lauded of Tour victories, Roger Walkowiak rode over the same climb, on his way to one of the most derided.

Most books paint Walkowiak as a virtual unknown before the Tour of 1956, but he had picked up wins every year of his professional career and had finished on the podium in Paris–Nice (1953) and the Critérium du Dauphiné (1955), two stage races that vie for the title of the second most important race in France.

Walkowiak took the yellow jersey in the 1956 Tour for the first time on stage 7, a 244km ride from Lorient to Angers. There, riding for the North-East Central regional team, he got himself in a 31-rider breakaway that crossed the line over 18 minutes ahead of the rest of the field. Walkowiak didn't win the stage but he was the best-placed rider in the breakaway and so took over the race lead. He held on to it for a few days before surrendering it to Gerrit Voorting of Holland. After losing more than fourteen minutes on the stage into Bayonne he slipped to seventh overall, over nine minutes back. And that looked to be that.

But Walkowiak wasn't done. He'd worn the yellow jersey and he liked the feeling. As the race gradually made its way through the Pyrenees, he started to gain time. A minute here, a minute there. Bit by bit the Frenchman slowly made his way up the overall classification. By the time the riders took to the start line in Turin for the stage to Grenoble, over the passes of Mont Cenis, the Croix de Fer and the Luitel, Walkowiak was in second place, 4 minutes 27 seconds off leader Wout Wagtmans.

The race was approaching its defining moment and Walkowiak rode it perfectly. Six kilometres from the top of the Croix de Fer he attacked, dragging with him the race's greatest climbers, notably Charly Gaul and

Federico Bahamontes. Over the top of the climb and on the descent into Allemont he tried to distance the climbing specialists, but in the valley they regrouped. On the Luitel, Gaul jumped away, launching a massive attack that would take him to the stage victory. Behind, Walkowiak stayed with Bahamontes, content in the knowledge that his earlier efforts would be sufficient to put him into yellow once more.

And so it proved. Walkowiak finished the stage fourth, eight minutes ahead of Wagtmans. He took the race lead and kept it until Paris. His win was met with disdain from some quarters. He had not won a stage and many thought he had only won because of tactical errors made by the favourites, not because he was the strongest. His win even coined a new term. Today a win "à la Walko" means a large upset caused by an unknown or unfancied rider.

● ● ●

After a descent of less than 100m I turn left and I am on to the slopes of the Croix de Fer. It is only 2.5km from the top of the Glandon to the summit of the Croix de Fer and in truth, after the hardship of the Glandon, it's a relatively easy ride. Surprisingly few of the cyclists I saw on the Glandon seem to be heading here, which is a shame, because the views from the top are spectacular. The horizon is filled with drama, from the three peaks of the Aiguilles d'Arves to the Cime du Grand Sauvage and the Saint-Sorlin glacier.

THE RACE WAS APPROACHING ITS DEFINING MOMENT AND WALKOWIAK RODE IT PERFECTLY. SIX KILOMETRES FROM THE TOP OF THE CROIX DE FER HE ATTACKED, DRAGGING WITH HIM THE RACE'S GREATEST CLIMBERS, NOTABLY CHARLY GAUL AND FEDERICO BAHAMONTES.

So here I am, sitting on a restaurant terrace, basking in the sun at the end of a difficult ride, gazing out on this glorious terrain. I'm enjoying a cold Coke and perhaps the best omelette I've ever had – certainly the hardest won. Even with all the pain, I realise I wouldn't want to be anywhere else today. The combination of the Glandon and the Croix de Fer might make you suffer, but the rewards they offer are rich indeed.

FAUSTO
COPPI

HE WON THE 1946 MILAN–SAN REMO BY MORE THAN 14 MINUTES, ATTACKING AFTER JUST 3KM, AND THE 1952 TOUR BY 28 MINUTES, A MARGIN THAT REMAINS A POST-WAR RECORD.

In 1949 Fausto Coppi, the *Campionissimo* (champion of champions), completed an unprecedented feat when he won both the Giro d'Italia and the Tour de France. Until Coppi's achievement the Giro/Tour double was considered an impossibility: the races were too long, too arduous and too close together for anyone to win both in the same year. But Coppi did the impossible, cementing his place in the sport's history and his native Italy's affections.

Angelo-Fausto Coppi was born in 1919, to Domenico and Angliolina Coppi, in the village of Castellania, in north-west Italy. Fausto was the fourth child in the family; a fifth, Serse, forever to be linked with Fausto, would be born four years later. The family lived a tough life, farming the land with their neighbours. It was an arduous existence that was to set the young Coppi up well for his life of suffering on the bike.

Leaving school at twelve years old, Coppi first laboured on the family farm before moving to work for a butcher 20km away. Missing his home, he moved back into the farmhouse and cycled to and from the butcher's every day, riding as fast as he could so that he could stay in bed for as long as possible. In his biography of Coppi, *Fallen Angel*, author William Fotheringham tells of the young Coppi sprinting past serious amateurs on his way to work, even beating a former professional rider up some climbs. Coppi was already beginning to show the talent that would whisk him away from the toil of rural life.

Coppi was introduced to a masseur and former cycling team manager, Biagio Cavanna, who by the late 1930s was completely blind. The meeting would change Coppi's life. Cavanna took the young Coppi under his wing and stayed with him throughout his entire career (barring a brief falling-out late on). Fotheringham highlights the importance of Cavanna to the young Coppi: "He taught him how to train, how to ride his bike, how to behave as a professional sportsman should. Eventually he provided him with team-mates, sympathy and magic mixtures to make him go faster." (Coppi would later freely admit the use of amphetamines to assist his performances, this at a time when such practices were not specifically outlawed.)

Coppi made startling progress under Cavanna's tutelage, turning professional in 1940, riding for the Legnano team, and claiming his first victory in the Giro d'Italia at just twenty. In 1941 he moved on to the team with which he is most famously linked: Bianchi. Over the course of his career he rode for the Italian team for a total of fifteen years over three separate periods.

Despite the disruption of the Second World War, Coppi would go on to win the Giro a further four times, the Tour de France twice, the Giro di Lombardia five times, Milan–San Remo three times, the world championships and Paris–Roubaix. He was a fearsome climber, a talented time-triallist and an expert in judging the solo breakaway. He won the 1946 Milan–San Remo by more than 14 minutes, attacking after just 3km, and the 1952 Tour by 28 minutes, a margin that remains a post-war record.

One of his most celebrated rides was a mammoth solo attack over five alpine passes in the 1949 Giro, which would land him his third pink jersey. Stage 17 took the riders over the climbs of the Maddalena, Vars, Izoard, Montgenèvre and Sestriere. As so often befits an epic day in the Alps, the weather was poor, with heavy rain greeting the peloton at the start line in Cuneo.

The race was meant to be a battle between Coppi and Gino Bartali, but it hadn't quite worked out that way. Coppi, just 43 seconds off the overall lead, was already nearly ten minutes ahead of Bartali going into the stage. If Bartali was to salvage his race, this was the stage he would have to do it on.

But he never got a chance. On the slopes of the Maddalena, Coppi broke away. The exact nature of how or why he did so seems to be unclear. Some accounts say he just sprinted clear, some that he reluctantly followed an attack by fellow Italian Primo Volpi, others that he had noticed Bartali struggling with mechanical problems and chose to strike. Whatever the circumstances of his solo escapade what is clear is that, by the top of the first climb, he had a lead of nearly three minutes. And that it continued to grow as the stage progressed.

For 190km Coppi ran amok in the Alps, gracefully gliding up the slopes, building more and more time as he went. It was a majestic display, and no one could make any impression on his lead. Bartali tried his damnedest and put in his own spectacular ride but the bare facts are chilling. The all-conquering Coppi arrived in Pinerolo after 9 hours and 19 minutes of riding. Nearly 12 minutes later Bartali crossed the line. Eight minutes after Bartali the third-placed rider came in. Coppi had destroyed the field, taken control of the race and confirmed his status as the best rider in the world.

Coppi was meticulous in his planning and training. Fotheringham tells of a training programme that would consist of long rides, for the final 100km of which Coppi would be joined by Cavanna's other charges, who would take turns to attack the Campionissimo and replicate racing conditions. Other training sessions involved riding as fast as possible for short distances before returning to a more steady tempo: interval training, long before the term was coined.

As well as being an innovator in training techniques, Coppi also turned conventional wisdom on its head when it came to diet. The cyclist's breakfast of steak was not for him: he would eat small amounts often, keeping his stomach light, and would also shun protein for carbohydrate. He paid particular care to tactics and back-up staff. He would isolate the key points, or stages, of a race and target those, choosing to defend his position at other times. He ensured he had the best mechanics to guarantee that his equipment was in the best possible condition.

Coppi was systematic and rigorous in his race preparations, but his riding style was characterised by graceful fluidity and panache. Fellow rider André Leducq spoke for many when he described Coppi as a man who rode "like a great artist", and Jacques Goddet came up with a memorable image for the smoothness and power of Coppi's technique: "Coppi climbing is like a ski lift gliding up its steel cable".

Coppi was defined not only by cycling but also by his relationships. His career is seen through the filter of his rivalry with Bartali (see pp166–171), the incumbent Italian champion when Coppi came on the scene. From the moment Coppi turned professional the two riders were linked. Bartali was the team leader at Legnano, Coppi's first team, where he was hired to ride in support of the proven champion. But it soon became clear that the team wasn't big enough for the both of them. In his first Giro, Coppi was due to ride for Bartali, only becoming team leader when his leader fell and lost time. Coppi went on to win the race and soon left for Bianchi.

After World War II, during which Coppi was captured by the British, both he and Bartali were at the peak of their powers. Italy's love was divided. You were either in Bartali's corner or Coppi's. Their rivalry prompted much debate

> **FOR 190KM COPPI RAN AMOK IN THE ALPS, GRACEFULLY GLIDING UP THE SLOPES, BUILDING MORE AND MORE TIME AS HE WENT. IT WAS A MAJESTIC DISPLAY, AND NO ONE COULD MAKE ANY IMPRESSION ON HIS LEAD.**

around the tables of Italy, making the two men the most famous of Italy's sportsmen. To this day the debate over who was the better rider still rages with undimmed passion.

Coppi was extremely close to his younger brother, Serse, who was also a rider on the same team as Fausto, riding as one of his *gregari* (*domestiques*). Serse's premature death, in 1951, hours after suffering a seemingly innocuous fall during a race in Turin, hit Fausto hard. At this point, his private life began to unravel.

Coppi's affair with the so-called "White Lady", Giulia Locatelli, led to the very public failure of his marriage and hers. At a time when adultery in Italy was punishable by imprisonment, there was public outcry as details of the affair were made known. Such was the extent of the scandal that the Vatican intervened to encourage Coppi to repair his marriage. The persuasion was unsuccessful: Coppi, who already had a daughter with his wife, fathered a son, Faustino, with Giulia. Italy was outraged, and even hardened Coppi supporters struggled with what their champion had done, particularly as they had backed him in his rivalry with the devoutly Catholic Bartali. The nadir came when the Pope refused to bless the peloton at the Giro because Coppi was there.

His career went into decline from 1957. Although he was still attracting big appearance money because of his past achievements, he won little. And, as befitted a man touched by misfortune

189

COPPI WAS SYSTEMATIC AND RIGOROUS IN HIS PREPARATIONS, BUT HIS RIDING STYLE WAS CHARACTERISED BY GRACEFUL FLUIDITY AND PANACHE.

If not for the outbreak of war, the imperious Coppi would almost certainly have won many more Grand Tours. Nevertheless, the hopes and aspirations of the Italian nation were raised by the magnificent successes of the enigmatic *Campionissimo*. He was an extremely photogenic athlete, and the dramatic images of him soaring high in the mountains of France and Italy helped a country that was in the process of dragging itself out of the pit of a war that had split the nation. And for this reason he remains Italian cycling's favourite son – which is why the highest point of each Giro is now named the Cima Coppi.

and scandal, his life was ended prematurely. Coppi was a keen hunter and was invited to join a trip to Africa to ride in some races and take in some hunting. While in Africa many of the party suffered mosquito bites and some, including Coppi, fell ill. Two weeks after his return, on January 2nd 1960, Fausto Coppi died of malaria in hospital. He was just forty years old.

FAUSTO COPPI SELECTED RESULTS:

1940: 1st overall and one stage win Giro d'Italia

1941: 1st Giro dell'Emilia

1942: 1st national championships
Hour record

1945: 1st Gran Premio di Lugano

1946: 1st overall and three stage wins Giro d'Italia
1st Milan–San Remo
1st Grand Prix des Nations
1st Giro di Lombardia

1947: 1st overall and three stage wins Giro d'Italia
1st national championships
1st Grand Prix des Nations
1st Giro di Lombardia

1948: Two stage wins Giro d'Italia
1st Milan–San Remo
1st Giro di Lombardia

1949: 1st overall and three stage wins Tour de France

1st overall and three stage wins Giro d'Italia
1st Milan–San Remo
1st Giro di Lombardia

1950: 1st Paris–Roubaix
1st La Flèche Wallonne

1951: One stage win Tour de France
Two stage wins Giro d'Italia

1952: 1st overall and five stage wins Tour de France
1st overall and three stage wins Giro d'Italia

1953: 1st overall and four stage wins Giro d'Italia
1st world championships

1954: 1st mountains classification and two stage wins Giro d'Italia
1st Giro di Lombardia
1st Trofeo Baracchi

1955: Two stage wins Giro d'Italia
1st Trofeo Baracchi

COL D'IZOARD

START POINT / Briançon
START ELEVATION / 1230m
FINISH ELEVATION / 2361m
LENGTH OF CLIMB / 19.5km
AVERAGE GRADIENT / 5.9%
MAXIMUM GRADIENT / 8.5%
FIRST TOUR / 1922
APPEARANCES / 33

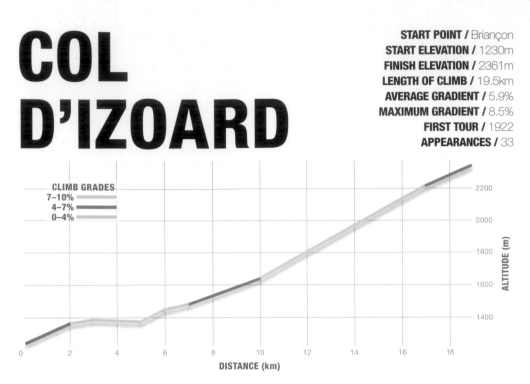

I'm in trouble. The weather is closing in, as the clouds above me darken from apathetic grey to a violent black. It's cold. Drizzle is turning to sleet, despite its being mid-June. Last night the peaks around me gained a fresh dusting of snow. This morning I was in two minds whether to attempt this climb today, but the forecast said the clouds would clear. If anything, exactly the opposite is happening.

I stop to fasten my jacket, my back hunched against the stiffening wind. A Frenchman dashes out from a campervan parked opposite, "Non, non monsieur," he shouts, pointing up the road, "it's the last kilometre. The summit," he's gesticulating wildly now, "the summit is around the corner." I smile and explain I have no intention of giving up but just need a rest. He seems reassured. I sip from my water bottle, munch a fruit bar, snap my shoes back into the pedals and get ready to ride the last slopes of the 20km-long, 2360m high Col d'Izoard. I'm sent on my way with hand claps and a "Bravo, allez!" The French understand what it means to ride these mountains. It's in their blood.

The climb to this point had been, in football parlance, one of two halves. The first 10km, from Briançon to Cervières, had been straightforward. After a lengthy climb out of Briançon, I was soon riding along a valley, escorted by a river that flows into the wonderfully named Lac du Pont Baldy. The valley was open and

the gradient kind, so I spun along quite happily, enjoying the view, excited that, after years of waiting, I was finally going to see the Casse Déserte: a barren wasteland pierced only by towering turrets of golden rock. A Tour de France temple built of stone and scree.

Ten kilometres in, at Cervières, the Izoard got all nasty on me. As I came out of the village the road turned to the right and pitched upwards sharply. Onwards, through the tiny conurbation of Le Laus, and the road remained steep as it entered a pine forest and started climbing through a series of hairpins. Five or six steep and arduous kilometres passed until I finally emerged from the tree line. Then I was hit by the wind full on, which eventually forced me to pull over for five minutes, using the handy excuse of the need to put on my jacket. That's when I meet the French campervan man.

With his cry of "allez" fresh in my mind, I slowly wind my way through the final sequence of hairpins, amid the wild and rocky slopes. It's tough, and he lied: I wasn't on the last kilometre – I have at least another two to go. I slowly turn the pedals, buffeted by the wind, until, on the point of cracking, I arrive at the top. I crest the Izoard, give a nod to the col sign, and go straight down the other side.

•••

The race has been to the Izoard 33 times so far. It first climbed the mountain in 1922 when the Tour moved the finishing town for the stage starting in Nice from Grenoble (where it had been since 1906) to Briançon. That meant taking on the Izoard.

That first ascent of the Izoard was claimed by Belgium's Philippe Thys, already a three-time Tour winner (1913, 1914 and 1920). He would go on to win the stage in Briançon, just out-sprinting fellow countryman Félix Sellier. It was one of five stage wins for Thys that year – he won twelve in all during his career.

The Tour was a regular visitor to the mountain throughout the 1920s. It was included for six straight years from 1922 through to 1927, with Luxembourg's Nicolas Frantz and Italy's Bartolomeo Aimo each leading over the summit twice. Frantz would go on to win Tours in 1927 and 1928, famously wearing yellow from start to finish in 1928, while Aimo would have to be content with two stage wins and a couple of podium positions over the course of his career. A handful of appearances during the 1930s then came before the Izoard's golden era of the late 1940s and 1950s.

• • •

I'm on my way down to the Casse Déserte and I am heady with anticipation. I have seen so many photographs of this mythical place, and spent hours examining countless images of the Tour passing through it, the riders dwarfed by the sheer scale of this cathedral of endeavour, where fans gather in their thousands to worship their heroes. It is the place I have most looked forward to seeing and, when I finally arrive, after descending for a couple of kilometres from the summit, I am not disappointed.

Pillars of serrated stone shoot upwards from the mountainside, towering over the road that weaves its way through this most desolate of landscapes. It's an eerie, mysterious place, made even more so by the slight scattering of snow coating the rocks higher up. For me there's an air of the Wild West about it. I almost expect to see a cowboy come riding along, greeting me with a "Howdy, stranger." But, in stark contrast to days when the Tour pays a visit, I have the place all to myself. The Casse Déserte is deserted – or almost. The only people I see are four other cyclists who come roaring down without stopping, heads down, knees pumping.

I spend a long time just wandering around, soaking up the unique atmosphere. It's quite unlike anywhere I've ever been before, or am likely to go. I leave my bike and scramble a short way down the scree towards a pillar of rock. I want to touch its roughness, to experience this place with all my senses. There, with Izoard rock in my hands and my ears enjoying the silence, I sit and think about what it would have been like up here when the Tour first arrived in 1922. This spot seems impossibly remote and otherworldly even today, when I know there's a café just a couple of kilometres away at the summit. It's hard to imagine what it must have felt like on that first foray into the

unknown. Finally I make my way back to the road and visit the simple memorial to two riders who have contributed more to the history of this place than anyone else: Fausto Coppi and Louison Bobet.

● ● ●

The race returned to the climb in 1947, the first Tour after the Second World War, and it was to be the scene of many terrific exploits over the next few years. First Jean Robic, then Gino Bartali and finally Fausto Coppi rose over its peak on their way to Tour victory in 1947, 1948 and 1949. Then Louison Bobet, the darling of France, led the peloton over the summit in 1950, the first of a record three times that he would lead the race here.

In 1951 Coppi was suffering a poor year by his standards. Injuries had limited him to just one stage win at the Giro d'Italia, where he'd finished fourth overall. Then a poor year became a tragic one. Five days before the start of the Tour, Coppi's brother Serse, a fellow rider and team-mate, crashed in Turin during the Giro del Piemonte. At first it seemed an innocuous enough accident, but Serse's condition quickly deteriorated and he passed away later the same night. Fausto was inconsolable. That he took to the Tour's start line in Metz at all was little short of miraculous, though in truth it was only the shadow of the great Fausto Coppi that rolled out that early July morning.

Three weeks later Coppi was still in the race, as the Tour set off for Briançon from Gap. The Italian was lying outside the top ten, well over thirty minutes behind race leader Hugo Koblet. But the race was about to go over his favourite climb, the Izoard. And Coppi felt his legs twitching in anticipation.

On the approach to the first climb of the day, the Col de Vars, Abdel-Kader Zaaf, a French national who had been born in Algeria and who would finish only one of the four Tours he started, launched a short-lived attack. With 110km or so still to ride, Coppi used the acceleration of Zaaf as a springboard. Joined by Roger Buchonnet, he headed up the road, striving to establish a gap.

And a gap was soon established. By the top of the Vars the pair had over eight minutes on the pursuing peloton. On the slopes of the Izoard, Coppi was too strong for Buchonnet. The great Italian champion was alone through the Casse Déserte, over the top of the pass and down into Briançon, where he crossed the line over three-and-a-half minutes ahead of his initial breakaway companion. The win was enough to move him up into the top ten overall, where he would stay for the rest of the race, finishing 10th in Paris. Even in his darkest hour, Coppi had it within him to illuminate the Tour on one of its toughest days.

Two years later both the Tour and Coppi returned to the Izoard. Only this time Coppi wasn't riding. Having won the 1953 Giro d'Italia, the Italian opted not to defend his Tour title. Instead he went to the Casse Déserte as a spectator, to watch the next great French champion commence his reign at the top of the Tour.

Louison Bobet had been close before: he'd finished fourth in 1947 and third in 1950 and had three Tour

EVEN IN HIS DARKEST HOUR, COPPI HAD IT WITHIN HIM TO ILLUMINATE THE TOUR ON ONE OF ITS TOUGHEST DAYS.

stages to his name by the time he started the 1953 Tour. The fiftieth anniversary of the Tour was set to be a show-down between the French, with Bobet facing challenges from within his own national team as well from riders such as Jean Robic, the 1947 winner, who was now an outcast riding for a regional team and hell-bent on revenge.

The in-fighting within the French team was put on hold when Robic took the race lead on stage 11. Now forced to work together in order to prevent a mere regional rider becoming a threat, the French team started to work for Bobet.

Going into the Izoard stage, the last major day in the mountains, Bobet was 3 minutes 13 seconds down on Jean Malléjac, another rider from a regional team. But all knew that this was the key stage. The night before, Bobet himself had said: "It's on the Izoard where the Tour will be played out. It's there that it will be won."

On the early part of the stage a three-man breakaway formed. Bernard Quennehen and Jean Dacquay of

the Nord-Est Centre team attacked, and were marked by Bobet's team-mate, Adolphe Deledda. As they approached the first climb of the day they had a lead of around nine minutes. Behind, Bobet stirred into action. He launched his chase on the slopes of the Vars and by the time he went over the summit he had reduced the gap to less than two minutes. But he was not done yet, not by a long way. Coppi was on the Casse Déserte, he had his camera, and Bobet wanted to put on a show.

In the valley between the Vars and Izoard, Bobet caught the three riders. Deledda then rode himself into the ground for his leader, towing Bobet along the valley roads, distancing Quennehen and Dacquay before dropping off at the foot of the climb. All of a sudden Bobet was on his own. Then he really went to work.

The Tour was there for the taking and wasn't to be found wanting. As he entered the open-air theatre of the Casse Déserte his rivals for the yellow jersey were in distress far away down the mountain. Bobet had put minutes into his adversaries on one of the Tours most storied passes. Bobet then passed by the Italian

maestro, later saying: "Fausto Coppi, after taking my photograph, gave me a friendly hand signal and a wink of the eye that said 'it's all sewn up'. It boosted my morale and I thank him [for it]."

Indeed it was all sewn up. Bobet went over the summit more than three minutes ahead, a lead that he had stretched to 5 minutes 28 seconds by the time he crossed the line in Briançon. His overall lead was now over eight minutes on Malléjac; when they reached Paris, it was more than fourteen. Louison Bobet had won his first Tour. He would win two more. (See p199–201 for more.)

● ● ●

Humbled by the Casse Déserte, I make my way slowly back up to the top of the Izoard. Despite the weather, there are still some glorious views back down towards Briançon and I stand there, braving the wind and sleet peering over the mountains. I try to savour the view, striving to make myself appreciate what I'm looking at. But, in all honesty, my mind is still 2km back down the road with Coppi and Bobet.

THE NIGHT BEFORE, BOBET HIMSELF HAD SAID: "IT'S ON THE IZOARD WHERE THE TOUR WILL BE PLAYED OUT. IT'S THERE THAT IT WILL BE WON."

LOUISON BOBET

HE WON THE FINAL TIME TRIAL IN NANCY TO CLAIM THE TOUR BY OVER FIFTEEN MINUTES. IT WAS THE FIRST TIME THAT A FRENCHMAN HAD SUCCESSFULLY DEFENDED HIS TOUR TITLE SINCE LUCIEN PETIT-BRETON WAY BACK IN 1908.

Louison Bobet was the first rider to win the Tour de France three times in succession, and from 1953 until 1955 he was the darling of France, as he dominated the annual loop around the country. And he really did dominate: the average margin of his three wins was more than eleven-and-a-half minutes.

Bobet was born in 1925 in the village of Saint-Méen-le-Grand in the centre of Brittany. The son of a baker, Bobet initially took to a bicycle to deliver bread to his father's customers, but his obvious talent on two wheels meant that soon he was delivering race wins rather than the daily baguette.

His first win of note came in 1946 when, at the age of 21, he won the French amateur national championships in Vincennes. The following year he turned professional with the Stella team and took seven race wins, including the Tour du Finistère, the Course à la Mer (his first stage-race win) and the 280km Boucles de la Seine-Saint-Denis, which he won after striking out alone with 70km still to ride.

He rode his first Tour that same year, abandoning on stage nine having lost over 35 minutes on the preceding stage into Briançon, the town that would one day become the site of some of his greatest exploits. But all that was still six years away.

He fared far better at the 1948 Tour, finishing fourth overall and claiming stage wins at Biarritz and Cannes. He also spent nine days in the yellow jersey, only losing it when he and Gino Bartali raged a fierce battle on two tough days in the Alps, over the mightiest mountains that the range can offer (see pp167–169). Mixed fortunes in the Tour followed. An abandonment on stage 10 in 1949 was followed with third overall, the King of the Mountains title and another stage win (his first of three triumphant arrivals into Briançon) in 1950.

Bobet's first Tour win came in 1953, the sixth time he started the race. Once again he won the stage over the Izoard and into Briançon, this time grabbing the yellow jersey as well (see p196 for more on Bobet's 1953 win). Arguably his greatest period would come between July 1954 and August 1955.

First of all he defended his Tour title in the face of stiff competition from the Swiss pair of Ferdi Kübler and Fritz Schaer. Bobet took three stage wins en route to claiming his second Tour title, holding the yellow jersey for five days early on before losing it for a week. He got it back after stage 14 into Millau, when he, Kübler and Schaer were all in a 23-man breakaway that crossed the finish line more than four minutes ahead of a peloton that contained the previous leader, Gilbert Bauvin. The stage was won by Kübler but Bobet now had a four-minute lead overall, a lead he progressively increased through the Alps, once again winning in Briançon. As the race exited the mountains, Bobet had a lead of nearly thirteen minutes. Then he won the final time trial in Nancy to claim the Tour by over fifteen minutes. It was the first time that a Frenchman had successfully defended his Tour title since Lucien Petit-Breton, way back in 1908.

After his second Tour triumph Bobet went to the world championships in Solingen, Germany. It was a tough course, 16 laps of a 15km route, including a 3km climb. Fausto Coppi, the reigning champion, had constructed his season around defending his title and, with little more than a quarter of the race to go, launched an attack in pursuit of two riders who had broken away: Robert Varnajo of France and Michele Gismondi of Italy. Soon on to Coppi's wheel were Jacques Anquetil, Fritz Schaer, Charly Gaul, Jean Forestier and Bobet.

The six caught and passed the breakaway and then, over the course of the next few laps, a process of attrition wore the leaders down. With Bobet now setting a fierce pace, first Forestier and Anquetil fell away, then Coppi tumbled, ruling him out of the final reckoning. Soon Gaul lost touch. With two laps to go it was just Bobet and Schaer left.

Then, right at the end of the penultimate lap, Bobet suffered a puncture on the big climb and had to stop for a wheel change. There was only 15km to go. With Schaer now an ever-diminishing speck on the horizon, Bobet remounted and launched a furious pursuit. Amazingly, he caught the Swiss rider within 2km of the finish, blasted right past him and took the win by twelve seconds. France had her first world champion for eighteen years.

Bobet's great form continued into 1955. Wearing the rainbow jersey of the world champion he surprised many by winning the Tour of Flanders, one of the toughest one-day classics. Pierre Chany described his win as "stunning", saying that some spectators dropped their cartons of chips in shock as they watched Bobet beat Hugo Koblet, Rik Van Steenbergen and Bernard Gauthier in the sprint. The win was not without controversy, though. It was initially judged that the breakaway had broken race rules by riding through a closed level crossing, an offence for which the penalty was disqualification. After the intervention of Bobet's manager Antonin Magne, and protests from many Bobet supporters, the result was allowed to stand.

The best twelve months of Bobet's career ended with yet another Tour win, again set up by a terrific performance in the mountains, this time on Mont Ventoux (see pp108–109). He took the yellow jersey seven days before the end of the race, winning by just under five minutes in Paris. Unlikely though it seemed at the time, that stage win over the Ventoux was to be Bobet's last Tour stage victory.

Bobet was to gain wins in Paris–Roubaix and Bordeaux–Paris, and a stage victory at the Giro d'Italia (where he came second overall in 1957, just 19 seconds behind Gastone Nencini), but he completed only one more Tour, in 1958, finishing seventh. In 1959 he rode his last Tour, abandoning at the top of the Col de l'Iseran. The mountains were at last too much for the ageing champion.

He carried on riding until 1962, then set up a thalassotherapy centre on the south coast of Brittany. He died in March 1983, aged 58.

LOUISON BOBET SELECTED RESULTS:

1946: 1st amateur national championships

1947: 1st Tour du Finistère
1st overall Course à la Mer

1948: 4th overall and two stage wins Tour de France

1949: 1st overall Tour de l'Ouest

1950: 3rd overall, 1st mountains classification and one stage win Tour de France
1st national championships

1951: One stage win Tour de France
One stage win and 1st mountains classification prize Giro d'Italia
1st Milan–San Remo
Two stage wins Paris–Nice
1st Critérium International
1st national championships
1st Giro di Lombardia

1952: 1st overall and four stage wins Paris–Nice
1st Grand Prix des Nations

1st Critérium International

1953: 1st overall and two stage wins Tour de France
One stage win Tour de Romandie

1954: 1st overall and three stage wins Tour de France
1st world championships
One stage win Critérium du Dauphiné

1955: 1st overall and two stage wins Tour de France
1st Tour of Flanders
1st overall and three stage wins Critérium du Dauphiné

1956: 1st Paris-Roubaix

1957: 2nd overall and one stage win Giro d'Italia

1959: 1st Bordeaux-Paris

1960: 1st overall and six stages Roma–Napoli–Roma

COL DE JOUX-PLANE

START POINT / Samoëns
START ELEVATION / 702m
FINISH ELEVATION / 1691m
LENGTH OF CLIMB / 11.6km
AVERAGE GRADIENT / 8.5%
MAXIMUM GRADIENT / 11.2%
FIRST TOUR / 1978
APPEARANCES / 11

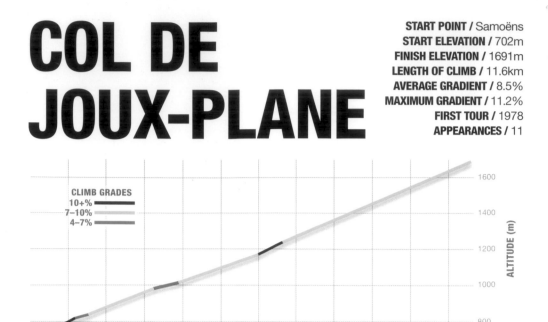

The Col de Joux-Plane starts hard and it ends hard. And the middle bit is no picnic either.

Samoëns is going through its morning routines as I make my way through the pretty town. A lorry is hoisting a communal bin high into the air and tipping it slowly; men and women in high visibility jackets are tending to the streets and paths; café owners are setting out tables and chairs, propping up menus, preparing for the day's trade. The town has an air of muted contentment. The sun is shining, there's a cooling breeze, people are smiling and chatting. Everything is very pleasant indeed. Yes, it is going to be a lovely day in Samoëns. Pity I won't be here to enjoy it.

THE COL DE JOUX-PLANE STARTS HARD AND IT ENDS HARD. AND THE MIDDLE BIT IS NO PICNIC EITHER.

The road to the Joux-Plane climbs steeply out of the town and I'm quickly clicking through the gears to find one that feels comfortable. Alarmingly, that already seems be the lowest one I have. Five hundred metres in and already I've nowhere to run to when the going

gets tougher. The Col de Joux-Plane is over 11km long. It does not bode well.

And then an incident occurs that very nearly stops my assault on the Joux-Plane before it has barely started. Coming towards me is an open-backed 4x4. It hits a bumpy part of road, the jolt sending a large circular container high into the air. Imagine a solid plastic paddling pool, about two metres in diameter, half a metre deep, bouncing on to the road and then rolling right towards me. And gathering an alarming amount of pace as it does so. We are on a collision course.

Well, you might say, why don't you just stop? Indeed, but I'm cleated into my pedals. My cleats and I have an interesting relationship. I'm scared of them because they make me fall over if I don't concentrate. I have to plan each stop with some precision to prevent myself from toppling off my bike. So I just keep twisting and turning and hoping. Eventually, with about twenty metres to spare, the big plastic thing rolls into the ditch at the side of the road. I'm saved. At least it took my mind off the climb for a few moments.

Places to rest and recover are few on this climb. The only chances to do so come early when, in theory at least, I should be fresh. With under 5km ridden, the road flattens slightly as I go through Cessonax. I try

to take advantage because I know that from here on it is arduous all the way to the top, but even here I'm finding the Joux-Plane a tough proposition.

With about 6km gone I come to the hardest stretch of the climb. The next section averages nearly 11% and has points where it touches 13%. It is leg-breaking work and I am out of the saddle, trying to find some sort of decent cadence. Somehow I manage to haul myself up and, just as I am at breaking point, the road at last relents just enough for me to sit back down.

The Joux-Plane entered the Tour in 1978. Christian Seznec was the first rider over the mountain and went on to win the stage in Morzine. In fact, every rider that has gone over the summit first on the Tour's eleven visits has gone on to win the stage. In the early 1980s the race couldn't stay away from the climb, taking the peloton over its precipitous peak for five consecutive years from 1980 to 1984. In the 28 years since it has only been back five times. Maybe familiarity bred contempt. Certainly its most recent visit left a bad taste.

That came on stage 17 of the 2006 race, which was to become one of the most infamous stages of recent Tour history. Phonak's Floyd Landis had been humiliated the day before on the climb to La Toussuire. Wearing the yellow jersey, he had cracked, losing over eight minutes on the final ascent and dropping out of the top ten overall. His Tour was surely over.

Stage 17 was another big day in the mountains, from Saint-Jean-de-Maurienne to Morzine, with the Joux-Plane the last of five mountains. On the first climb of the day, the Saisies, with a break already up the road and nothing to lose, Landis sent his Phonak team to the front of the bunch and ordered them to increase the pace. Then, with the other favourites struggling and Oscar Pereiro, the man who had taken the yellow jersey on La Toussuire, out of the leading group, Landis attacked alone and set the race on fire. By the top of the Saisies he had a gap of over three minutes. On the Aravis he caught the breakaway and promptly rode by them. Over the Colombière and Côte de Châtillon-sur-Cluses, Landis surged on. Only T-Mobile's Patrik Sinkewitz could stay with him on the way to the Joux-Plane, but as soon as the race hit the final climb even he was too cooked to stick the heat that Landis was dishing out.

Turning a huge gear and continuously dousing himself in water, Landis ground his way up the Joux-Plane. Behind him it had dawned on the peloton that they had made a mistake in letting him go. Initially confident of being able to bring him back into the bunch, the teams of the main contenders suddenly

LANDIS, A FORMER MOUNTAIN BIKE RIDER AND TERRIFIC DESCENDER, INCREASED THAT GAP ON THE DESCENT INTO MORZINE. HE FINISHED NEARLY SIX MINUTES AHEAD OF SASTRE AFTER A 128KM ESCAPADE.

realised they weren't gaining time quickly enough. The frantic chase conducted by the CSC team soon blew the peloton apart, but Landis would not be stopped. Over the top of the Joux-Plane he had a gap of more than five minutes over CSC's Carlos Sastre, who was desperately trying to get himself into yellow.

Landis, a former mountain bike rider and terrific descender, increased that gap on the descent into Morzine. He finished nearly six minutes ahead of Sastre after a 128km escapade. He was now only thirty seconds off the race lead, a gap he made up on the final time trial to stand on top of the podium in Paris. But the drama was not over. It later emerged that Landis had tested positive after the Morzine stage and his Tour win was taken away. It was a sad conclusion to what had been one of the most dramatic Tours in recent memory.

• • •

This climb presents a tough challenge, and the reward for your effort is that you're on a road that offers what must be some of the most picturesque views in the Alps. The first part of the ride is through a glorious pine forest, granting views of Mont Blanc through the trees. It feels wonderful to be riding under the gaze of western Europe's most intimidating peak. The small villages I pass through are also a delight – tiny clusters of rustic, cramped chalets, with piles of logs outside. Despite the odd rooftop solar panel, it feels like this part of the world hasn't changed essentially for many years.

Finally the summit comes into sight. There is still 2km to go and the climbing is difficult, with no slackening off. The top appears and vanishes as the road twists up this final section. I round a corner expecting the summit to be very close, but instead I am confronted with a long ribbon of tarmac winding its way up to the pass. It is an onerous conclusion to the climb, but eventually I make it.

And what's at the top of the Col de Joux-Plane? A café, shut of course; inspiring views; a ski-rental shack; and ducks. Now, it might be that ducks are a fairly common occurrence at this altitude, over 1700m up an alp, but in all the years I've been riding up mountains I've never seen one. Here there are two, a couple, happily tottering around, then flitting about over my head with wings flapping twenty to the dozen. I sit and watch them for an age. For some reason I find it hard to leave these two birds, kin to those that waddle around the field at the back of my house all day long. It's odd what these mountains can do to you.

BRADLEY WIGGINS

ON STAGE 15, TO THE SWISS SKI RESORT OF VERBIER, VANDE VELDE FELL AWAY AND, ALL OF A SUDDEN, WIGGINS WAS SCALING THE ALPS WITH THE LIKES OF ALBERTO CONTADOR, CADEL EVANS, ANDY SCHLECK AND CARLOS SASTRE – THE SPORT'S BEST CLIMBERS.

In 2012 Bradley Wiggins became the first British rider to win the Tour de France. Prior to the 2012 Tour, Wiggins was already a cycling superstar in Britain, but for his accomplishments on the track rather than on the road. Until his Tour win the public at large knew Wiggins because he had won three Olympic gold medals on the track: one at Athens 2004, two at Beijing 2008. From 2000 to 2008 the velodrome was where Wiggins did his best work, as he became the world's premier pursuit rider.

Wiggins was born in Gent, Belgium, in 1980. His British mother, Linda, had moved to the Belgian city to be with his father, Garry, an Australian who was trying to make his way on the Belgian six-day racing scene. Garry left the family when the young Bradley was just two and Wiggins and his mother moved to London. It was the TV coverage of Chris Boardman winning gold in the Barcelona velodrome in 1992 that inspired young Wiggins to take up cycling. Just six years later he took a track silver in the Commonwealth Games and a gold at the junior world championships. A bronze medal in the team pursuit at Sydney 2000 followed.

In 2002 Wiggins signed for the French team La Française des Jeux and in 2003 rode his first Grand Tour, the Giro d'Italia. He lasted until stage 18 before bowing out, no small achievement for a first major stage race of any kind. In truth, with Wiggins focusing on the track until 2008, there was little in way of results on the road to suggest that people were looking at a future Tour champion. It wasn't until 2009, after the Beijing Olympics, when Wiggins switched his focus to the road, that an assault on Paris looked even remotely possible.

By then Wiggins was riding for the Garmin-Chipotle team. He entered the Tour with some good results behind him, having finished second in time trials at the Critérium International, Paris–Nice and Giro d'Italia, but his role at the Tour was as a support rider for the team's leader, Christian Vande Velde. That position was turned on its head as the race progressed. On stage 15, to the Swiss ski resort of Verbier, Vande Velde fell away and, all of a sudden, Wiggins was scaling the Alps with the likes of Alberto Contador, Cadel Evans, Andy Schleck and Carlos Sastre – the sport's best climbers. By the end of the Verbier stage Wiggins was third overall, just 1 minute 46 seconds behind Contador and over two minutes ahead of Vande Velde. Bradley Wiggins was the new leader of the team. Wiggins couldn't quite stick with the top riders in the following days, but he still finished fourth in Paris, equalling Robert Millar's result of 1984.

A protracted move to Team Sky came at the end of the year and the British team installed him as their team leader. But 2010 didn't turn out quite as planned: he finished 24th in Paris. Perhaps, some thought, 2009 had been a flash in the pan.

But no. After a tough winter training schedule, Wiggins started the 2011 season in the condition of his life. A podium position at Paris–Nice followed by his first stage race win at the Critérium du Dauphiné saw him installed as an outside favourite at the Tour. Misfortune struck on stage 7, however, when a crash left him with a broken collarbone. He finished the year taking

third at the Vuelta a España behind team-mate Chris Froome. That Vuelta featured some severe climbing, including the insanely steep Angliru, once again proving that Wiggins could climb with the best. While Wiggins could beat almost anybody that mattered in a time trial, he could now match them in the mountains as well.

October 2011 brought the unveiling of the 2012 Tour route. Heavy on time trials and relatively light on summit finishes, it suited Wiggins perfectly. His hopes were heightened further when it emerged that Contador, the sport's best climber and a very good time trial rider as well, would not be riding (see p237). Wiggins promptly started 2012 in scintillating form. He won Paris–Nice and the Tour de Romandie, and he defended his Critérium du Dauphiné title, becoming the first

rider to hold those three titles at the same time. He had proven his team-leadership credentials and, along with 2011 winner Cadel Evans, was the main favourite for the Tour.

His team's performance at the Dauphiné had been particularly impressive, marshalling the peloton at key moments and controlling the race. Everything was set up for a Wiggins offensive. And so it proved: Sky were too powerful for the rest of the peloton. Wiggins took the yellow jersey on stage 7 and never looked like losing it. He won both time trials with ease, defended stoutly in the mountains and even had the strength to lead out team-mate Mark Cavendish to win the race's final stage on the Champs-Élysées. The Brits had conquered France. Bradley Wiggins was the new king of Paris.

BRADLEY WIGGINS SELECTED RESULTS:

1998: 1st junior world championships individual pursuit

2nd Commonwealth Games team pursuit

2000: 3rd Olympic Games team pursuit

2001: 1st overall and two stage wins Cinturón Ciclista Internacional a Mallorca

2002: 2nd Commonwealth Games individual and team pursuits

2003: 1st world championships individual and team pursuits

One stage win Tour de l'Avenir

2004: 1st Olympic Games individual pursuit

2nd Olympic Games team pursuit

2005: One stage win Circuit de Lorraine

One stage win Tour de l'Avenir

2007: 1st world championships individual and team pursuits

One stage win Quatre jours de Dunkerque

One stage win Critérium du Dauphiné

2008: 1st Olympic Games individual and team pursuits

1st world championships individual and team pursuits and madison

2009: 1st national championships

One stage win Driedaagse van De Panne

1st overall and one stage win Herald Sun Tour

4th overall Tour de France

2010: One stage win Giro d'Italia

1st national championships

2011: 1st overall Critérium du Dauphiné

1st national championships

3rd overall Vuelta a España

2012: 1st overall and two stage wins Tour de France

1st Olympic Games individual time trial

1st overall and one stage win Paris–Nice

1st overall and two stage wins Tour de Romandie

1st overall and one stage win Critérium du Dauphiné

LA PLAGNE

START POINT / Aime
START ELEVATION / 661m
FINISH ELEVATION / 2080m
LENGTH OF CLIMB / 21.4km
AVERAGE GRADIENT / 6.6%
MAXIMUM GRADIENT / 10.4%
FIRST TOUR / 1984
APPEARANCES / 4

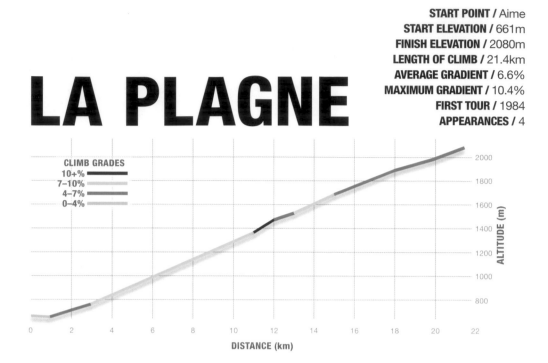

CLIMB GRADES
10+%
7–10%
4–7%
0–4%

ALTITUDE (m)

DISTANCE (km)

It's 11.20am on a Sunday morning and I am in Aime, at the foot of the climb to La Plagne. As I prepare myself the sky is clear and the day quickly warming, so I decide to ride light, carrying only a wind-proof jacket, which I stuff into one of my jersey pockets. It's a decision that I will regret.

After only a kilometre or so I pass through the village of Mâcot, to be greeted by the sound of an accordion. A small fête is in full swing. People are milling around, chatting with drinks in hand, listening to the music. Everyone looks jolly in the Sunday morning sunshine, and people wave as I ride by, lifting my spirits.

But soon my spirits plunge. I'm only four kilometres into this climb and already my legs are giving some worrying signals – I'm less than one fifth of the way through this climb and even at this early stage I can feel trouble brewing. I drag myself up a steep section and approach the next kilometre marker. I'm hoping for some good news, praying that the stone will announce an easing of the gradient.

But no, it only gets worse. The marker says 10% for the next stretch. I need to rest. I feel bad.

• • •

La Plagne has featured only four times in the Tour de France, always as a summit finish. The first, in 1984, was won by Laurent Fignon. It was Fignon again who triumphed when the Tour paid its next visit three years later. But in 1987, while the Frenchman was powering to victory, the destiny of the yellow jersey was being fought out further down La Plagne's slopes.

Ireland's Stephen Roche had already won the 1987 edition of the Giro d'Italia, and going into the stage to La Plagne he was just 25 seconds adrift of the Spanish rider Pedro Delgado. With the rest of the field over two minutes back, the 1987 Tour was coming down to two men. Delgado was the better climber but Roche had the edge riding against the clock. With one time trial to come, Roche knew that if he was within touching distance of his rival coming out of the Alps, he'd stand a great chance of winning the race.

But instead of riding conservatively, Roche attacked Delgado early. It was to prove costly. After the second mountain of the day, the Madeleine, Roche was caught. At the foot of La Plagne, Delgado opened a gap that grew alarmingly. With 10km to go Roche trailed by more than two minutes. It looked as though his Tour was over. Then with 5km left, Roche steadily began to claw his way back.

With the television cameras concentrating on the battle for the stage win between Fignon and Anselmo Fuerte, no one quite knew where Roche was in comparison to Delgado. When Fignon crossed the line, the latest time checks had Roche over a minute in arrears. Delgado arrived in fourth place, and just as he reached the finish a figure appeared behind him. "Just who is that rider coming up behind?" exclaimed an incredulous Phil Liggett, commentating on the race, "because that looks like Roche, that looks like Stephen Roche. It's Stephen Roche! He's come over the line! He almost caught Pedro Delgado, I don't believe it!"

Roche promptly collapsed on the roadside, needing oxygen after his heroic fight-back. In one of the great Tour-saving rides of all time he'd limited his losses to just four seconds. Four days later he would stand on the top of the podium.

I've eight kilometres still to go and my legs are killing me. My thighs are burning, I've got sweat gushing into my eyes and I feel sick. This climb is proving to be much harder than I had ever anticipated – I am fighting just to keep the pedals turning over, concentrating on trying to haul myself up this bloody mountain. I haven't felt this awful since the Marie-Blanque. The road surface isn't helping either: it's rutted and pitted, sapping my energy with every bump.

I pass through La Roche and, for the first time, I can see La Plagne, the resort towering above the bobsleigh track that was used when Albertville hosted the Winter Olympics in 1992. As I ride on, gazing out over the track, I notice the sun has disappeared. Thankfully, it's clouding over. The cooler air should make for a much more comfortable ride.

I approach hairpin number five. I am completely shattered but I've still got about four and a half kilometres to go. I find my mind wandering back to Liggett's 1987 Tour de France commentary and, in my fatigued state, start to wonder what his famous voice might say if he was watching me now: "He's gone. The legs have gone. It looks like his ride could be finished here on the road to La Plagne."

But luckily he isn't watching my wretched performance. No one is. I haven't seen a single cyclist all day. I struggle on, and then spots of rain begin to fall lightly.

● ● ●

His ride on La Plagne saved the Tour for Stephen Roche in 1987, and the same can be said of Miguel Indurain the next time the resort hosted a stage finish.

Indurain had dominated the Tour since 1991 and, in 1995, he was looking to become only the fourth man to claim five Tour wins, and the first to do so in consecutive years. Stage 8 of the 1995 Tour took the riders from Le Grand-Bornand, over the Saisies and the Cormet de Roselend, and up to La Plagne. Indurain was more of a specialist against the clock than a climber (see pp216–219) and had

taken hold of the yellow jersey during the previous stage, a 54km time trial. But his lead was slender heading into the mountains, with just 23 seconds separating him from second-placed Bjarne Riis.

But on the road to La Plagne, Riis was the least of Indurain's problems. Swiss rider Alex Zülle had attacked on the day's first serious climb, the Saisies, going clear with two other riders. By the time he crested the Cormet de Roselend he was alone, with a lead over Indurain of a little less than five minutes. Had the stage stopped at that point, Zülle would have been leading the Tour de France.

ON THE SLOPES OF LA PLAGNE INDURAIN MADE A MOCKERY OF THOSE WHO ACCUSED HIM OF BEING A BORING TIME-TRIAL SPECIALIST WITH NO PANACHE.

On the slopes of La Plagne, however, Indurain made a mockery of those who accused him of being a boring time-trial specialist with no panache. For 12km he rode at a ferocious pace and pulled back nearly three minutes. He left the peloton's supposed climbing specialists, men such as Marco Pantani and Laurent Jalabert, gasping in his wake. The Spaniard crossed the line just two minutes behind Zülle. Not only did he keep hold of his yellow jersey, but he gained significant time over everyone other than Zülle, whose victory propelled him into second overall, a position he would hold until Paris, where he stood on the podium below Indurain, the winner for the fifth time.

● ● ●

At long last I enter the outskirts but I calculate I still have about two kilometres to go. I'm in so much pain that the ride has turned into a war against this mountain. I'm fighting against the urge to climb off and admit defeat. It's been a horrible day on the bike. And then it gets even worse.

Thunder crashes and the heavens open. I'm riding in the middle of a cloudburst the likes of which I have rarely seen. It's as though someone is standing right above me, emptying bath after bath over my head. There is nowhere to shelter. I have no option but to press on.

I come up to a roundabout. I've no idea where to go. There are no signs to indicate the route of the official climb and I can't ask anyone because I am the only idiot out in this weather. I decide take the road for La Plagne Centre. I just want to finish this climb and go back down.

I ride through the thunderstorm for another fifteen minutes. The rain turns to hail as I search in vain for the end of this wretched climb. I've reached the centre of La Plagne, where the streets are now cascading with rainwater. This will have to do. I don't care any more. I'm heading back to the car.

But things go from bad to worse. The descent is a challenge, to say the least. I brake cautiously and try to ride slowly, but still the wind-chill – which always makes for a cold descent, even when you aren't drenched – quickly freezes me to the bone. I'm shaking, my hands are numb and I can't feel my feet at all. My arms are shuddering and my teeth chattering. My head feels like it's been stuck in a freezer. In short, all is not good and it dawns on me that I might be in a spot of trouble. I curse myself for casually discarding my wet-weather clothing a few hours ago.

With ten kilometres still to ride I pull over at a bus shelter. At last it has stopped raining, but I need to try to warm up and get some feeling back into my limbs. So I jog on the spot, flap my arms about, rub my legs, blow onto my hands; anything to get the blood pumping. Eventually I begin to feel a little better and re-start the descent.

The air temperature gradually rises as I get further down the mountain. At last I reach the outskirts of Aime. I make straight for the car and, paying no notice to who might be around, I strip off my sodden clothes as quickly as I can. The whole day has been little short of a nightmare. La Plagne – an unforgettable experience.

MIGUEL
INDURAIN

Miguel Indurain, or Big Mig as he was to become known, was the first rider to win five consecutive Tours. He ruled the event with an iron fist from 1991 to 1995, when no one ever really came close to challenging him. His Tour tactics can be summed up thus: win the time trials, don't lose time in the mountains, win the Tour.

And that is what Indurain did for five straight years. He was accused of killing the Tour, of riding like a metronome. Always in complete control, never riding on instinct, never with aggression, never with panache. He was the antithesis of the great champions of yesteryear (with the exception of Jacques Anquetil, who faced similar criticisms), the exact opposite of Coppi, Bobet, Merckx, Hinault: those seen as the true greats. The manner in which he achieved his successes was somehow seen to have diminished his achievements. Instead of being lauded for riding to a strategy that made the most of his abilities, he was often derided for it, even when he won the Giro/Tour double for the second successive year in 1993, something no other rider has ever done.

Such criticism was not quite fair. True, during his five-year reign of the Tour, Indurain never won a stage that wasn't a time trial. (In previous years he'd won two mountain stages – 1989 to Cauterets and 1990 to Luz-Ardiden – but finished down in the overall standings.) Yet, without some fine performances over the mountains, Big Mig would never have prevailed.

For a cyclist, Indurain was a big man: over six feet tall and weighing more than twelve stones. It's often been observed that losing weight in the run-up to the 1991 Tour was the key to the improvement in his climbing ability, but though this was undoubtedly a factor, Indurain had already shown that he could climb well enough to win mountain stages, and not just at the Tour – at the 1990 Paris–Nice race he won the stage to

Mont Faron, a climb that averages a leg-testing 9% over 5.5km. Furthermore, a comparison of his performances before and after his Tour victories points to a marked improvement in that area as well. As late as 1990 his total combined deficit to the various time-trial winners was nearly three minutes. To go from that to winning all but three time trials in his five winning Tours was a quite remarkable turnaround.

Miguel-Maria Indurain Larraya was born on July 16th 1964 in Villava, northern Spain. He started cycling aged ten and took to the sport quickly. A popular story tells of the young Miguel, distraught at the theft of his cherished second-hand bike, going to work in the fields with his father in order to save enough money to buy a replacement. The reality would seem to be slightly different. Writer Stuart Stevens travelled to Indurain's home town and spoke to Aitor David, the man who ran Indurain's official fan club. David told Stevens that when the bike was stolen Indurain's father simply bought another one. "People like to say Miguel was a poor farm boy," he said. "Farm, yes. Poor, no."

Indurain rode for his local club, Club Ciclista Villavés, with promising results. By the time he was 18 he had won the amateur national championships and, in the following year, 1984, he turned professional with the Reynolds team. Stage wins in the 1984 and 1985 Tour de l'Avenir followed, as did his first win in a stage race – the 1986 Vuelta Ciclista a Murcia. Later in the same year, he took the overall win at the Tour de l'Avenir, a race that's seen as the testing ground for Tour prospects. He took to the Tour start line in 1985. He only lasted four stages, but it was to be the first of twelve straight Tour appearances.

Initially, while working loyally for the various leaders of his team, including 1988 winner Pedro Delgado, Indurain recorded generally unspectacular results. In 1989 and 1990,

however, that changed. Those two mountain-top wins in Cauterets and Luz-Ardiden, coupled with 17th- and 10th-place finishes in Paris, showed glimpses of what was around the corner.

Indurain's first yellow jersey – and overall title – came in 1991. Belying his reputation as purely a time-trial rider he took yellow in the Pyrenees, after a difficult 232km stage from Jaca, in Spain. The route took the riders over the climbs of the Pourtalet, Aubisque, Tourmalet and Aspin and up to Val Louron. Going into the stage Indurain was 4 minutes 44 seconds down on leader Luc Leblanc, and more than two minutes behind Greg LeMond, the pre-race favourite, who had picked up his third Tour win the year before.

At the foot of the Tourmalet, LeMond attacked, a move that Indurain countered. Then, towards the top of the climb, LeMond lost some ground. He could have reasonably expected to regain that time on the descent, but it was not to be. Indurain edged away and, by the time he reached the climb of the Aspin, he was on his own. Then, having got wind that Claudio Chiappucci was chasing hard, he waited for the Italian climber to reach him. At the time Chiappucci was out of the top ten and so was no threat to Indurain.

Once together, the two set to work. Up the Aspin, down the Aspin, along the valley and up to Val Louron they rode together, taking turns to tow the other. Behind, LeMond was labouring, even hitting the deck after having his rear wheel clipped by a rival team's car.

On the final climb LeMond was in all sorts of trouble. Team-mate Eric Boyer dutifully brought the American up the climb but they crossed the line 7 minutes 18 seconds behind Chiappucci and second-placed Indurain. Indurain took over custody of the yellow jersey, defended his three-minute lead over Gianni Bugno all through the Alps and then secured it with a second time-trial win on the penultimate day of the Tour. It was Indurain's first Grand Tour win, the first of seven (five Tours, two Giri d'Italia) that he would win in the next five years.

These devastating displays in time trials were occasionally matched by rip-roaring rides in the mountains, not least his incredible ascent of Hautacam in 1994 (see pp48–51). But it was in the mountains when his hold over the Tour finally wavered. In 1996, on stage 7 to Les Arcs, Indurain, having started the stage just a single second behind eventual winner Bjarne Riis,

DEVASTATING DISPLAYS IN TIME TRIALS WERE OCCASIONALLY MATCHED BY RIP-ROARING RIDES IN THE MOUNTAINS, NOT LEAST HIS INCREDIBLE ASCENT OF HAUTACAM IN 1994.

cracked on the final ascent to the ski station. With a little over 3km still to ride, Indurain, who had tried to match an acceleration by Riis's team mate Jan Ullrich, fell away. As the main contenders for the Tour powered up the mountain, the great man was left to fight his way alone to the top. Eventually he crawled over the line having lost over four minutes to stage winner Luc Leblanc and three minutes to Riis.

His Tour was all but over. Champion that he was, Indurain kept fighting all the way to Paris but he was fighting a losing battle. He would finish 11th overall, more than fourteen minutes behind Riis. It was Indurain's final Tour.

A few weeks later Indurain took gold in the Olympic Games time trial. It was a last hurrah. On January 2nd 1997, Miguel Indurain announced his retirement, saying: "My family are waiting."

MIGUEL INDURAIN SELECTED RESULTS:

1983: 1st amateur national championships

1984: One stage win Tour de l'Avenir

1985: Two stage wins Tour de l'Avenir

1986: 1st overall and three stage wins Tour de l'Avenir

1st overall and one stage win Vuelta Ciclista a Murcia

1987: 1st overall and three stage wins Vuelta a los Valles Mineros

1988: 1st overall and one stage win Volta Ciclista a Catalunya

1989: One stage win Tour de France

1st overall Paris–Nice

1st overall and one stage win Critérium International

1990: One stage win Tour de France

1st Clásica de San Sebastián

1st overall and one stage win Paris–Nice

1991: 1st overall and one stage win Tour de France

1st overall and one stage win Volta Ciclista a Catalunya

2nd overall Vuelta a España

1992: 1st overall and three stage wins Tour de France

1st overall and two stage wins Giro d'Italia

1st national championships

1993: 1st overall and two stage wins Tour de France

1st overall and two stage wins Giro d'Italia

1994: 1st overall and one stage win Tour de France

World hour record

1995: 1st overall and two stage wins Tour de France

1st overall Midi–Libre

1st overall and one stage win Critérium du Dauphiné

1st world championships Individual Time Trial

1996: 1st overall and two stage wins Critérium du Dauphiné

1st Olympic Games Individual Time Trial

LES DEUX ALPES

START POINT / Barrage du Chambon
START ELEVATION / 1044m
FINISH ELEVATION / 1650m
LENGTH OF CLIMB / 9.8km
AVERAGE GRADIENT / 6.2%
MAXIMUM GRADIENT / 10.7%
FIRST TOUR / 1998
APPEARANCES / 2

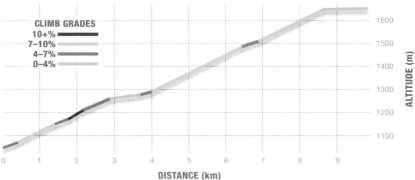

The climb to the ski resort of Les Deux Alpes has been used by the Tour just twice. It is a victim of its neighbour's success – the iconic hairpins of Alpe d'Huez are just along the valley road. The Alpe is a legendary Tour climb and a Tour de France without a visit to its theatre of pain is often regarded as being all the poorer for it. It is longer, higher and harder than Les Deux Alpes, and the Tour can't really accommodate both.

So why should a book devoted to the great climbs and climbers of the Tour de France include a chapter on a mountain that the Tour has visited only twice? Well, Les Deux Alpes is here for personal reasons and I make no apologies. Without the first of those two visits there's a good chance that this book wouldn't exist.

●●●

The road up to Les Deux Alpes veers off from the Col du Lautaret. The Lautaret is a busy, unpleasant road that links Bourg d'Oisans with Briançon. It passes through a number of long, frightening tunnels and is always full of traffic itching to overtake on blind bends. I hate it. So it's a relief when I finally turn off near the Barrage du Chambon, a hydroelectric dam, and at last start the climb.

At just over 9km and with an average of around 6%, Les Deux Alpes should be a relatively straightforward

ride. No mountain is ever easy – not for me anyway – but although my legs are soon feeling the gradient and my breathing is getting heavier, it's not devilishly hard. As Tour de France climbs go, Les Deux Alpes is even proving to be a reasonably comfortable experience.

Like its famous neighbour, the road to Les Deux Alpes winds its way up the mountain through a series of hairpins. There are ten in this case, each numbered with a sign that tells you how far there is to go to the top. As I ride on, counting down the hairpins and enjoying the views over the Romanche valley, my mind drifts off, back to the 1998 Tour and stage 15. Back to Monday July 27th 1998. Back to the day I fell in love with the Tour de France.

●●●

Marco Pantani won the Tour in 1998 and he did so by winning stage 15, the toughest stage of the race, 189km from Grenoble to Les Deux Alpes. The route took the peloton over the Croix de Fer, Télégraphe and Galibier, before the final climb to this ski resort. It was the first time that Les Deux Alpes had featured on the Tour route. And it was a classic.

If any edition of a Tour needed a classic stage, 1998 was it. The race had been plagued by scandal. The Festina affair had rocked the sport (see p179). Team hotels and buses had been raided. Whole squads had been taken

in for questioning. Riders threatened to go on strike and staged sit-ins over what they saw as invasions of privacy. The Tour was descending into bedlam. For a while it looked like the race might not even get to Paris.

As the race left Grenoble, Pantani, who had won a stage four days previously in the Pyrenees, was in third spot overall, more than three minutes behind 1997 winner and favourite Jan Ullrich. It was a terrible day: the peloton was battered by wind and rain for the entire stage and temperatures dropped to below five degrees on some of the climbs. At the foot of the Galibier a break that included Christophe Rinero and Rodolfo Massi, who had led over the Croix de Fer and the Télégraphe, still had a gap of over two minutes on the favourites. Then Pantani decided his time had come.

The little Italian shot up the road like a motorbike and, in no time at all, he had distanced the yellow jersey and was gaining on the breakaway. Standing on the pedals

IN THE END, PANTANI FOUND ALMOST FOUR MINUTES MORE THAN THAT. IN A DEMONSTRATION OF SUPREME CLIMBING HE WALTZED UP THE FINAL MOUNTAIN. HE WAS UNTOUCHABLE.

in his unique, crouched way, he scaled the steep slopes of the Galibier like they were a minor hindrance. By the top he had not only caught and passed the breakaway but had built an advantage of more than two minutes on Ullrich. As he started the descent of the Galibier, Pantani needed to find one extra minute on the final climb to take the yellow jersey.

In the end, Pantani found almost four minutes more than that. In a demonstration of supreme climbing he waltzed up the final mountain. He was untouchable. Clad in soaking wet and lurid Lycra, his shaven head covered with a bandana, his face grim with pain, Pantani rode to the stage win and Tour de France glory. In the gloom of the sodden Alps he crowned one of the most spectacular breakaways of the modern era by taking the yellow jersey. He went on to win his one and only Tour.

THIS CLIMB HAS A FEARSOME REPUTATION. ALTHOUGH DIFFICULT UPHILL, IT IS FEARED MORE FOR ITS TECHNICAL AND PRECIPITOUS DESCENT. A NUMBER OF RIDERS HAVE CRASHED ON THEIR WAY OFF THIS MOUNTAIN.

Back in the UK, sitting in front of a television, I was transfixed. Despite all of the problems surrounding that year's race, 1998 was the year I got the Tour. And it was Marco's performance on that day that did it. It was simply one of the greatest pieces of sporting drama that I had ever seen, and from that moment I was hooked. Despite all that followed, and of that there was plenty (see p224–227), on that day in 1998 Marco Pantani showed me just what drama the Tour could offer. And for that I will always be grateful.

• • •

I enter the ski town. For an out-of-season resort it is surprisingly busy. Sure, most shops are closed, but there are people out collecting their Sunday newspapers, stocking up on bread and walking their dogs. Les Deux Alpes is bustling with weekend life.

Then I see it.

Over to my left is a memorial that commemorates Pantani's virtuoso performance. I had no idea that it existed and it crowns what has already been an emotional ride for me. The monument itself is a simple carving of a cyclist hunched over his bicycle, engaged in a fierce tussle with the mountain. For a long time I sit near it, remembering the flawed genius of Pantani. In the end I have to tear myself away. The skies are clouding over and the wind is picking up. It's time to leave Les Deux Alpes.

This may not be the longest nor the most difficult of climbs. It may not have the mythical status of Alpe d'Huez. But it does have history. Les Deux Alpes and the little Italian climber Pantani together provided one of the great stories of the modern Tour – a feat that saved a Tour from oblivion and started a television viewer back in Somerset on a journey that would ultimately bring him here.

So why is Les Deux Alpes worthy of place in this book? That's why.

In 1998 Marco Pantani became only the seventh rider to win both the Tour de France and the Giro d'Italia in the same year, adding his name to those of Eddy Merckx, Bernard Hinault, Fausto Coppi, Jacques Anquetil, Miguel Indurain and Stephen Roche. Although they were the only two Grand Tours the little Italian would win, his impact on the sport was far greater than mere numbers suggest.

Born in Cesenatico in January 1970, Pantani joined the Fausto Coppi Sports Club as a young boy and entered his first race aged eleven. Though he had to borrow an old lady's bicycle for the race, he noticed he was faster than most on the hills: a sensation that would stay with him for the entirety of his career.

Pantani steadily rose up the Italian amateur ranks. Third in the 1990 Baby Giro (the amateur version of the Giro d'Italia) became second in 1991 and first in 1992. Pantani was ready for the professional scene. He joined Carrera in 1992, but no more wins came for two years. When they finally came, however, what wins they were.

Pantani would devote his career to two races: the Giro and the Tour. He was a Grand Tour rider and that was it. The classics were not for him, nor even week-long stage races like the Critérium du Dauphiné. He needed long, high, steep climbs to shine. The peaks of the Alps and the Pyrenees were his playground.

His first ride in the Giro came in 1993. He rode well into the final week, in the service of his team-leader Claudio Chiappucci, who would go on to finish third. For his part Pantani was lying in 18th position overall when he was forced to abandon with tendinitis. Nonetheless, he had given more than an indication that he could cut it at the highest level.

MARCO PANTANI

IN THE SPACE OF TWO DAYS PANTANI HAD ANNOUNCED HIMSELF NOT ONLY AS THE WORLD'S FINEST CLIMBER BUT A SERIOUS GRAND TOUR CONTENDER AS WELL.

He returned to the Giro in 1994 to take his first wins, back to back on stages 14 and 15, two unbelievably tough days in the Dolomites. Stage 14 was 235km from Lienz to Merano. The route took in four climbs but it was on the last of these that Pantani showed for the first time what he was really capable of. On the climb of the Passo Monte Giovo, a regular 20km ascent with stretches of upwards of 9%, Pantani flew away, overhauling the stage leader, Pascal Richard, to solo to the win.

But he wasn't satisfied with that. Stage 15 was an even tougher day, featuring the terrible twosome of the Stelvio and the Mortirolo. Pantani waited until the start of the Mortirolo to launch his attack. There, as the 15km climb ramped up (the first 3km averages a thigh-burning 11%), Pantani went for it. Through the dappled shade of the early slopes of Italy's killer climb, the Carrera rider left the pink-jersey group in his wake. He ploughed through the leftovers of an earlier escape group, now split into ones and twos all over the mountainside, overhauled Franco Vona, who had been leading the stage, and rode on by. In front of enormous crowds, he conquered the Mortirolo alone.

On the descent he was caught by Miguel Indurain, who was desperately trying to defend his 1993 Giro win. The pair rode to the final climb of the day, the Santa Cristina, where, Pantani lit the afterburners once again. No one could hold him back as he scaled the day's final peak in solitude. It had been a stunning display. Pantani won his second Giro stage in Aprica by just under three minutes and climbed to second overall. And there he would stay. In the space of two days Pantani had announced himself not only as the world's finest climber but a serious Grand Tour contender as well.

One month later he was riding his first Tour de France. No stage wins came his way, but he still rode impressively. Third at Hautacam, second at Luz-Ardiden, eighth at Alpe d'Huez, third at Val Thorens, fifth at Cluses, second at Avoriaz and third overall in Paris – it all pointed to a man on his way to Tour success. Surely the age of the pure climber was just around the corner.

Pantani would be dogged by crashes throughout his career and 1995 was to prove his worst year. Early in the season he collided with a car, ruling him out of the Giro. He recovered in time to take the start line at the Tour, winning his first stages: one in the Alps at Alpe d'Huez and one in the Pyrenees at Guzet-Neige. He finished 13th overall.

Then, after he claimed third spot at the world championships, there came a sickening accident during the Milano–Torino semi-classic. A 4x4 was permitted on to the course just as Pantani and fellow Italian riders Davide Dall'Olio and Francesco Secchiari rounded a corner. There was a head-on collision that left Pantani with multiple leg injuries. He wouldn't ride again until 1997.

After nearly twenty months of recuperation, Pantani returned to the Giro. This time a cat ran out in front of him on stage 8. He crashed again and abandoned, only to rise again at the Tour, claiming two stage wins (Alpe d'Huez and Morzine) and finishing third overall. His win at Alpe d'Huez entered him in the record books for the fastest ever ascent of the mountain, at just 37 minutes 35 seconds.

Pantani's greatest year was 1998. He entered the Giro with no real expectation of a win. But the diminutive climber was still ninth, 1 minute 20 seconds down, as the race headed into stage 14, a 165km affair from Schio to Piancavallo. On the final climb, Pantani launched his bid for the Giro. Initially Mapei's Pavel Tonkov, who was just one second behind Pantani, went with him. But

the relentless pace of the Italian soon had the Russian gasping and Pantani was left to ride the rest of the stage alone. He sprinted across the finish line, arms aloft. It was his first Giro stage win since Aprica in 1994 and it lifted him to second place overall, just 22 seconds behind Alex Zülle.

Pantani lost time in the following time trial but got it back in spades two days later, during the tough 217km of stage 17, over four mountain passes. Pantani arrived at the stage finish with Giuseppe Guerini, who took the stage. Pantani, having distanced all of his other rivals, took the race lead, and consolidated it on stage 19. With around 3km to go on the final climb to Plan di Montecampione, the last mountain of the entire race, Pantani looked over his shoulder. There he saw the face of Pavel Tonkov, the man who had

been shadowing him throughout the mountains, the man who had won this race in 1996 and finished second in 1997, the man who was a better time-trialler than he, and therefore the man Pantani had to get rid of if he was to win the Giro.

Pantani turned back, lifted his backside out of the saddle and went. For the final 3km he barely sat down as he waltzed up the steepest sections of the climb. Tonkov cracked, with nothing left to give. Pantani crossed the line 57 seconds ahead of the Russian, securing a lead of 1 minute 28 seconds overall: a lead he would keep all the way to Milan. Marco Pantani had won his first Grand Tour.

Il Pirata – a nickname prompted by his bandana and earring – was now a hero in his homeland, and his reputation soared even higher when he went

PANTANI TURNED BACK, LIFTED HIS BACKSIDE OUT OF THE SADDLE AND WENT. FOR THE FINAL 3KM HE BARELY SAT DOWN AS HE WALTZED UP THE STEEPEST SECTIONS OF THE CLIMB. TONKOV CRACKED, WITH NOTHING LEFT TO GIVE.

to the Tour looking to complete a rare Giro/Tour double. A win at Plateau de Beille and an incredible ride to Les Deux-Alpes (see pp220–223) secured an amazing win over pre-race favourite Jan Ullrich. Pantani had set the cycling world on fire.

But then it all came crashing down. In 1999, just two days from the end of the Giro, and wearing the pink jersey of race leader, Pantani failed a "health-check". His haematocrit level breached 50% and he was declared "unfit" and suspended from the race; raised haematocrit levels are one indication of EPO abuse. Later investigations identified a link between Pantani and Francesco Conconi, an Italian sports doctor who was charged with "sporting fraud" for allegedly supplying riders with EPO in the 1990s. Although Conconi was formally acquitted in 2004, the judge described him as "morally guilty".

Pantani, humiliated, claimed innocence. Although he returned to the Tour, winning two stages in 2000, including an enthralling duel on the slopes of Mont Ventoux with Lance Armstrong, he was never the same. His last race win came in 2000 at the Profronde van Stiphout criterium in the Netherlands. He rode his last Giro in 2003, finishing 14th, a great result for most riders, a disaster for him.

After the 1999 Giro expulsion, Pantani had descended into depression and drug abuse. Cocaine became his drug of choice. He was often rambling and incoherent, struggling to cope with what he saw as his persecution – at one point it was reported that there were no fewer than seven investigations into his affairs were in progress. That he was able to ride at all, let alone win, amid all this turmoil, speaks volumes for his talent.

He died on Valentine's Day 2004, alone in a cheap hotel in Rimini. He was just 34 years old. Cerebral and pulmonary oedema was the official cause of death, with the coroner's report stating it had been brought on by "acute intoxication from cocaine."

Marco Pantani was a complex individual, a rare talent who illuminated races whenever the road tilted upwards. In an era when racing was becoming more and more predictable and controlled, Pantani was an irrepressible force, a free spirit, a rider who rode according to what his instincts told him. He was perhaps, as Lance Armstrong said upon learning of his death, "more of an artist than an athlete."

MARCO PANTANI SELECTED RESULTS:

1992: 1st Baby Giro

1994: 3rd overall and best young rider Tour de France

2nd overall and two stage wins Giro d'Italia

1995: Two stage wins and best young rider Tour de France

3rd world championships

1997: Two stage wins and 3rd overall Tour de France

1998: 1st overall and two stage wins Tour de France

1st overall, two stage wins and 1st mountains classification Giro d'Italia

1999: Four stage wins Giro d'Italia

2000: Two stage wins Tour de France

COL DE LA COLOMBIÈRE

START POINT / Le Grand-Bornand
START ELEVATION / 930m
FINISH ELEVATION / 1613m
LENGTH OF CLIMB / 11.8km
AVERAGE GRADIENT / 5.8%
MAXIMUM GRADIENT / 9%
FIRST TOUR / 1960
APPEARANCES / 19

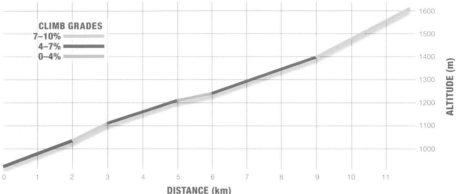

Professional road cycling is very much a team sport, something that often comes as a surprise to those new to the sport. Moreover, that team spirit, that feeling of togetherness, extends beyond the professional peloton into the cycling community as a whole. There is a bond between us cyclists, no matter what our abilities or our steed of choice: we are first and foremost cyclists, and we look out for each other. On the Col de la Colombière today I witnessed a fine example of that spirit of fellowship.

• • •

In 1968 the Tour took in the Colombière for only the second time. Its first visit had been in 1960 when Fernando Manzaneque, a Spanish rider, had gone over the climb first. Manzaneque stayed away and won the stage. In a career spanning eleven years he would go on to win two more Tour mountain stages, winning at Val d'Isère in 1963 and Luchon in 1967.

The Colombière featured on stage 19 in 1968, the penultimate climb in a 200km stage from Grenoble to Sallanches. Only three Britons have ever won stages that have finished at the summit of a mountain. Super-climbers Robert Millar (Guzet-Neige 1984 and Superbagnères 1989) and Chris Froome (La Planche

THERE IS A BOND BETWEEN US CYCLISTS, NO MATTER WHAT OUR ABILITIES OR OUR STEED OF CHOICE: WE ARE FIRST AND FOREMOST CYCLISTS, AND WE LOOK OUT FOR EACH OTHER.

des Belle Filles 2012) are two of them. But those two mountain experts followed in the wake of Barry Hoban, a sprinting ace who just happened to pick up his first real stage win in the cool mountain air of the Alps.

By 1968 Hoban was riding his third Tour. He had already crossed a finish line first the previous year, but that was the day after the tragic death of Tom Simpson (see p112) when the stage was neutralised and the British team allowed to win. In 1968 it was a very different story.

On the road to Sallanches, Hoban escaped on a descent into Albertville. Well down in the overall classification, and considered to be only in search of points at the upcoming intermediate sprint, he was left to go. After all, there were three big mountains still to scale. Hoban quickly gained a gap, picked up the sprinters points and then kept going on to the climb of the Aravis. When he reached the top he had a lead of over seven minutes.

The Colombière was the next climb. The climbers in the peloton were now chasing, but Hoban hung in there, losing little of his advantage. He was comfortable on the regular pitch of the Colombière and the road was not steep enough for the true specialists to reel him back. By the top of the climb he still had six minutes. Hoban descended well on the steep and technical drop into Cluses and battled up the final climb to win by 4 minutes 6 seconds.

Hoban would win eight stages during his career, the best tally of any British rider until Mark Cavendish came on the scene. He is the only rider ever to have won in Sallanches, as the race has never returned for a stage finish.

I'd made it to the top of the Col de la Colombière without too much difficulty. I'd chosen to ride the southern ascent from the ski village of Le Grand-Bornand, an attractive enough if somewhat clichéd alpine place – all low-rise, wooden ski chalets. If truth be told, the climb from Le Grand-Bornand is the easier side of the climb. I chose this route, you understand, only because it is the side that the Tour has used most often (thirteen times, compared to six times for its north side) and certainly not because my legs were still aching from the previous day's exertions.

The ride up from Le Grand-Bornand had been extremely pleasant, not an adjective I often use in conjunction with a Tour climb. The views over the Aravis chain of mountains were spectacular and I was perfectly content, gently spinning my legs and absorbing the alpine ambience as I climbed through meadows of wild flowers, accompanied only by other cyclists and the clanging of cow bells.

Four or five kilometres into the ride a cyclist overtook me. Clearly out training, he had no time to take breath or pause to exchange pleasantries. He was obviously a honed athlete with calves that looked like they had

been carved from oak: strong and golden, glistening with sweat as he sprinted off up the road. Unfortunately for him, he was soon joined by a dog, dragging a chain along with it.

The dog had broken free from its tether and was celebrating its new-found freedom by chasing cyclists. Irritated by this interloper, Oak Calves Man tried to shoo it away without breaking rhythm but the dog was having none of it and stuck by his side, throwing in an occasional bark for good measure. This carried on for a few hundred yards. It reminded me of those fanatical supporters in the mountains who run alongside the professionals as they ascend to glory. Often you'll see a rider flick an arm out or fix an angry glare at these people, usually to no avail. Well, that was exactly what was happening here. It was, I have to admit, amusing to watch for a while. But then, like so many of his human counterparts, the dog quickly tired and flopped down on the verge, exhausted.

• • •

Stage 7 of the 2007 Tour finished in Le Grand-Bornand, after climbing the tougher northern slopes of the Colombière, which was the day's only significant climb. German cyclist Linus Gerdemann used the climb to propel himself to his first (and to date only) Tour stage win.

Gerdemann had been part of a day-long, fifteen-man breakaway that splintered on the early slopes of the Colombière as a flurry of attacks were made. Eventually, with 11km of the climb still to go, the T-Mobile rider was at the front of the race along with Credit Agricole's Dmitriy Fofonov. Over the course of the next six kilometres the two worked together to extend their gap while all the time cagily looking each other over, trying to gauge the other's condition.

As they approached the 5km marker, Gerdemann decided it was time to fly. He drifted behind Fofonov to have a final look at the Kazakh, glanced back down

the road to make sure no-one else was coming up, and then sprinted off. Fofonov quickly fell away (he would finish 40th on the stage, well over three minutes down) but, as Gerdemann continued his ride to the top, Inigo Landaluze of Euskaltel-Euskadi started off in pursuit of the German. As Gerdemann neared the summit, waves of crowds parting before him, Landaluze was gaining. The German's advantage at the top was a slender 18 seconds.

What followed was a breakneck descent into the stage finish. Driving a massive gear, Gerdemann fearlessly flew down the Colombière, risking everything to open up a gap. After 15km of madcap racing, Gerdemann crossed the line 40 seconds ahead of Landaluze. The win was also enough to give him one day in the yellow jersey.

• • •

The climb maintained its steady gradient, never really rising beyond 6% or so until 2km from the top. Then it steepened and became hard going, forcing me out of my saddle for the first time. The pitch remained difficult, through a testing series of hairpins, all the way to the top, rising still further in the last 500m. That last half a kilometre was by far the hardest stretch of the entire climb for me and for the first time my legs were beginning, if not exactly scream, then murmur discontent. But it was only a very brief moment and at the top I was left to reflect on a thoroughly enjoyable ride – hard enough to be a bit of a challenge but not so tough that I wasn't able to enjoy the fantastic mountain scenes that were all around me.

As you might expect on a gorgeous weekend, at the top I joined a throng of other cyclists, among them a group of four Frenchmen who ranged in age from mid-40s upwards. They had clearly been up there

a while. After excitedly discussing their various rides, they appeared to grow concerned and started peering back down the mountain. Then, after a few more minutes they packed up their cameras and rode off back down towards Le Grand-Bornand. I thought nothing more of it and continued wandering around, taking photographs and generally taking the time to bask in another Tour de France mountain ascent completed, before slowly making my own way back.

And then, about a kilometre or so into the descent, who should I pass but the four Frenchmen. Only now there were five, one of whom was clearly in some distress. But his mates were with him. Not only had they ridden back down the climb to find him, they wanted him to make it too, so – not satisfied with just riding alongside him – they were all taking it in turns to gently push him up the Col de la Colombière, the others shouting words of encouragement as they went. Everyone was helping, everyone involved, all working together. Sure, the guy receiving the help looked a bit embarrassed, and there would probably be some good-natured ribbing about it later but, right then, all that mattered to this group of friends was that they all made it to the top, so that they could say that they rode up the Col de la Colombière together. No one was to be left out.

It was a quite wonderful display of self-sacrifice. I have rarely seen a better example of cyclists looking out for each other. More than anything else, it's that display of teamwork, that spirit of camaraderie, that show of togetherness, that I'll take away from the Colombière.

DRIVING A MASSIVE GEAR, GERDEMANN FEARLESSLY FLEW DOWN THE COLOMBIÈRE, RISKING EVERYTHING TO OPEN UP A GAP. AFTER 15KM OF MADCAP RACING, GERDEMANN CROSSED THE LINE 40 SECONDS AHEAD OF LANDALUZE. THE WIN WAS ALSO ENOUGH TO GIVE HIM ONE DAY IN THE YELLOW JERSEY.

AVORIAZ

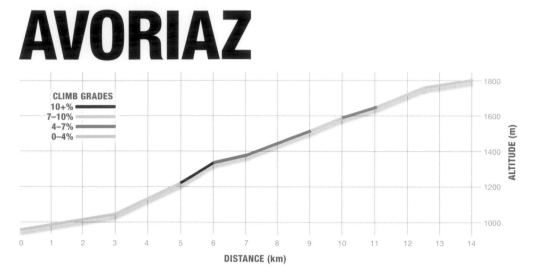

CLIMB GRADES
10+%
7–10%
4–7%
0–4%

ALTITUDE (m)

DISTANCE (km)

I'm 5km into the climb from Morzine to the ski station of Avoriaz when what must be the fifteenth lorry, bursting with building materials, thunders past. It's mid-afternoon on a weekday at the end of May and I expected this road to be quiet. Silent actually. This road goes nowhere other than to the out-of-season resort. I thought I might see a few fellow cyclists, perhaps a walker or two. But no. I've seen no one on bikes, no hikers, just lorries. Plenty of loud, filthy, fully loaded lorries.

• • •

The road from Morzine to Avoriaz has been used seven times by the Tour. The first was in 1975, the finale of a 225km stage from Valloire, which was won by Vicente Lopez Carril, a Spanish climber who would record five top-ten overall placings at the Tour, including a podium spot in 1974, when he finished third.

The next three visits all took the form of time trials. Two – 1977 and 1983 – were won by Lucien Van Impe on his way to two of his six polka-dot jersey wins. Those Van Impe stage victories sandwiched one by Bernard Hinault, who used the 54km time trial from Évian to Avoriaz in 1979 to secure his second Tour win.

As the riders prepared at the start in Évian, Hinault was lying second overall, 49 seconds behind Joop

Zoetemelk, who had come second to Hinault the year before. There were three mountain stages in the Alps to come after the finish in Avoriaz, but such was the length of the time trial and difficulty of the final climb that large time gaps were expected.

Hinault set out like a rocket from Évian, immediately seizing control of the stage. Zoetemelk, who rolled out after the Frenchman, fell away alarmingly as Hinault powered away on the approaches to the Avoriaz climb. With just 23km gone, Zoetemelk was trailing by 36 seconds. Three kilometres later his pre-stage lead had been wiped out. Hinault was the yellow jersey on the road.

And the Frenchman roared on. At the bottom of the climb he had a 69-second advantage. At the top it was 2 minutes 37 seconds. It was a remarkable ride that put him in yellow for good. That Zoetemelk finished second, as close as he did, was in itself impressive, as he suffered a couple of mechanical problems on the stage, forcing him to change bikes. But the day, and the stage, belonged to the Frenchman.

• • •

The first part of the climb is a lot of fun. The road ascends in a series of tight hairpins that gradually get further and further apart. I like hairpins. First of all

START POINT / Morzine
START ELEVATION / 965m
FINISH ELEVATION / 1796m
LENGTH OF CLIMB / 13.6km
AVERAGE GRADIENT / 6.1%
MAXIMUM GRADIENT / 11.1%
FIRST TOUR / 1975
APPEARANCES / 7

they are often relatively flat and so give the opportunity for a few easier metres of riding. Secondly, if they are not flat, and the roads are quiet enough, you can get a bit of a boost by riding up on to the high part of the bend before turning down sharply, picking up a small bit of speed before carrying on up the climb (it all helps). Thirdly, I like the feeling of approaching a hairpin, out of the saddle, gazing around the corner, as if I'm planning to launch an attack, the way I've watched countless professionals do.

ON MOUNTAINS LIKE THIS I LIKE TO ADAPT AN OLD SAYING: "LOOK AFTER THE HAIRPINS AND THE SUMMITS WILL LOOK AFTER THEMSELVES."

But I like them mainly because they break the climb into manageable chunks. I don't have to worry about the enormity of the climb above me, I just have to worry about getting to the next hairpin. And then the one after that. On mountains like this I like to adapt an old saying: "Look after the hairpins and the summits will look after themselves."

And that's how I'm dealing with this climb. Hairpins come and hairpins go as Morzine, nestled in the Aulps valley below, gradually gets smaller and smaller as I steadily gain height.

● ● ●

One of the few occasions that Avoriaz has been used as a finish to a normal road stage was in 1985. Colombian rider Luis Herrera had already written his name in Tour history the year before by winning on the Alpe d'Huez. In 1985 he had eyes on the polka-dot jersey.

Stage 11, from Pontarlier to Morzine-Avoriaz, was the first of that year's mountain stages. One hundred and ninety five kilometres in length, it went over climbs of the Pas de Morgins and Corbier, before heading up to the ski resort.

On the first climb, with over 60km still to ride, Bernard Hinault, now chasing his fifth Tour win and already in yellow, was at the front of the peloton, setting a fast tempo. His pace was too high for most and he gradually opened a gap. Sensing an opportunity to tighten his grip on the mountains competition, Herrera went with the race leader. Over the top of the first climb, with the Colombian leading, the pair had a lead of one minute. Over the course of the rest of the stage the two worked together: Herrera on the slopes, Hinault in the valleys. By the foot of the climb to Avoriaz, with Herrera having led over the Corbier as well, their gap had extended to over two-and-a-half minutes.

The two riders saw their advantage whittled down as the race approached the top and their efforts, under the baking sun, began to tell. Pedro Delgado was in hot pursuit, but Herrera and Hinault managed to hold on. As they approached the line, Herrera sprinted away to take the stage, increasing his lead in the King of the Mountains. Hinault had a firm grasp on yellow. Their escape had worked for both men and each would keep hold of his jersey until Paris.

● ● ●

Eventually Avoriaz comes into view. At a guess I would say it is still five or six kilometres away but the distinctive shapes of this purpose-built resort are clearly identifiable. From this point the climb gets

tough, on the mind as much as on the body. This road goes on and on. Drifting in and out of view for an interminable amount of time, Avoriaz remains just beyond my grasp. It's clouding over and threatening rain. Lorries continue to roar by. I'm getting tired and irritable. When will this climb end?

Finally, I approach a building on a bend. I'm crawling along on a steep section and can't really see beyond the corner but I fully expect to round it and see a sign welcoming me to Avoriaz. But no. My heart sinks. There is a sign, in fact there are two. One denotes the top of the Col de la Joux-Verte, a barricaded road off to my left that would take me down to Montriond, the other helpfully tells me that Avoriaz is still another two kilometres away. It may not sound a lot, but two thousand metres on a steep mountain can sometimes be enough to break the spirit.

But not in this case. Thankfully, those final kilometres are relatively easy. The gradient at last slackens and, after 12km or so of tough going, my legs suddenly don't know how to stop turning. It actually feels, for the first time, like I am sprinting towards the top of an Alpine ascent, like a true Tour de France rider. As I approach the town I let fantasy take over. In my altitude-affected mind I've been part of a breakaway all day and have attacked decisively. No one has been able to match the explosive pace I've set and now here I am, riding to Tour glory and the yellow jersey. Then another lorry-load of building blocks and timber rumbles by, waking me from my dream.

As I tear into town a couple in a car pass me, heading down the mountain. I catch the driver's eye as we cross and he gives a nod of approval. For some reason that nod means a lot to me. A simple gesture it may have been, but I felt like it validated my whole ride up. It was a nod that said: "Look at that fella, he's going well." I was pleased with that nod. It was as close to a "chapeau" as I would get on this trip.

AVORIAZ IS STILL ANOTHER TWO KILOMETRES AWAY. IT MAY NOT SOUND A LOT, BUT TWO THOUSAND METRES ON A STEEP MOUNTAIN CAN SOMETIMES BE ENOUGH TO BREAK THE SPIRIT.

At the top it is immediately evident why I had been overtaken by so many lorries. Avoriaz is a building site. There are builders and diggers and cranes and lorries and rubble everywhere. I try to cycle through the town but get caught in a maze of diversions, temporary one-way systems and gravel-strewn pathways. Instead I turn my back on the place and concentrate on the views back down the valley, to Morzine, now far below, and the mountains of the Portes du Soleil. With clouds continuing to converge around the peaks, it's an impressive and dramatic view. Occasionally the sun finds a gap in the clouds and pours through, illuminating a solitary summit, a beacon of light in the gathering gloom. It is, though, all somewhat ruined by the constant racket of construction going on behind me. I leave with the hammering and sawing and drilling still ringing in my ears.

Alberto Contador is the finest climber in the professional peloton today. While other riders come close (Andy Schleck and Joaquim Rodriquez, to name just two), no one can match Contador's ability to deliver when it really matters. His capacity to vary his pace, with repeated violent accelerations in the course of long climbs, sets him apart from the best of the rest.

Contador was born in Madrid in 1982. He turned professional in 2003 with ONCE-Eroski team, where top tens in the Vuelta a Castilla y Leon, the Deutschland Tour and the Clásica Ciclista a los Puertos were followed by his first professional win at the tour of Poland. It was a promising start but his 2004 season was cruelly cut short when he collapsed during a stage of the Vuelta a Asturias and required surgery to stop bleeding on the brain. He didn't race again that year.

Contador returned to the professional peloton in January 2005, winning a stage at the Tour Down Under. Victories at the Setmana Catalana, Vuelta al País Vasco and the Tour de Romandie followed. He also rode his first Tour that year, placing 31st overall.

It was in 2007 when he really exploded into the top league, having joined the Discovery Channel team. He won Paris–Nice and the Vuelta Castilla y Leon, and when July came around he travelled to the Tour with hopes for a top-five finish and a win in the young riders' competition.

Going into stage 14 to Plateau de Beille in the Pyrenees, the Spaniard was lying in third place overall, 2 minutes 31 seconds behind the yellow jersey of Michael Rasmussen. In a frenzied stage, the climbers attacked and counter-attacked for kilometre after kilometre, until, with five kilometres to ride, Contador and Rasmussen had dropped Mauricio Soler, Carlos

ALBERTO CONTADOR

Sastre and Cadel Evans. It was just the two of them now, chasing a lone breakaway rider, Antonio Colom. They caught him with just over 3km to go. Over the rest of the climb the two matched each other stroke for stroke. Contador jumped ahead of the Dane with less than 100m left, crossing the line with his now trademark pistol gesture. It was his first Tour stage win. Two days later he would inherit the yellow jersey as Rasmussen was thrown off the race (see p194). In only his second Tour, Contador had reached cycling's pinnacle.

The following year Contador went on to win the Giro and the Vuelta, becoming only the fifth rider in history to have won all three Grand Tours (Eddy Merckx, Bernard Hinault, Felice Gimondi and Jacques Anquetil are the others).

He returned to the Tour in 2009, facing competition from Lance Armstrong, who had come out of retirement and joined the Spaniard's Astana team. Despite infighting within the squad, Contador prevailed, winning impressively at the ski resort of Verbier and taking the time trial around Lake Annecy. After the race Contador said: "The situation in the team before the Tour wasn't perfect. But for me it simply made me want to win the Tour even more. I used them all as extra motivation, and in the end I've achieved my goal. Psychologically, it was a difficult Tour. But every day I was telling myself there is just one more day to go."

In 2010 he again stood on the top step in Paris having defeated Andy Schleck by 39 seconds (see p82) but then tested positive for the use of the banned substance Clenbuterol. A protracted legal case followed, with Contador claiming that the substance had been unknowingly ingested from a piece of contaminated steak. Eventually the Court of Arbitration for Sport (CAS) ruled against him, imposing a two-year ban backdated to July 2010, meaning that he was stripped of his 2010 Tour and 2011 Giro wins. Contador continues to maintain his innocence.

He returned to racing in August 2012, straight away winning the Vuelta for the second time. At the time of writing he is the favourite for the 2013 Tour.

ALBERTO CONTADOR SELECTED RESULTS:

2002: Two stage wins Vuelta a Palencia

2003: One stage win Tour de Pologne

2005: One stage win Tour de Romandie

One overall and one stage win Setmana Catalana de Ciclismo

2006: One stage win Tour de Romandie

2007: 1st overall and one stage win Tour de France

1st overall and two stage wins Paris–Nice

1st overall and one stage win Vuelta Castilla y Leon

2008: 1st overall Giro d'Italia

1st overall and two stage wins Vuelta a España

1st overall and two stage wins Vuelta Castilla y Leon

2009: 1st overall and three stage wins Tour de France

1st national championships

1st overall and two stage wins País Vasco, Zalla

2010: 1st overall Tour de France*

1st overall and one stage win Paris–Nice

1st overall and one stage win Vuelta Castilla y Leon

2011: 1st overall and two stage wins Giro d'Italia*

2012: 1st overall and one stage win Vuelta a España

*Contador was stripped of these results following his positive test. The wins were awarded to Andy Schleck (Tour 2010) and Michele Scarponi (Giro 2011).

COL DU TÉLÉGRAPHE

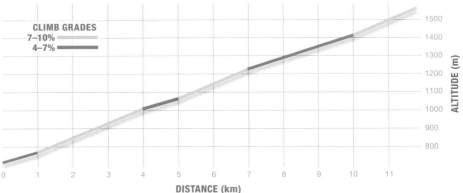

CLIMB GRADES
7–10%
4–7%

ALTITUDE (m)
1500
1400
1300
1200
1100
1000
900
800

DISTANCE (km)
0 1 2 3 4 5 6 7 8 9 10 11

Early Sunday morning in Saint-Michel-de-Maurienne. It's September but already it is hot. The road through the town is busy with bicycles and motorbikes and campervans. The main holiday season may be over but the place is still busy with people wanting a taste of the mountains. In a month or so the snow will come and the passes will start to close for the winter. Time is running out to travel the high roads of France. I join a long queue at the *boulangerie*. They are doing a roaring trade, not surprisingly, as it is the only place in town that's open. Above me peaks loom large. I look skyward, to the rarefied air of the Tour's famous passes. For the last time. Today is my last day in the mountains, and it's a big one.

I reach the front of the queue and stock up. Sandwiches, sugary drinks, a cake or two. I'm anxious to ensure I have enough energy for this last adventure. I'm heading to the top of perhaps the Tour's greatest climb, certainly the favourite of founder Henri Desgrange, the one climb he said surpassed all others. I'm heading to the top of the Col du Galibier, 35km away to the south. But to get there I've the no small matter of the Col du Télégraphe to battle first.

● ● ●

It was 1911 when the Télégraphe was first climbed by the Tour (see p19), and the first man to scale its heights

was Émile Georget, who is more celebrated for leading the way over the Galibier a few hours later. Georget, already a multiple Tour stage winner, went on to win the stage in Grenoble and finish in third in Paris. Away from the Tour his best results would be two wins in the mammoth, and now defunct, Bordeaux–Paris classic.

If this climb were positioned anywhere else it would rightly be regarded as a serious mountain in its own right. As it is, the Télégraphe is often just regarded as the support act for the Galibier, the soup before the steak. But I've always had a soft spot for this climb, because it was the very first mountain pass from which I watched a Tour stage. In 2005, after years of watching the race on TV, I finally went to France to see the spectacle for myself. My friends and I had naively planned to drive up the Galibier to watch the stage from Courchevel to Briançon. When, the night before, we announced this plan to an English guy dressed resplendently in a white suit (whom I subsequently discovered was none other than Johnny Green, ex-manager of The Clash and cycling writer), he laughed his head off. "Good luck," he said. "The road's been closed for days."

So we settled for the Télégraphe instead. We sat on a high bank with a French family, watched a three-man breakaway consisting of Santiago Botero, Oscar Pereiro and Alexandre Vinokourov being pursued by a peloton headed by the entirety of Lance Armstrong's Discovery

START POINT / Saint-Michel-de-Maurienne
START ELEVATION / 732m
FINISH ELEVATION / 1566m
LENGTH OF CLIMB / 12km
AVERAGE GRADIENT / 7.1%
MAXIMUM GRADIENT / 9.7%
FIRST TOUR / 1911
APPEARANCES / 24

Channel team, then ran back down the mountain to a bar, just in time to see Vinokourov crest the Galibier and descend to the stage win. It was a wonderful day.

That day Vinokourov was just pipped to the summit of the Télégraphe by Botero. You have to go back to Julio Jiménez in 1966 to find the last rider to top the Télégraphe and then go on to win the stage. But in the 55 years from 1911 to 1966, the Tour climbed the Télégraphe from Saint-Michel-de-Maurienne thirteen times, and on eight of those occasions the leader over the Télégraphe went on to win the stage. On the eleven occasions that the climb has been tackled since 1966, on the other hand, not a single rider has repeated the feat. It's an interesting illustration of how the Télégraphe is now perceived. Racing has become far more conservative and everyone is now too wary of what lies further up the valley.

• • •

I roll out of the town centre, cross a bridge over the Arc river and start the climb to the Col du Télégraphe. Twelve kilometres to go.

The road initially weaves its way up the mountain in a series of hairpins. The sun is beating down on me and soon I'm sweating heavily. I pass through the village of Les Petites Seignères. Ahead is a hulking mass of rock topped by some TV transmitters and the Fort du Télégraphe, built in the late 1800s to protect access to the Galibier and the valleys beyond.

• • •

In 2011 the Télégraphe featured on the last day in the mountains. It was a short stage, just 109km from Modane to Alpe d'Huez. The day before, Andy Schleck had won on top of the Galibier (see p250), distancing the defending champion Alberto Contador. Now Contador wanted revenge.

As soon as the race hit the slopes of the Télégraphe, Contador attacked. There were still more than 90km to race but the Spaniard wanted to spring a surprise. He was joined by team-mate Daniel Navarro, who went straight to the front and started to pace his leader up the climb. Behind, Andy Schleck and his brother Frank were stirred into action and soon a group of four riders formed.

Contador, Navarro and the Schleck brothers weren't the leaders on the road, because an attack of fourteen riders had gone right from the gun, but it looked like this was the group from which the Tour winner would come. And Australian Cadel Evans, the overnight favourite, wasn't in it. Drama was unfolding on the Col du Télégraphe.

Evans eventually got back to Contador and the Schlecks. Frank Schleck couldn't hold the pace much longer, leaving Andy to fend for himself. Then Contador attacked again. And again. And again. The sporadic but explosive accelerations from the Spaniard distanced Evans and the yellow jersey of Thomas Voeckler, who had come back to the group with Evans. But Andy Schleck would not crack.

Contador and Schleck bridged across to the remnants of the breakaway just as they reached the summit of the Télégraphe. The pair then flew up the Galibier

and on to the descent, while Evans launched a furious pursuit. By the time the riders reached the foot of the final climb he was back. Contador's efforts on the Télégraphe had ignited the race, but had ultimately been in vain. Evans would go on to win the Tour.

FRANK SCHLECK COULDN'T HOLD THE PACE MUCH LONGER, LEAVING ANDY TO FEND FOR HIMSELF. THEN CONTADOR ATTACKED AGAIN. AND AGAIN. AND AGAIN.

the most picturesque mountain scene. The Maurienne valley is harsher than others. It is busy and industrial, with the A43 autoroute and its hectic traffic easily visible from here.

• • •

On to the last third of the climb and my legs are beginning to tire. Every time I feel my muscles starting to complain I rein things back a bit. Now I hear voices. Three French riders are slowly coming up to me, talking non-stop. Here I am, trying to ration every last scrap of energy, concentrating hard on my breathing, and these guys are rabbiting away as if they're down the local bar, chewing the fat over a couple of *demis*. It takes an age for them to pass and not one of them pauses for breath. I find it intensely irritating. The air is full of inane chatter when all I want is to be left alone to suffer. Eventually they depart and peace descends. Once more the hills are alive only with the sound of my gasping.

Towards the top of the pass the views across and down the Maurienne valley open up. It's impressive, but not

The pitch rises again, a final test to overcome before the summit finally comes into view. I toil my way up and join the throng of cyclists and motorbikers basking in sumptuous sunshine. After the weeks spent cycling in the mountains of France I thought I knew what to expect at the top of climbs like this: the obligatory col sign, perhaps a café, a shop selling fluffy marmots. But I never expected a large, raging dragon, baring razor-sharp teeth and with claws like prongs. But that's what I get. Even if it is made of straw.

I sit in the sun and recover. I like this climb. At 12km it's not too long, it takes you past some pleasant villages, through the coolness of a pine forest. There are a few hairpins and sweeping bends. Tough sections and places to recover. And there's a dragon at the top. What's not to like?

Onwards to the Galibier. Now, that's likely to be a very different prospect.

CHARLY GAUL

Charly Gaul had two very different nicknames for two very different reasons. For his exploits in the rarefied air of the peaks of Italy and France he was called *L'Ange de Montagne* (the Angel of the Mountains). For his exploits in the bushes during the 1957 Giro d'Italia he was dubbed, somewhat less flatteringly, *Chéri Pi-pi* (Dear Wee-wee).

Born in 1932 in Plaffenthal, Luxembourg, Gaul was a talented amateur who learned his trade by attending training camps run by Charles Pélissier – a multiple Tour stage winner in the 1920s and 1930s – before turning professional in May 1953 with the Terrot team.

As at least one of his nicknames suggests, Gaul was a genius when the road tilted upwards, but he was also a complicated, often irritable man. Les Woodland describes him as a "little flea who got on everyone's nerves," writing that his fellow riders used to describe him as "making up in ego what he lacked in inches."

But his rivals in the peloton also recognised his talent. Raphaël Géminiani, French national champion in 1953 and winner of seven Tour stages, described Gaul as "a murderous climber... turning his legs at a speed that would break your heart, tick tock, tick tock, tick tock."

By the time the 1956 Giro d'Italia came around, Gaul, now riding for Faema-Guerra, was already known as one of the best climbers in the peloton. He had a string of victories behind him and had claimed third place and the mountains prize at the 1955 Tour. He opened his Giro account on stage 7, winning the 205km stage from Pescara to Campobasso, and secured a second win seven days later in a mountain time trial. However, he was still outside the top ten overall, more than 16 minutes down on the leader Pasquale Fornara, as the peloton started stage 18, a 242km haul from Merano to Monte Bondone. It was to be a momentous day that

RAPHAËL GÉMINIANI, FRENCH NATIONAL CHAMPION IN 1953 AND WINNER OF SEVEN TOUR STAGES, DESCRIBED GAUL AS "A MURDEROUS CLIMBER. . . TURNING HIS LEGS AT A SPEED THAT WOULD BREAK YOUR HEART, TICK TOCK, TICK TOCK, TICK TOCK."

would enter cycling legend and secure Gaul his first Grand Tour victory.

As the stage progressed the heavy rain that had been falling all day turned to snow. On the descent of the penultimate climb conditions worsened still, brakes iced up and riders, on the verge of hypothermia, were forced from their bikes. Fornara, the wearer of the leader's pink jersey, gave up and sought refuge in the sanctuary of a farmer's kitchen. It was unheard of for a leader of the Giro d'Italia to abdicate in such fashion, but this was no normal day.

But Gaul was at his best in the cold and wet. With the weather deteriorating with every passing minute, onwards he went, up the slopes of the Bondone. Still wearing his red, short-sleeved Faema jersey, Gaul climbed through the deepening snow, as the wind whipped the falling flakes into a blizzard. The crowds, who were huddled under umbrellas, roared him on as he weaved his way up the mountain in a demonstration of amazing defiance in the face of apocalyptic conditions. After a mighty battle against the mountain and the elements, Gaul finally crossed the line over seven minutes ahead of Giuseppe Fantini and more than twelve minutes before Fiorenzo Magni. (Magni's own performance was perhaps even more spectacular, given that he was riding with a shattered collarbone, the pain of which was so great that he'd been able to ride a time trial a few days earlier only by attaching a piece

of rubber to his handlebars and gripping it with his teeth.) Some riders only managed to cross the line curled up in team cars; the race organisers took pity on them and allowed them to start the next day.

On a day when over half the players in the field abandoned, Gaul had gained over twenty minutes and seized the pink jersey. Gaul easily kept hold of the race lead to the finish in Milan just two days later. The Angel of the Mountains had won his first Grand Tour.

It was at the same race, on the same stage, one year later, that Gaul earned his second, less complimentary nickname. The Luxembourger had what can only be described as a hate/hate relationship with French rider Louison Bobet. At the Giro in 1957 it was to cost him dearly.

Going into stage 18, again to Monte Bondone, Gaul was in pink, leading the race by nearly one minute from Gastone Nencini, with Bobet a further 21 seconds down. Halfway through the stage, Bobet and some other French riders opted to take a "natural break" – that is to answer the call of nature. There is an unwritten code of conduct among riders that no one will attack at such times. So Gaul carried on, maintaining a modest pace, before deciding to stop as well. As Bobet and his team-mates passed Gaul, by now in the bushes, turned to make an indecent gesture towards Bobet. The Frenchman was incensed and immediately ordered his team to ratchet up the pace.

Gaul flew into a rage, and set off in a desperate attempt to catch them. But it was to no avail. By the finish he had lost ten minutes, dropped out of the reckoning and earned his new nickname. Although Gaul would gain some measure of vengeance later, helping Nencini win the Giro by guiding him through the mountains, purely to ensure Bobet wouldn't win, he would have to wait another year to exact his full revenge.

Before the 1958 Tour the French team was in disarray. The French had an embarrassment of riches but those gems sat uneasily together. Jacques Anquetil, the 1957 Tour winner, told the team management that he would only ride with either Louison Bobet or Raphaël Géminiani, but not both. Bobet was selected by manager Marcel Bidot, leaving a furious Géminiani to ride the race with the Centre-Midi team, but not before he had posed for photographs alongside a donkey he'd called Marcel. Former team-mates were now at war.

Despite winning two time trials, including one on Mont Ventoux (see p111), Gaul was not threatening the overall classification as the riders prepared for stage 21, 219km from Briançon to Aix-les-Bains, taking in the Lautaret and the Luitel before three climbs in the Chartreuse. Géminiani, who had been making a point by riding aggress-ively all race, was in yellow by nearly four minutes. At the start line, Gaul was happy – it was raining. He found his hated rival Bobet and taunted him, saying that he was going to attack on the Luitel. He even told him on which hairpin.

And sure enough, when the race reached the appointed moment, Gaul attacked. In the cold and the rain, he turned the Tour upside down. At first the race leaders were unconcerned: they considered the man from Luxembourg to be too far down to be a threat to them, believing instead he was only going after points for the mountains prize. But as the gap increased they realised that something more serious was afoot.

At the summit of the Porte, the first of the Chartreuse climbs, Gaul had 5 minutes 50 seconds over Géminiani. At the top of the Cucheron it was 7 minutes 50 seconds. As he crested the Granier it was 12 minutes 35 seconds. Gaul was simply riding a different race from everyone else. Géminiani was frantically trying to seek support, asking his former teammates for assistance. It was not forthcoming, with Bobet and company either unwilling or simply unable to help. Gaul rolled into Aix-les-Bains 14 minutes 35 seconds ahead of Géminiani. The Frenchman, distraught, rounded on his countrymen: "Judases," he cried, "[you're] all Judases."

HE FOUND HIS HATED RIVAL BOBET AND TAUNTED HIM, SAYING THAT HE WAS GOING TO ATTACK ON THE LUITEL. HE EVEN TOLD HIM ON WHICH HAIRPIN. AND SURE ENOUGH, WHEN THE RACE REACHED THE APPOINTED MOMENT, GAUL ATTACKED. IN THE COLD AND THE RAIN, HE TURNED THE TOUR UPSIDE DOWN.

Gaul was now trailing the new race leader, Vito Favero, by just 1 minute 7 seconds. But the Luxembourger was a fine rider against the clock and knew he was favourite for the final time trial. Sure enough, there he took hold of the yellow jersey, to claim his one and only Tour de France win.

Another win at the Giro d'Italia came in 1959. He retired from professional cycling in 1965 and disappeared from public life for nearly twenty years, living as a hermit in a forest. He reappeared in the 1980s, working in the archives of a sports museum, remarrying and having a daughter before passing away in December 2005, aged 72 years.

CHARLY GAUL SELECTED RESULTS:

1953: 1st Fleche du Sud
2nd Critérium du Dauphiné
3rd Tour du Luxembourg

1954: 1st Circuit des 6 Provinces
2nd Tour du Luxembourg

1955: 1st overall and one stage win Tour Sud-Est
3rd overall, 1st mountains classification and two stage wins Tour de France

1956: 1st national championships
1st overall and three stage wins Giro d'Italia
1st overall and one stage win Tour du Luxembourg

1957: 1st national championships
4th overall and two stage wins Giro d'Italia

1958: 1st overall and four stage wins Tour de France
3rd overall and one stage win Giro d'Italia

1959: 1st overall, 1st mountains classification and three stage wins Giro d'Italia
1st overall Tour du Luxembourg
One stage win Tour de France

1960: 1st national championships
3rd overall and one stage win Giro d'Italia

1961: 1st national championships
1st overall and one stage win Tour du Luxembourg

1962: 1st national championships

COL DU GALIBIER

START POINT / Valloire
START ELEVATION / 1434m
FINISH ELEVATION / 2645m
LENGTH OF CLIMB / 17.5km
AVERAGE GRADIENT / 6.9%
MAXIMUM GRADIENT / 10.5%
FIRST TOUR / 1911
APPEARANCES / 58

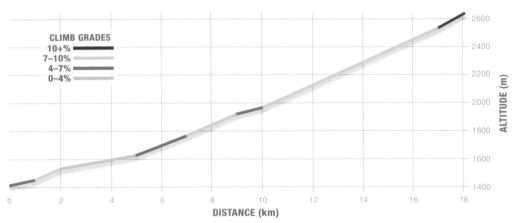

CLIMB GRADES
10+%
7–10%
4–7%
0–4%

ALTITUDE (m)

DISTANCE (km)

I descend from the top of the Télégraphe into Valloire, the ski resort at the foot of the Galibier. The town is quiet as I pass through. A handful of people are enjoying an early picnic on the grass at the side of the road; others are peering into restaurant windows or examining menus, wondering what to do for lunch. I stop by a small chapel on the outskirts, where I eat a sandwich and refill my bottle with cool water from a fountain. I sit there, absent-mindedly chewing my cheese and ham baguette, staring ahead. Up there, 17km away, is the Galibier. I've been here before. This is one of the Tour's very toughest summits: it's high, it's long and it's steep. In short, it's brutal.

An old woman, sitting on a bench a few metres away, follows my gaze.

"C'est la route du Galibier," she says.

"Mmm," I reply lost in thought. I can't take my eyes off the road.

Eventually I rouse myself, take a last swig of drink, refill my bottle for the final time, swing my leg over the saddle, cleat in, and get ready for my hardest ride yet.

• • •

When the climb was first introduced in 1911, Henri Desgrange was moved to write: "Oh Sappey, oh Laffrey, oh Col Bayard, oh Tourmalet! I shall not fail in my duty to proclaim to the world that you are like pale and common wine compared to the Galibier: all one can do before this giant is doff one's hat and bow." From that point on the Galibier was his favourite. It is no surprise that the southern slope of this grand climb was chosen as the spot for a memorial celebrating the life of the Tour founder. (See p19 for more on the Galibier's first stage.)

The Tour was captivated by this Alpine giant and returned every year up to and including 1948 (the race was not run during the two world wars). Since 1948 the Galibier has featured a further 31 times, including twice in 2011, when the race celebrated the centenary of the Tour's arrival in the Alps with climbs of both the southern and northern ascents, including the highest summit finish in Tour history. More on that later.

Surprisingly for a climb that has featured so frequently, no rider has ever led over its summit on more than two occasions, although no fewer than seven riders can lay claim to having been first over the top twice, one of them being Charly Gaul. Prior to 1955 the

Tour had not been a happy hunting ground for Gaul. The Luxembourger had started twice and abandoned twice. But 1955 was to be different. And the stage over the Galibier was to be the day when Gaul introduced himself properly to the Tour de France.

Stage 8 was the first big day in the mountains. A gruelling 253km, over the summits of the Aravis, Télégraphe and Galibier, from Thonon-les-Bains to Briançon, were on the agenda. Early in the stage the Dutchman Jan Nolten escaped from the peloton. Gaul, well out of the top ten already, went after him and, as the pair approached the first climb of the day, they had already built a healthy lead over the bunch.

Gaul led Nolten over the Aravis by a bike length. The peloton was already over four minutes behind, seemingly not bothered by the escape. Then, on the slopes of the Télégraphe, Nolten could no longer hold the wheel of Gaul, the expert climber. As the Dutchman fell back, the Luxembourger powered on,

and in less than 12km of the Télégraphe he put more than five minutes into Nolten. Gaul, the Angel of the Mountains, had flown free on his way to the roof of the Tour. There was no let-up on the Galibier. Cruising up the steep ramps of this monster, Gaul was untouchable. At the summit his lead was nearly sixteen minutes. He would lose a couple of those on the descent into Briançon but he had ripped the Tour apart on one of the race's toughest stages.

His first Tour stage win was followed by another in the Pyrenees twelve days later. He would finish the 1955 Tour on the podium and as the winner of the mountains competition.

● ● ●

As expected, the opening kilometre is hard. The road rises straight out of Valloire, 8% right away, dead straight, no respite. It's a long, difficult drag out of the town towards Les Verneys. Here the Galibier shows some pity, and the gradient relaxes – two or three kilometres of only 3%. It's tempting to drive forward, to get a move on while the going is good. But I don't. I know that this is the only easy section on this entire climb and so I maintain a steady pace, turning an easy gear very slowly. I know I'm going to need all my energy later. Soon enough the pitch rises again.

CRUISING UP THE STEEP RAMPS OF THIS MONSTER, GAUL WAS UNTOUCHABLE. AT THE SUMMIT HIS LEAD WAS NEARLY SIXTEEN MINUTES. HE WOULD LOSE A COUPLE OF THOSE ON THE DESCENT INTO BRIANÇON BUT HE HAD RIPPED THE TOUR APART ON ONE OF THE RACE'S TOUGHEST STAGES.

The road is pretty straight. Only slight twists as I follow a dried-up river bed prevent me from seeing far up the valley. Peaks glower high above. It's a harsh and hard landscape. Yes, it's impressive and grandiose. But pretty it is not. Summits like daggers wait to take their slice of flesh. And I'm not even halfway.

● ● ●

From its first visit the Tour had taken the riders through a tunnel that had been blasted through the mountain when the pass had been constructed in the late 1800s. But in 1976 part of the tunnel collapsed, forcing its closure, so a new road was built 89m above the tunnel, adding another kilometre to the climb. In 1979, with the new road complete, the Tour returned to scale the augmented heights of the Galibier.

Fittingly it was Lucien Van Impe, the best climber of that era, perhaps of any era, that was the first over the new road. On the 166km from Moûtiers to Alpe d'Huez, Van Impe led over the Madeleine and the Galibier but fell away on the approach to the summit finish. He crossed the line over five minutes behind eventual stage winner Joaquim Agostinho, who recorded the biggest win of his career.

● ● ●

At last I reach Plan Lachet, the auberge just before the road swings right into a series of tight and steep hairpins. Eight kilometres to go and I don't feel too bad, all things considered. But then things go downhill. Metaphorically. Quickly.

As I start the first of the arduous banks that have been thrown up the mountain, something inside snaps. Quite suddenly I have no energy. My legs are lame, my shoulders sagging, my heart deflated. My head is willing me on but my body is broken. I've felt like this on other climbs, but never quite this bad. I don't know how I'm going to get up the rest of this climb.

I continue to turn my legs slowly, pulling myself painfully up each hairpin. I stand, I sit. Then I stand again. No position is comfortable. A campervan drives by. The woman in the passenger seat looks at me pityingly. I almost expect the brake lights to come on and for her to hop out and offer me a lift. I'd like to think that had she done so I would have had the strength of character to turn her down. But to be honest I'm not sure I would have. Luckily my resolve is not tested as the van carries on up the mountain. I have no choice but to continue under my own steam.

● ● ●

In 2011 the Tour marked the centenary of the first stage on the Galibier with two stages over the mountain, including a first ever Galibier summit finish, making it the highest point the Tour has ever drawn a finish line.

The decision to hold a finish at the summit of the Galibier was a bold one. The road narrows to little more than a car's width at the top and there is precious little space to house all of the normal post-stage paraphernalia. Still, the decision was made. The TV trucks and team buses stationed themselves on the Col du Lautaret, 8km from the top of the Galibier, and everyone got ready for what promised to be an historic stage. Thanks to Andy Schleck, nobody was disappointed.

Schleck, starting the stage 2 minutes 36 seconds behind the yellow jersey of Thomas Voeckler, but more crucially 1 minute 18 seconds down to his main rival Cadel Evans, caught everyone napping and attacked on the climb of the Col d'Izoard, more than 60km from the finish. It was a throwback to the days of yesteryear. To the days of Coppi and Bartali, when they tore up the Izoard.

As Schleck powered up the climb, looking to get across the gap to a breakaway that had gone earlier in the day, no one behind stirred. Evans, Voeckler, Contador – they all just sat there, unwilling to chase so early in the stage. By the time Schleck had descended the Izoard and started the climb of the Lautaret, on the way to the Galibier, he had joined the remnants of the breakaway to form a group of six. In the peloton things were getting nervous. Schleck had nearly four minutes. It was too much. The chase was on.

On to the Galibier, where Schleck's only companion, Maxim Iglinskiy, immediately cracked. Suddenly Schleck was left to climb alone to the highest finish in Tour history. He had to dig deep, and as the final

kilometres ticked by his advantage came tumbling down. Evans was leading the pursuit. At times, in the final few hundred metres, Schleck almost appeared to come to a halt. But slowly, agonizingly, the finish line appeared. Andy Schleck had produced one of the great rides of the modern era to win the centenary stage on top of the Galibier, matching his effort twelve months earlier, when he'd done the same thing on the Tourmalet. It wasn't enough to put him in yellow, Voeckler having completed his own heroic ride to keep his hold on the jersey for another day. It wasn't enough to eventually get him to the top step in Paris – Evans would take that, rewarded for his pursuit on the Lautaret and Galibier. But it was enough to write him into history as the winner of the only stage to finish on top of Desgrange's beloved Galibier.

● ● ●

I'm taking it one kilometre at a time now. I'm so tired that I can't think beyond the next one thousand metres. I pass through Les Granges, a small cluster of buildings that operates as a cheese co-operative. I pass signs offering a kilo of Beaufort for less than 14 Euros. I ignore the temptation – I really don't need the extra weight. Around the corner, and there's a glass and metal monument on the right. It's as good an excuse

as any to stop. I pull over and wander over to take it look. It's in memory of Marco Pantani, the great Italian climber; it was on these slopes that he launched his bid for the 1998 Tour title (see pp224–227).

With just over four kilometres to go I remount and try to pedal. It's nothing less than torture. The sun is still beating down remorselessly and most of the sky is blue, but away to the west angry clouds are looming large. Thunder booms from summit of the Galibier, which is now visible high above.

Three kilometres. Two kilometres. The sound of thunder again slams off the rock all around me. The road ramps still further. Past the reopened tunnel – open to cars but not to bikes. One kilometre. Steeper still, more hairpins, over 10%, keep on going, keep on going... got to make it... got to make it... got to make it.

The last kilometre of the Galibier is relentless. Finally the road hairpins round to the right for the final stretch. There are fantastic 360-degree views, with the 3228m peak of the Grand Galibier standing stoutly away to the east, lording it over the narrow roadway that serves as the pass.

I am so tired. The Télégraphe and Galibier together have taken their toll. I had planned to cycle down the other side of the Galibier to visit the Desgrange memorial that stands on the mountain's southern slope but I simply can't face the ride back up. I decide that the monument can wait until next time. Because there will undoubtedly be a next time. In spite of how tough this mountain is, regardless of how bad it makes you feel, it cannot be resisted. You are in the presence of greatness and that feeling is addictive. So, safe in the knowledge that one day I will be back on this mountain, I turn around and start the long descent back to Saint-Michel-de-Maurienne.

The Col du Galibier, the Tour de France's epic climb, Desgrange's favourite. It had been a fitting end to my mountain adventures.

ANDY SCHLECK HAD PRODUCED ONE OF THE GREAT RIDES OF THE MODERN ERA TO WIN THE CENTENARY STAGE ON TOP OF THE GALIBIER, MATCHING HIS EFFORT TWELVE MONTHS EARLIER, WHEN HE'D DONE THE SAME THING ON THE TOURMALET.

CORK CITY
LIBRARIES

FURTHER READING

Les Alpes et Le Tour,
edited by Thierry Cazeneuve, Philippe Court and
Yves Perret (Le Dauphiné Libéré, 2009)

Bad Blood – The Secret life of the Tour de France,
Jeremy Whittle (Yellow Jersey Press, 2008)

Blazing Saddles: The Cruel and Unusual History
of the Tour de France,
Matt Rendell (Quercus, 2007)

Born to Ride: The Autobiography of Stephen
Roche, Stephen Roche (Yellow Jersey Press, 2012)

Cycling Heroes, Les Woodland
(Springfield Books, 1994)

The Death of Marco Pantani, Matt Rendell
(Phoenix, 2007)

The Eagle of Toledo – the Life and Times of
Federico Bahamontes, Alasdair Fotheringham
(Aurum Press, 2012)

Eddy Merckx: The Cannibal, Daniel Friebe
(Ebury Press, 2012)

Every Second Counts, Lance Armstrong,
with Sally Jenkins (Yellow Jersey Press, 2003)

Fallen Angel – The Passion of Fausto Coppi,
William Fotheringham (Yellow Jersey Press, 2010)

In Pursuit of Glory, Bradley Wiggins (Orion, 2009)

In Search of Robert Millar, Richard Moore
(HarperSport, 2008)

Inside the Tour de France, David Walsh
(Stanley Paul & Co Ltd, 1994)

It's Not About the Bike: My Journey Back to Life,
Lance Armstrong, with Sally Jenkins
(Yellow Jersey Press, 2001)

La Fabuleuse Histoire du Cyclisme,
Pierre Chany (Editions O.D.I.L, 1975)

La Fabuleuse Histoire du Tour de France,
Pierre Chany and Thierry Cazeneuve (Minerva, 2003)

Lance Armstrong – Tour de Force,
Daniel Coyle (HarperSport, 2006)

Le Tourmalet – Sommet des Tourments,
Patrick Fillon, Jacques Hennaux, Gerard Schaller
and Philippe Le Men (L'Équipe, 2010)

Merckx: Half Man Half Bike, William Fotheringham
(Yellow Jersey Press, 2012)

Le Mont Ventoux, Arsène Maulavé (Alan Sutton, 2010)

Mountain High, Daniel Friebe and Pete Goding
(Quercus, 2011)

The Official Tour de France Centennial 1903–2003,
edited by Matt Rendell and Nicolas Cheetham
(L'Équipe and Weidenfeld & Nicolson, 2003)

Racing Through the Dark – the Fall and Rise of
David Millar, David Millar, with Jeremy Whittle
(Orion, 2011)

Sex, Lies and Handlebar Tape: The Remarkable
Life of Jacques Anquetil, Paul Howard
(Mainstream Publishing, 2011)

Slaying the Badger: LeMond, Hinault and the
Greatest Ever Tour de France, Richard Moore
(Yellow Jersey Press, 2012)

The Story of the Tour de France Volume 1,
Bill and Carol McGann (Dog Ear Publishing, 2006)

The Story of the Tour de France Volume 2,
Bill and Carol McGann (Dog Ear Publishing, 2008)

Le Tour, Geoffrey Nicholson
(Hodder & Stoughton, 1991)

Le Tour – A History of the Tour de France,
Geoffrey Wheatcroft (Pocket Books, 2003)

Le Tour de France et les Pyrénées,
Dominique Kérébel (Éditions Cairn, 2010)

The Unknown Tour de France, Les Woodland
(Van der Plas Publications/Cycle Publishing, 2005)

Tour Climbs, Chris Sidwells (Collins, 2008)

Tour de France – the History, the Legend, the
Riders, Graeme Fife (Mainstream Publishing, 2006)

Uphill Battle – Cycling's Great Climbers,
Owen Mulholland (Velopress, 2003)

We Were Young and Carefree: The Autobiography
of Laurent Fignon, Laurent Fignon, translated by
William Fotheringham (Yellow Jersey Press, 2010)

The Yellow Jersey Companion to the Tour de
France, edited by Les Woodland
(Yellow Jersey Press, 2003)

AUTHOR ACKNOWLEDGEMENTS

This book has drawn on a wide range of sources, some of which can be found in the Further Reading section. However, I'd like to give special thanks to the following writers: Graeme Fife, Richard Moore, Chris Sidwells, Les Woodland, Daniel Friebe, Matt Rendell, William Fotheringham, Bryan Malessa, and the late Pierre Chany. Their work has served not only as invaluable reference material but as a real inspiration to me as I have tried, in my own small way, to follow in their footsteps. I'd also like to acknowledge *Sport et Vie* magazine, plus the Tour's website, letour.fr, and the other websites I have used extensively while writing this book: climbbybike.com, cyclingarchives.com, memoire-du-cyclisme.net, bikeraceinfo.com, cyclingrevealed.com, bestofthepyrenees,com, outsideonline.com and cyclingfever.com.

I'd like to thank Jonathan Knight, Jonathan Buckley, Matt Swann and all at Punk Publishing for their unwavering enthusiasm and support, and for turning my text and photographs into this book. I'd also like to thank Harriet Yeomans and Sophie Dawson, who were instrumental in shaping the project – I hope you both like the end result.

Thanks to Chris Shepherd in the Pyrenees and Melanie Smith in the Alps. Chris was a wonderful host in her charming Chambre d'Hote (maisonpyrenees.com) at the foot of the Tourmalet: as well as providing me with delicious food and wine, she unearthed volumes of *Sport et Vie* magazine in her loft – these were an invaluable resource. At the peaceful Ferme Noemie campsite (fermenoemie.com), near Bourg d'Oisans, Melanie kindly offered me a beautiful caravan as my temporary home from home. It was a perfect base from which to ride, and a splendid sanctuary in which to write.

I'd like to thank all my friends and family for all their interest and offers of help. I'd also like to thank my managers, who understood what this meant to me and made arrangements that gave me the necessary time.

But most of all I want to thank my wonderful partner, Karen. Without her unstinting support and enthusiasm, her ability to pick me up when I needed it most, and her willingness to be left alone for weeks on end, finishing a half-finished kitchen while I went off and chased my dream, I simply couldn't have done this. Karen, thank you.

INDEX

Author: Giles Belbin

Managing Editor: Jonathan Knight

Editor: Jonathan Buckley

Initial design: Harriet Yeomans

Typesetting, artwork, image production and further design: Matt Swann (21stBookDesign.blogspot.com)

Picture research: Jo St Mart

Proofreaders: Leanne Bryan, David Jones

Indexer: Diana LeCore

PR: Fiona Reece

Published by: Punk Publishing Ltd, 3 The Yard, Pegasus Place, London SE11 5SD

All photographs © Giles Belbin except as follows:

Pg 6, Rene Vietto (front) and Vicente Trueba (back) climb Col du Tourmalet, July 1934/©UCL Archive; Pg 9, top Luz-Ardidien/©UCL Archive, bottom, Iseran ©Tour de France; Pg10, Andy Schleck/©123RF; Pg 11 ©Corbis; Pg 12, Fausto Coppi/©UCL Archive; Pg 13, Galibier/©UCL Archive; Pg 14-15 ©UCL Archive; Pg 18, Joux Plane/©UCL Archive; Pg 26, Maurice Garin/©Library of Congress; Pg 36, Vicente Trueba/©UCL Archive; Pg 38, Vietto (front) and Trueba (back) climb Col du Tourmalet, July 1934/©UCL Archive; Pg 46, 47, Robert Millar/©123RF; Pg 54, 56 Luis Ocana/©UCL Archive; Pg 62, Bernard Hinault/©Tour de France; Pg 64, Bernard Hinault/©123RF; Pg 66, Laurent Fignon and Bernard Hinault, Tour de France 1984/©123RF; Pg 74, Van Impe/©123RF; Pg 84, Eddy Merckx/ ©Tour de France; Pg 86, 88, Eddy Merckx/©UCL Archive; Pg 96, Julio Jiménez/©Corbis; Pg 102, 104, Laurent Fignon/©UCL Archive; Pg 114, Bernard Thevenet/©123RF; Pg 116, Bernard Thevenet and Eddy Merckx, Tour de France 1975/©123RF; Pg 124, 126 Jacques Anquetil/©123RF; Pg 128 Jacques Anquetil/©Tour de France; Pg 137, Greg Lemond and Bernard Hinault/©UCL Archive; Pg 138, Greg Lemond/©123RF; Pg 146, Lance Armstrong/©123RF; Pg 148, Lance Armstrong/©Tour de France; Pg 156, Frederico Bahamontes/©UCL Archive; Pg 158, Bahamontes (1) with Anquetil, Tour de France 1963 /©UCL Archive; Pg 166, 168, 170, Gino Bartali/©UCL Archive; Pg 178, Richard Virenque/©Corbis; Pg 183, Col du Glandon/©123RF; Pg 186, 188, 190, 191 Fausto Coppi/©UCL Archive; Pg 198, 200, Louison Bobet/©UCL Archive; Pg 206, 208, 209, Bradley Wiggins/©123RF; Pg 216, 218, 219 Miguel Indurain/©123RF; Pg 221, Les Deux Alpes/©123RF; Pg 224, 226, Marco Pantani/©123RF; Pg 236, 237 Andy Schleck (L) with Alberto Contador, 2010/©UCL Archive; Pg 242, 244, Charly Gaul/©UCL Archive.

Extracts from *Eddy Merckx: The Cannibal* by Daniel Friebe, published by Ebury Press; *The Yellow Jersey Companion to the Tour de France* by Les Woodland; *Fallen Angel – The Passion of Fausto Coppi* by William Fotheringham; *We Were Young and Carefree: The Autobiography of Laurent Fignon* by Laurent Fignon (translated by William Fotheringham); *Born to Ride: The Autobiography of Stephen Roche* by Stephen Roche; *Merckx: Half Man Half Bike* by William Fotheringham; *It's Not About the Bike: My Journey Back to Life* by Lance Armstrong, all published by Yellow Jersey Press.
Reprinted by permission of The Random House Group Limited.

Extracts from *Sex, Lies and Handlebar Tape: The Remarkable Life of Jacques Anquetil* by Paul Howard; *Tour de France – the History, the Legend, the Riders* by Graeme Fife.
Reprinted by permission of Mainstream Publishing.

Extracts from *Le Tour de France et les Pyrénées* by Dominique Kérébel.
Reprinted by permission of Éditions Cairn.

Extracts from *Blazing Saddles: The Cruel and Unusual History of the Tour de France* by Matt Rendell.
Reprinted by permission of Quercus Books.

Extracts from *Racing Through the Dark – the Fall and Rise of David Millar* by David Millar, with Jeremy Whittle.
Reprinted by permission of Orion Books.

Extracts from *The Official Tour de France Centennial 1903–2003* edited by Matt Rendell and Nicolas Cheetham.
Reprinted by pemission of L'Equipe and Weidenfeld & Nicolson/Orion

The publishers and authors have done their best to ensure the accuracy of all information in *Mountain Kings*, however, they can accept no responsibility for any injury, loss or inconvenience sustained by anyone as a result of information contained in this book.